CURSE OF THE BLUMENTHALS

PHYLLIS KARAS

New York Times bestselling author

A POST HILL PRESS BOOK
ISBN: 979-8-89565-431-6
ISBN (eBook): 979-8-89565-432-3

Cover design by Jim Villaflores

This is a work of nonfiction. All people, locations, events, and situations are portrayed to the best of the author's memory and knowledge. Although adequate research was undergone concerning criminal cases, real-life people and perceptions, and authentic situations and incidents, the author and publisher do not assume and hereby disclaim any liability concerning any legal or criminal details present in this book.

This book, as well as any other Post Hill Press publications, may be purchased in bulk quantities at a special discounted rate. Contact orders@posthillpress.com for more information.

Post Hill Press
New York • Nashville
posthillpress.com

Published in the United States of America
1 2 3 4 5 6 7 8 9 10

Advance Praise for *Curse of the Blumenthals*

"A tragic car accident, a mistress's murder and a long reckoning with intergenerational trauma—these are the sorts of crises Tolstoy must have meant when he wrote 'each unhappy family is unhappy in its own way.' And yet, through compassionately dogged reporting, Phyllis Karas, a Blumenthal cousin herself shows how with love, patience and time, family curses can be, if not broken, at least absorbed."

—**Michael Kimmel**,
author of *Playmakers: The Jewish Entrepreneurs Who Created the Toy Industry in America*

"In fiction, curses are supernatural punishment from a sorcerer. In real life, curses are more akin to serious bad luck, the kind of misfortune that, when familial, can tear a clan apart. Phyllis Karas's *Curse of the Blumenthals* is the uplifting story of a family that might've splintered but persevered due to the cohesiveness of faith and love. Part genealogy, part family scrapbook, part true-crime reporting, this fascinating memoir is a near-obsessive examination of just how meticulous the agonies of chaos must become before one suspects the cards of fate are stacked."

—**Michael Benson**,
author of *Gangsters vs. Nazis*

"Whether we like it or not, family forms the fabric of every human being. In *Curse of the Blumenthals*, an honest and meticulously researched account of the author's family, Phyllis Karas reveals how two tragedies, nineteen years apart, can have reverberations decades later. This is a mesmerizing tale of how an ordinary American family can carry sorrow, resilience, and ultimately triumph in the face of tragedy."

—**Shirley Russak Wachtel,**
author of *The Baker of Lost Memories*
and *A Castle in Brooklyn*

To the Blumenthal family, past and present.

To my precious grandchildren, Jason, Danny,
and Belle Karas, our family's future.

To Jack, whose love for my Blumenthal
family makes me love him even more.

To my adored beautiful sister, Toby Klasky Bondy, a
vital part of every story of my life, whose absence seems
impossible. Good night, Tobe. I'll see you in the morning.

"Only people who are capable of loving strongly can also suffer great sorrow, but this same necessity of loving serves to counteract their grief and heals them."

—Leo Tolstoy

CONTENTS

INTRODUCTION

"What is a cousin, anyhow?"

Personally, I wear the word "cousin" as a badge of honor. While I have fourteen first cousins on my father's side, it is the thirteen first cousins on my mother's side, the Blumenthal side, including three I never met, who have imprinted that word deep within my soul. The ten I know have been locked together so firmly that no matter where we grew up or wherever we moved or whomever we married, nothing could keep us apart.

For we Blumenthals are survivors of two nightmares. The first nightmare claimed the lives of six of our relatives in 1935, when a drunk driver destroyed their car. The drunk driver survived; none of my relatives did. Thus, we were taught from an early age that when you lose six members of your family all at once, you will do everything humanely possible not to lose another.

Less than two decades later, in 1954, our cousin Ronnie tested that vow and triggered the second nightmare, when, at age eighteen, he confessed to a hideous crime.

In 2015, when I began my search for the truth about these two devastating, life-altering events in my family, I never expected how much I would unravel. Every family has secrets and ghosts—but so many?

Because these events happened so many years ago, I lost the opportunity to speak directly to many who were personally involved in them. Through the help of an expert genealogist and several extraordinary Providence, Rhode Island; Connecticut; and Boston-area librarians and researchers, I have been able to find papers, interviews, and family trees that proved indispensable as I worked to piece together these events.

However, my deepest thanks belongs to my Blumenthal cousins, who at the time of this writing were in their seventies and eighties, along with one in his fifties, and who searched their memories and photograph albums and miraculously remembered details of what they saw or heard about both the Accident and what my family always called the Incident, perhaps trying to sanitize the hideous event.

Undeniably, some of what I learned from all these generous sources has been altered in my telling. Conversations we shared have inevitably changed. Above all, I need to express that this is my family's story and that I am merely the storyteller. I accept that this is a huge responsibility and that I am far from a perfect narrator. But never would I stray from the fact that it is love that has propelled me to take that role and to lead the search for the true story of the Blumenthals, my imperfect, cursed, brave, loving, and adored family. As Tolstoy so aptly put it in *Anna Karenina* in 1878, "All happy families are alike; each unhappy family is unhappy in its own way." This seems uniquely true more than 140 years later.

And below is my glorious Blumenthal family, minus Phillip and Rose's great-grandchildren and great-great-grandchildren and even their great-great-great-grandchildren. I would need a forest, not a mere tree, to list all these precious branches.

Blumenthal Partial Family Tree

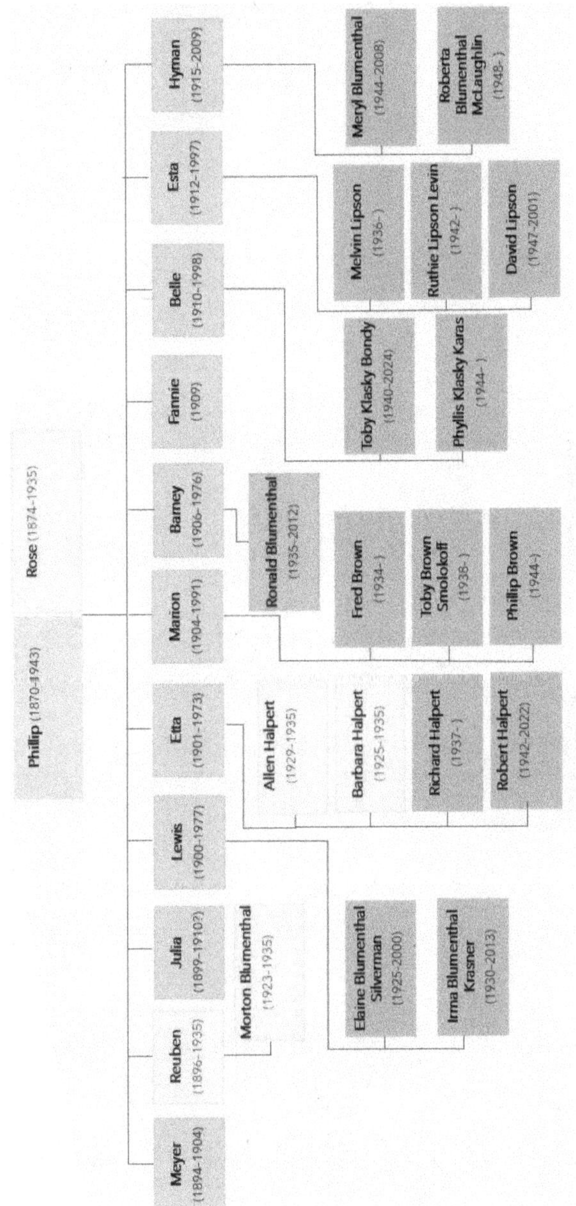

Credit: Robert Krock

CHAPTER ONE
A Family Like Any Other Family

So who were my Blumenthal relatives? How did they arrive in America, and where were they living before the Accident?

These Blumenthals all lived in Providence, the capital city of Rhode Island. While I was not born until 1944, nine years after the Accident, these Blumenthals were my relatives: my mother Belle Blumenthal Klasky's parents, sisters, brothers, aunts, uncles, and cousins. Although I never had the chance to meet the six we lost on that May day in 1935, I have held their memories, as well as my band of cousins and their families, dear to my heart for as long as I can remember. Indeed, nearly ninety years after the Accident, I gratefully acknowledge the blessed presence in my life of fifteen first cousins, thirty-four second cousins, and an ever-increasing crew of third cousins. I suppose this was not all that unusual considering that my mother had ten siblings. Even though three of them died before the age of ten, the remaining seven, like my mother, reproduced wonderfully.

My uncle Reuben (Ruby), born in 1896, was the driver of the car in the Accident. His parents were Phillip and Rose (known as Teibe) Blumenthal, who had arrived in New York from Russia through Ellis Island—Phillip in 1890 and Rose in 1889, and they married in 1893. They came from the Riga area, which was once a part of the former Tsarist Russian empire and is now a port in Latvia, the capital and largest city in the Baltics.

Rose Blumenthal

Phillip Blumenthal

The Blumenthal family are Litvaks, Lithuanian Jews, and in Europe were considered to be more intellectual and stoic than their rivals, Galitzianers, the more emotional Jews from Galicia (western Ukraine and southeastern Poland). My cousin Mel always joked that our grandmother Teibe, who had produced eleven children in twenty-one years, from 1894 to 1915, had been what some might consider a typical Litvak, successful in the bedroom as well as in the kitchen.

The Blumenthal family, arriving in the first wave of Jewish immigrants from Eastern Europe that began in the 1880s, left New York and settled in Providence, Rhode Island, in a section of the city that was north of the downtown area. By that time, the German Jews who had arrived earlier had moved away from the downtown area and settled in the neighborhood off the South Side. Jews of the North End had come to Providence from the small villages (shtetls), towns, and cities of Eastern Europe, primarily Poland, Lithuania, and Russia.

Of Phillip and Teibe's eleven children, three—Fannie, Julia, and Meyer—did not survive into adulthood. Meyer, born in New York in 1894, died in Providence in1904 at age ten; while Fannie, born in Providence on March 12, 1909, died at ten months on December 1, 1909. Julia, born in October 1899 in Rhode Island, died sometime between 1900 and 1910. Yet the eight who remained, four boys and four girls, grew up strong, attractive, and close-knit in their Orthodox Jewish family home on 7 Overhill Road in Providence, Rhode Island. Belle, my mother, born in 1910, was the fifth of those eight. In truth, I feel guilty about even mentioning the year of her birth. Fanatical about never revealing her actual age, my mother made us promise that we would never reveal her birthdate on her tombstone. Indeed, when she died in 1998, the granite marker on her gravesite revealed only the facts that she was a loving wife, mother, grandmother, and great-grandmother, all of which, indeed, she was.

My mother Belle's father, my grandfather Phillip Blumenthal, had been a house painter but later earned a living as a tailor with his own business. He was a tall, handsome man, for whom I was named, following the tradition of naming a child after a beloved deceased relative. My grandfather's height was passed on to many of his grandchildren, and even to his grateful great-grandchildren, many of whom used this advantage in excelling in sports such as basketball, football, and lacrosse, though none of them ever had the chance to thank the donor of this gift.

I wish so much that I knew anything about my grandmother Teibe, who died before I and most of my cousins were born. I do remember my mother telling me that Teibe was always working, which is understandable considering the size of her family. Apparently, my mother was extremely thin growing up, so much so that my grandmother sent her to a relative's house in the country to fatten her up. The "country" could well have been a few miles away, but my mother remembered drinking fresh milk from the cows while she was there. "Since all the food in our house was strictly kosher," my mother related, "I worried that since the milk I was drinking at our relative's house came straight from the cow, it might not have been kosher. But my mother insisted I eat everything that our relatives gave me. So, I did, and it was all so delicious. When I got home my mother said I looked so much better. She had never complimented my looks before then, so I felt especially happy. My older sister Marion was always known as the beauty in the family, but for a little while I felt pretty, too."

How I wish I had asked my mother for more stories about this woman who will always be an enigma to me. Indeed, there is so much more I would love to know about the lives of the Blumenthals who began their lives in the former Tsarist empire. But what I do know for sure is that everything in those lives changed in an instant one horrible day in May 1935.

CHAPTER TWO

The Accident: What Can Six Graves Mean?

So much of the Blumenthal family history can be illuminated in the six well-tended and clearly marked graves consecrated in 1935 in Lincoln Park Cemetery in Warwick, Rhode Island. To be specific, in Section 39, Plot 37: Grave 2, Grave 3, Grave 4, Grave 5, and Grave 6. The sixth grave is in Section 07, Plot 63, Grave 1.

For as long as I could remember, my mother marked all the major events of her life in relationship to what she named the Accident. In "The Accident," as the May 1935 headline in the *Providence Journal* explains, "Six Residents of Providence Lose Lives in Auto Crash Near Willimantic, Conn." Those residents were my mother's mother, Rose Blumenthal, 61; her brother Reuben Blumenthal, 39, who was driving the car; her nephews, Morton Blumenthal, 12, and Allen Halpert, 6; her niece, Barbara Halpert, 10; and her sister's mother-in-law, Jennie Halpert, 60. Both Rose and Jennie were the grandmothers of the three children in the car.

The six Blumenthal relatives had been returning to Providence after visiting thirty-five-year-old Dave Halpert, the father of Barbara and Allen, who was recuperating from a recent heart attack at Mt. Sinai Hospital in Hartford, Connecticut, about a seventy-five-mile trip. My mother, twenty-four and recently divorced, was the one who answered the call from the Connecticut State Police informing the family of the deadly crash. Living at her parents' home at 7 Overhill Road in Providence with her mother and father, Belle had spent the last month caring for her sister Etta Blumenthal Halpert's two children, Barbara and Allen. When Dave became ill, he and Etta had already been in Connecticut for several weeks working on a possible new business opportunity there. Etta had been at her husband's bedside since his heart attack and would remain until he was strong enough to return to their home in Providence. Only three days after his heart attack, Dave had asked to see his adored two children since it had been at least a month since he had seen them.

My mother was devoted to her niece and nephew and vividly remembers braiding Barbara's wavy, light-brown hair for the afternoon visit to Connecticut, as well as finding just the right pants and shirt for Allen. "The children looked especially beautiful that day," she told me more than once. "They were so excited to be driving to Connecticut to see their father, who they missed terribly."

The Blumenthal family shortly before the accident. Seated, front row: Morton (Morty) Blumenthal (killed in the Accident), Allen Halpert (killed), Elaine Blumenthal Silverman, Irma Blumenthal Krasner, Barbara Halpert (killed). Second row: Jeanette Blumenthal (Ruby's wife), Ruby Blumenthal (killed), my grandmother Tillie (Teibe) Rose Blumenthal (killed), my grandfather Phillip Blumenthal, Etta Blumenthal Halpert and David Halpert (Etta's husband). Top row: Barney Blumenthal, Edythe Frank Blumenthal (Barney's wife), Lewis Blumenthal, Sally Feldman Blumenthal (Lewis's wife), Hyman (Hy) Blumenthal, Esta Blumenthal Lipson, Herman Kaufman (my mother's first husband), my mother—Belle Blumenthal Kaufman, Jack Brown (Marion's husband) and Marion Blumenthal Brown.

During the month before the crash, while her sister and brother-in-law remained in Connecticut, my mother had helped the children write daily letters to their father, and, along with her mother, had cared for all their needs. She had hoped to go to the hospital with Rose, Reuben, Morton, Allen, and Barbara that May afternoon, but when Dave's mother, Jennie, decided to take the ride to see her son, the sixth seat would be occupied. Belle was disappointed as she was equally anxious to see her brother-in-law, but, as things turned out, she stayed back in Providence…and lived.

In an especially punishing turn of fate, my aunt Etta had already heard about the crash before my mother received that life-altering call. After his six relatives left the hospital, my uncle Dave was understandably exhausted and drifted off to a deep sleep. My aunt asked the nurse to bring his dinner a bit later so he could get a little rest. Energized by the visit, though sad to watch her precious children and other family members leave the hospital, Etta left her sleeping husband and retreated to the hospital cafeteria for a cup of tea. While she was sitting there, she heard an announcement over the radio that there had been a fatal crash on the Providence-Willimantic Road. "I knew it was my family," she said years later. It was never surprising to me that she knew that, that she felt a sharp pain deep inside her heart, the beginning of her own heart condition that would plague her for the rest of her life, eventually killing her thirty-eight years later.

After the crash, heartbroken beyond words, my mother wrote the children's daily letters to Dave as he recovered in the Connecticut hospital unaware that his two children, along with his mother, had died in the crash. In her deepest despair, my mother forced herself to write loving and happy letters to him from a six-year-old and a ten-year-old who no longer lived. I have never stopped marveling at the strength it must have taken her to write those letters, to write the words the two children she so adored might have wanted their father to read.

In one of our rare conversations about that unforgettable day, my mother told me that so often she had to rewrite some of the letters because the ink with which she wrote the words was smeared by her tears. I could visualize my mother, in her childhood room, shattered by her own divorce, devastated by the loss of her niece and two nephews as well as her mother and brother, trying to take care of her equally heartbroken father, forcing herself to write of simple everyday events from the point of view of two children who missed their parents. She even managed to draw funny little pictures that Allen and Barbara would have drawn for their father. Knowing their father was an artist, they had always worked hard to send him pictures he would have admired. For their mother it was particularly agonizing, knowing the truth, to watch her husband smile as he read each word and happily studied each picture. I would never stop being awed and shaken by the courage of my aunt and my mother. Their shared love for Dave Halpert compelled them to do everything humanly possible, as well as incomparably painful, to keep him alive.

Recently, I learned one particularly poignant detail concerning the attempt to keep the news about the death of his children, along with those of his mother, brother-in-law, mother-in-law, and nephew from my uncle Dave. On the morning of Thursday, May 16, two days after the Accident, my extraordinary aunt Etta left her ill husband in the Mt. Sinai Hospital in Hartford, Connecticut, and was driven the eighty-two miles to Lincoln Park Cemetery in Warwick, Rhode Island, by her brother Lewie for the funeral of their two children, as well as of her mother, brother, and nephew. When she returned to her husband's bedside hours after the funeral, he noticed that she was wearing a black dress. He commented briefly on the "fancy dress," but she shrugged it off as nothing special. It is so hard to believe he did not sense that a tragedy had happened in his life, but on that infinitely sad day, his wife, dressed in black, her face inevitably tinged in unutterable sadness, never offered even a hint of such a hideous possibility.

For most of my aunts and uncles, speaking about the Accident—at least by the time I was old enough to begin to comprehend what had happened—was rare. Some words were impossible to say. My cousin Ruthie remembered that her mother, my aunt Esta, who was exactly, to the day, two years younger than my mother, talked a little bit about it. "She was engaged to my father at the time and planning their upcoming wedding," Ruthie said. "As a matter of fact, she, too, was in the kitchen at 7 Overhill Road when the phone call came from the state police. She said she was cooking something on the stove. I know the wedding she and my father were planning never happened. There had been too much sadness to even think about it. So, they eloped instead. Three months later. On August 9, 1935."

It was just around that time, nearly two months after the Accident, when the doctors deemed my uncle Dave well enough to leave the hospital and return to Providence. The day before his discharge, his Providence rabbi came to his hospital bedside to deliver the news about the Accident. By some miracle, Dave's heart withstood the shock, and he and my aunt Etta returned to their home. "Dave had to have known or at least suspected that something was horribly off," my mother told me. "No matter how hard I tried to make the kids' drawings exactly like the ones that they had always sent him, I couldn't do the impossible."

While her father had the meticulous eye of an accomplished artist, Barbara, at ten, already had the beginnings of a gifted sketcher. Still, Dave would have noted even a minute difference. Unquestionably, the whole hospital staff had to have been deeply shaken by the accident. "Dave was a sensitive man," my mother said. "He would have picked up the colossal change in the atmosphere surrounding all of them." But my mother also believed that Dave's love for my aunt had compelled him to continue to play the hideous charade they were both performing, hoping in some small way that he was sparing her having to tell him the unspeakable truth. "More than once," said my mother, "I'd been tempted to ask him if he had known or suspected what had happened before the rabbi told him. But I knew there was no point in causing him any more pain by discussing that nightmare. He was such a special person. There are no words to adequately describe my brother-in-law."

During the four years following his release from the hospital, Dave and Etta Halpert miraculously and joyfully produced two more sons, my cousins Dick and Bob. When Bob was twenty-two months old, Dave died of a massive heart attack. Etta survived and lovingly raised her sons, while never failing to lavish love on each of her many nieces and nephews. She was, without question, my favorite aunt. She always convinced me, along with all my other cousins, that each of us was her ultimate favorite.

As for my mother, from that day on, her future life as a wife and the mother of two daughters was tainted by that May day. Her anxiety level was permanently stuck at an often-crippling high. Every letter or phone call to me once I'd reached a certain age ended with these words, "Love you. Be careful driving." And why not? From the time she was twenty-four until her death sixty years later, the world was a dangerous and unreliable place. Bad things could suddenly and unexpectedly happen to innocent people, especially to those she loved. Heartbreakingly, they did.

Indeed, that one hideous event in her family's life was impossible to ignore. Numerous newspaper stories from all over the country reported the shocking news of the Accident.

WEATHER

The Providence Journal

Founded as a semi-weekly in 1820; as a daily in 1829

VOLUME CVII. NO. 114 TWENTY-SIX PAGES PROVIDENCE, WEDNESDAY, MAY 15, 1935 PRICE TWO CENTS

SIX PROVIDENCE RESIDENTS MEET DEATH IN AUTO CRASH; THREE OTHER PERSONS HURT

SPEEDING AUTOS COLLIDE ON ROAD IN CONNECTICUT

Three Members of Blumenthal Family, Three of Halpert Family Are Killed.

UNDERTAKER AMONG HURT

He and Two Companions, in Second Auto, Suffer Severe Injuries; Both Heading for Home

Six persons returning to this city after visiting a relative in a Hartford hospital met death early last night in a head-on collision of automobiles on the Providence-Hartford highway in the centre of the village of North Windham, Conn., near Willimantic.

Three Willimantic men, occupants of the second automobile, were injured, one of them critically.

The light sedan in which the Providence party was riding collided with the heavier car containing the Willimantic men in front of the North Windham Post Office, the collision telescoping the two automobiles and crushing the lighter car.

At midnight, Connecticut authorities adjourned their investigation until today without establishing officially the cause of the accident, but two men in an automobile following the Willimantic car were declared ready to tell police it was being driven erratically and swerved in front of the Providence-bound vehicle.

The six dead were two elderly women, a man and three children. One of the women was the mother of the man and grandmother of one of the children. The other woman was grandmother of the two remaining children who were the son and the daughter of the man the party had visited in the Hartford hospital.

The dead:

MRS. ROSE BLUMENTHAL, 61, of 7 Overhill road, this city. Killed instantly.

MORTON BLUMENTHAL, 10, her grandson, of 15 Taft avenue, this city. Killed instantly.

REUBEN BLUMENTHAL, 39, of 15 Taft avenue, this city, son of Mrs. Blumenthal and father of Morton Blumenthal. Reuben Blumenthal was the driver of one of the cars. He died at Windham Community Memorial Hospital, Willimantic, at 11:45 last night, of a fractured skull and shock.

MRS. JENNIE HALPERT, about 60, of 111 Eleventh street, this city. Died a short time after the accident.

BARBARA HALPERT, 10, granddaughter of Mrs. Halpert, who was living temporarily with her grandmother. Killed instantly.

ALLEN HALPERT, 6, grandson of Mrs. Halpert, and also living temporarily with her. Killed instantly.

The injured:

THOMAS H. KILLOUREY, 45, Willimantic undertaker and driver of the other car. In critical condition with fractured skull at Windham Hospital, Willimantic.

DENNIS F. HAGGERTY, 38, Willimantic postal employe, who was riding with Killourey. In hospital at Willimantic. Condition not serious.

JOSEPH OSSO, 48, Willimantic merchant who also was riding with Killourey. In hospital at Willimantic. Possible leg fracture.

Visit at Hospital

The Providence party went yesterday morning to Hartford to visit David Halpert, son of Mrs. Jennie Halpert and father of Barbara and Allen Halpert. Formerly of New Bedford, he recently went to work

Continued on Page 2, Column 2

THE PROVIDENCE JOURNAL, WEDNESDAY, MAY 15, 1935

SIX RESIDENTS OF PROVIDENCE LOSE LIVES IN AUTO CRASH NEAR WILLIMANTIC, CONN.

The Party Was Returning From Hartford and in Passing Through North Windham Collided with Another Auto Driven by Thomas Killourey, a Willimantic Undertaker. All in the Providence Car Were Either Killed Outright, or Died Later from Injuries. Killourey Was Seriously Injured, and Two Other Men Riding with Him Were Less Seriously Hurt. Mrs. Jennie Halpert, 111 Eleventh Street, Upper Left, Was Instantly Killed. On Her Right Is Reuben Blumenthal, 15 Taft Avenue, Driver of the Car, Who Died in a Willimantic Hospital; Morton Blumenthal, 10-Year-Old Son of Reuben; and Mrs. Rose Blumenthal, 7 Overhill Road, Mother of Reuben Blumenthal. Below, Allen Halpert, 6, and Barbara Halpert, 10, Grandchildren of Mrs. Jennie Halpert.

SIX PROVIDENCE RESIDENTS KILLED

Continued from Page 1, Col. 8.

in Hartford. His wife and two children came to Providence to stay with his mother.

Last Friday, David Halpert suffered a heart attack and was taken to Mt. Sinai Hospital, Hartford. His wife joined him and Monday he asked to see his children.

Reuben Blumenthal, Pawtucket druggist and World War veteran, drove David Halpert's car to Hartford, taking his mother, Mrs. Rose Blumenthal, his son, Morton, and the three members of the Halpert family. Reuben Blumenthal was a brother of Mrs. David Halpert.

Still seriously ill last night, David Halpert was not told of the tragedy.

Killourey, Haggerty and Osso had been to a Superior Court session at Putnam, where Osso had applied for naturalization, with the two other men his witnesses. His petition was refused.

The accident occurred about 6:30 o'clock. The two groups were returning to their homes.

The scene of the accident was a comparatively straight stretch of the two-lane concrete highway (U. S. No. 6). The car driven by Blumenthal was descending a slight grade.

The automobiles are believed to have come together almost directly head-on. The Blumenthal car was turned violently around so that its right side went against the left side of Killourey's car. Both automobiles were facing north, and were on that side of the highway, in front of the postoffice, when they came to rest.

One of the elderly women was thrown from the Providence car. The five other persons were caught inside.

Reuben Blumenthal Conscious

Reuben Blumenthal was conscious after the accident, although his skull, both arms and right leg were fractured. He was able to partly identify for Dr. C. E. Simonds, medical examiner, those who had been riding with him.

Mrs. Halpert died a short time after the accident. The four other victims were killed outright.

Dr. Simonds and State Policemen Kenneth Stevens and James A. Buckley of the Stafford Spring barracks questioned Haggerty and Osso at the Windham Community Memorial Hospital in Willimantic, where they, Killourey and Reuben Blumenthal were taken.

"Everything occurred so suddenly I don't know what happened," Haggerty said.

Capt. James S. Thompson of Camp Fernow, CCC at Hampton, Conn.; Stanley Kogut, Connecticut Park Development Commission employe attached to the camp, and two other men were in an automobile following the Killourey car.

Police had not questioned them at midnight, but Capt. Thompson and Kogut were reported to have declared that Killourey's automobile was zig-zagging in front of them.

Dr. Simonds said the primary cause of the deaths of all victims was fractured skulls. Deputy Coroner Louis A. Woisard of Danielson will conduct an inquest today.

Victims Widely Known

Mrs. Blumenthal, her son, and Mrs. Halpert were widely known in this city.

Morton Blumenthal was the only son of Mr. and Mrs. Reuben Blumenthal. The latter was at her husband's store in Pawtucket when other relatives told her of the accident.

Barbara and Allen Halpert were the only children of Mr. and Mrs. David Halpert.

Positive identification of the victims was not made until late last night, after relatives had gone to Willimantic from this city.

The automobiles are believed to have come together almost directly head-on. The Blumenthal car was turned violently around so that its right side went against the left side of Killourey's car. Both automobiles were facing north, and were on that side of the highway, in front of the postoffice, when they came to rest.

One of the elderly women was thrown from the Providence car. The five other persons were caught inside.

Reuben Blumenthal Conscious

Reuben Blumenthal was conscious after the accident, although his skull, both arms and right leg were fractured. He was able to partly identify for Dr. C. E. Simonds, medical examiner, those who had been riding with him.

Mrs. Halpert died a short time after the accident. The four other victims were killed outright.

Dr. Simonds and State Policemen Kenneth Stevens and James A. Buckley of the Stafford Spring barracks questioned Haggerty and Osso at the Windham Community Memorial Hospital in Willimantic, where they, Killourey and Reuben Blumenthal were taken.

"Everything occurred so suddenly I don't know what happened," Haggerty said.

Capt. James S. Thompson of Camp Fernow, CCC at Hampton, Conn.; Stanley Kogut, Connecticut Park Development Commission employe attached to the camp, and two other men were in an automobile following the Killourey car.

Police had not questioned them at midnight, but Capt. Thompson and Kogut were reported to have declared that Killourey's automobile was zig-zagging in front of them.

Dr. Simonds said the primary cause of the deaths of all victims was fractured skulls. Deputy Coroner Louis A. Woisard of Danielson will conduct an inquest today.

Victims Widely Known

Mrs. Blumenthal, her son, and Mrs. Halpert were widely known in this city.

Morton Blumenthal was the only son of Mr. and Mrs. Reuben Blumenthal. The latter was at her husband's store in Pawtucket when other relatives told her of the accident.

Barbara and Allen Halpert were the only children of Mr. and Mrs. David Halpert.

Positive identification of the victims was not made until late last night, after relatives had gone to Willimantic from this city.

"BURGLARY RING" PREYING ON FILM STARS REVEALED

Woman and Four Men Arrested; Linked to $500,000 Loot.

Los Angeles, May 14. — (UP) — A nation-wide "burglary ring" which preyed on Hollywood film notables and distributed stolen goods through "fences" in New York, Chicago and Mexico, was disclosed tonight by police after the arrest of a woman and four men.

More than $500,000 worth of jewelry, furs and other valuable loot was taken from homes of prominent film stars and executives by members of a "burglary school" who studied private lives of film stars as a background for systematic burglaries, police said.

Names, addresses and unlisted telephone numbers of many well-known members of the film colony were found in a little black book seized by arresting officers, police said. The names included Jean Harlow, Peter Arno, Marion Davies, John Barrymore, Eddie Cantor and District Attorney Burton Fitts.

PROBE CONTINUES INTO FATAL CRASH

Survivors of Tragedy That Took Six Lives Questioned by Coroner.

NO CHARGES YET PLACED

Joint Funeral Services Will Be Held Here Today for Victims of Connecticut Accident

As relatives of the victims made arrangements for a joint funeral service this morning, the State of Connecticut yesterday continued its inquiry into the automobile collision Tuesday evening at North Windham which took the lives of six Providence-bound motorists.

The services will be conducted at 11 o'clock at the Max Sugarman funeral home, 150 Randall street. It was expected last night that Rabbi Israel M. Goldman of Temple Emanu-El would officiate. Rabbi Goldman was in New York when informed of the tragedy.

Burial in Warwick

Five of the victims will be buried in a single plot in Lincoln Park Cemetery, Warwick. In an adjacent plot the sixth, Mrs. Jennie Halpert, will be buried next to her husband.

In the other plot will be buried Mrs. Rose Blumenthal; her son, Reuben Blumenthal; the latter's son, Morton Blumenthal, and Barbara and Allen Halpert, grandchildren of both the elderly women who were killed.

Full military honors will be paid Reuben Blumenthal by Rhode Island Post, No. 23, Jewish War Veterans of the United States, of which he was a member, and former officer-of-the-day. He enlisted in the Rhode Island National Guard in 1913, and was a member of the Coast Artillery when the guard was federalized in the World War.

Military services will be in charge of Commander Barney Taber, Aide Paul J. Robin, Chaplain Charles M. Hoffman, Senior Vice Commander Max A. Cohen, Junior Vice Commander John J. Rouslin, with taps sounded by Esmond Borod. The firing squad at Lincoln Park Cemetery will be in charge of Irving D. Paster.

Bearers will be Past Commanders Charles M. Hoffman, Max A. Cohen, Paul J. Robin, Dr. Samuel I. Kennison and Dr. Maurice Mellion, Leo Wine, Aaron Cohen and Solomon Jacober.

Arthur G. Bill, Windham County coroner, yesterday took charge of the coroner's investigation begun Tuesday night by Assistant Coroner Louis A. Woisard.

Coroner Bill questioned Dennis F. Haggerty and Joseph Osso, the two passengers in the car driven by Thomas H. Killourey, Willimantic undertaker, who was injured critically.

Both Haggerty and Osso were kept at Windham Community Memorial Hospital at Willimantic.

Although Killourey was reported to have regained consciousness and to have recognized relatives, he was not questioned yesterday.

The three men, the only survivors of the crash, were on the front seat of Killourey's heavy sedan when it collided with the light car containing the Providence party, it was said.

No Charges Yet Placed

Coroner Bill declared no charges had been placed against anyone, and added that the completion of his investigation would depend on developments in Killourey's condition. The latter has a skull fracture, chest injuries and broken nose.

State Policeman Kenneth W. Stevens of the Stafford Springs barracks continued the police investigation yesterday, questioning several persons who were in the village of North Windham when the crash occurred.

The Accident was front page news in Providence, and the story was picked up in newspapers across the country.

As each one gruesomely reported, five of the occupants of the Blumenthal car had suffered fatally fractured skulls and died at the scene of the crash; one of the two grandmothers, sixty-year-old Jennie Halpert, was hurled from the car. If you look carefully at one of the photos of the aftermath of the crash, you can see a women's shoe at the front of the debris. Once noticed, this small but horrifying detail is impossible to forget. It could have been Mrs. Halpert's shoe, or that of my grandmother, Rose "Teibe" Blumenthal. How I wish that someone in the family had been able to collect that shoe, so that a small piece of one of the grandmothers might still exist. Incredulously, another item from the crash survived and made it back to the family: my uncle Ruby's wire-rimmed eyeglasses. When I was a child, I discovered them one day inside my mother's bedside table. When I put them over my own eyes, the world was way too blurry for me to see a thing. Tearfully, my mother explained to me that they had belonged to her older brother, that they were a miracle and she would never throw them away. Even at a young age, I understood that they were something precious and never tried to see through them again, just occasionally opening the drawer and touching them tenderly. I had no idea at that time just what a treasure they were—but I soon did.

The owner of those glasses, the sixth occupant of that car and its driver, my uncle Reuben, survived nearly three hours at the Windham County Memorial Hospital, with two broken arms, a fractured skull, and a broken right leg. He was, astonishingly, and with what had to be unbearable pain, physically able to provide the names of the five victims in his car before succumbing to the impact of his severely fractured skull and limbs. Yet, his eyeglasses survived, unscathed.

CHAPTER THREE

Thomas H. Killourey: Under the Influence

Over ninety years have passed since the Accident, and except for a brief mention in the hundreds of newspaper articles and one legal statement, there was little available about the driver of the hefty automobile that smashed into my relatives' smaller car. Thanks, however, to my no doubt unhealthy obsession about the man, I was able to uncover some information about Thomas H. Killourey of Willimantic, Connecticut, the man responsible for the deaths of six of my relatives. Perhaps by putting some light on this man, I could, in some small way, offer those six victims the gift of making certain their killer does not escape completely untarnished. Yes, Mr. Killourey was injured in the crash, and he served some time in prison for his crime, but those punishments, in my mind at least, were far from what he deserved. Perhaps the following account about Killourey might help at least one reader understand what might happen when a drunk gets behind the wheel of a car. Maybe, just maybe, another nightmare like the Accident might be prevented.

I found out surprisingly more information about this man than any of my cousins, including Dave and Etta's two sons, Dick and Bob, had previously learned. To my cousins, this information was obviously upsetting, yet, in some small way, each was grateful to understand even more about what had happened on that tragic day to the family they never got to know.

My greatest wish, of course, was that the driver had never been born, or, at the very least, had never become the funeral director of the successful Killourey Brothers undertaking firm, established by his father, John J. Killourey, in nearby Willimantic, Connecticut. Maybe then he would not have been able to afford the hefty, expensive, black Cadillac that he was driving on May 14, 1935.

While I obviously would never have a chance to meet the man, I overzealously discovered some facts about Thomas H. Killourey. Forty-five years old on Tuesday, May 14, 1935, Killourey was born in Willimantic, Connecticut, on August 25, 1891, the son of John and Julia McNamara Killourey. Thomas's father was born in Ireland. Thomas attended St. Joseph's School and Windham High School, which he left after two years to head to the Renouard School of Embalming in New York City, from which he graduated in 1909 at the age of eighteen. Then he joined his father and his brother, Daniel, in the Killourey Brothers family undertaking business, a business founded on May 2, 1883, when John began erecting its two-story building on Jackson Street in Willimantic.

The business was obviously profitable when, on June 4, 1913, twenty-two years before the Accident, twenty-one-year-old Thomas married Miss Margaret J. Hughes, a nurse, at St. Joseph's church in a fancy wedding. The reception and wedding breakfast were held at the bride's home.

After the festivities, the couple left in their automobile for a honeymoon in the Berkshire Mountains. Though the groom was behind the wheel of a different car from the one he was driving while intoxicated twenty-two years later on May 14, 1935, I wondered if the honeymoon car might have been a black Cadillac associated with the Killourey funeral home.

While I unearthed copious details about Thomas Killourey and his parents and his two wives and one daughter, I was saddened to learn that I would never find any living Killourey heirs. However, thanks to Connecticut State Prison records of inmate #13284, a.k.a. Thomas H. Killourey, I had descriptions of the day that ended Morty, Barbara, and Allen's lives, along with those of their grandmothers and my uncle Ruby. The descriptions are chilling. Of all the reports, the one that enrages me the most is the following description of the day and evening inmate #13284 spent on May 14, 1935.

As stated, Thomas H. Killourey's History of Offense in the Connecticut State Prison's records:

> The six occupants of the Blumenthal car had been to the Mount Sinai Hospital in Hartford, to visit David Halpert, father of the two Halpert children killed in the accident, who was suffering from heart trouble. He was the owner of the Chevrolet Sedan, Massachusetts Registration NO. 136932, operated by Reuben Blumenthal. It was traveling east on the state cement highway; width of cement, 16 feet, weather clear, highway dry. At this point there are three intersecting highways, Mansfield Road, Station Road, and the South Windham Road. A tire mark from the

left front Wheel of the Blumenthal car indicated that this wheel was at least 1 foot 5 inches south of the right of the center of the highway at the time of the accident.

Thomas Killourey, the accused, is 43 years old, married, lives at 260 Jackson Street, in Willimantic and conducts an undertaking business at 36 Union Street in Willimantic.

On the morning of May 14th, about 9 a.m. Killourey, with Dennis Haggerty and Joseph Osso, left Willimantic for Putnam in Killourey's Cadillac sedan car, to attend a session of the Superior Court where Mr. Osso was to have his final hearing on a petition for citizenship. Killourey and Haggerty went to act as witnesses for Osso. They attended the Superior Court and after a hearing, the petition for citizenship was denied by the Court. Mr. Killourey's own actions in court resulted in his being ordered to leave the courtroom by Deputy Sheriff McGarry, who testified before the Coroner that Mr. Killourey was under the influence of liquor, that his breath smelled of liquor and his eyes were blood-shot and he had a vacant stare. This was noted at 11:30 a.m.

All three men went to the Putnam Inn for dinner, there having several glasses of beer each. Coming out of the Inn, Mr. Killourey and companions met Curtis Dean, Clerk of the Superior

Court, who testified before the Coroner that Mr. Killourey was under the influence of liquor, that he smelled liquor on his breath, that he had a dazed look in his eyes and that he spoke incoherently.

The three men returned to the court house in the afternoon and it was noted by several other witnesses that they were all decidedly under the influence of liquor. Then they went to the Chickering Tavern, on Union Street, Putnam, where they had more beer to drink. They did shopping and indulged again. They left Putnam for Willimantic at about 4:15, in Killourey's car, Killourey driving. The next stop was at Sherman's Corner, Chaplin where they all had another glass of beer each. Leaving there for Willimantic, all three rode in the front seat, Killourey driving. Sherman's Corner is about one and one half miles east of North Windham Center, the scene of the accident.

As Mr. Killourey left Sherman's Corner, he was followed by a car containing Capt. James. S. Thompson, age 45, of Stratford, CT, Army Reserve, Officer in Command of 103rd Company.

<u>Captain Thomas states:</u> "After we left Sherman's Corner where we had stopped for gasoline, we noticed a Cadillac Sedan about two to three hundred feet ahead of us, traveling about 35

miles per hour. We noticed three men in the front seat. We attempted to pass this car several times but the Cadillac zigzagged to the left and right and it was dangerous to pass, so we dropped back to see what was happening. The Cadillac forced two cars off the highway which were coming in the opposite direction, nearly crashing into them, and in several instances, nearly hit the highway fence on the right side of the highway. All in our car came to the conclusion that the operator of the Cadillac was intoxicated.

As the Cadillac went down the slight grade into North Windham Center, its speed increased to about 50 miles per hour, increasing the distance between it and our car. As the Cadillac passed the Windham Line, it was zigzagging. I remarked, "I bet he hits the next car." At this time there appeared another car, coming in the opposite direction which was traveling on its right side of the State Highway. As the Cadillac approached this other, a Chevrolet, the Cadillac suddenly swerved to the left, directly in the path of the Chevrolet. The Chevrolet was on its right side of the highway.

As the two cars hit head on, a woman was thrown out onto the highway, both fronts rose into the air and the Cadillac pushed the Chevrolet around to the north side of the highway, both cars facing the Natchaug Grocery Store and Post Office. We stopped our car and went to the scene of the accident. There we found several people had been killed or injured. We first assisted the people in the Chevrolet. I talked with Mr. Blumenthal, asked him where he lived. He later gave the names of the children and other occupants of the car to Dr. Simonds and said they came from visiting someone in a hospital. I assisted Mr. Killourey, who was badly injured and hanging out of his car, head down on left running board, his feet caught in the gear shift. I noticed an open bottle on the left running board of Killourey's car containing what I assumed to be a small amount of liquor. I picked it up and put [it] on the front floor boards. I was sitting on the right side of Stanley Kogut, driver of our car and had a clear vision everything that transpired."

Kogut corroborated Thompson's account. He also talked with Reuben Blumenthal, who stated, "That fellow ran right into me." Kogut also saw the whiskey bottle and smelled liquor on Killourey's breath.

The Accident occurred on a straight road in Windham, Connecticut.

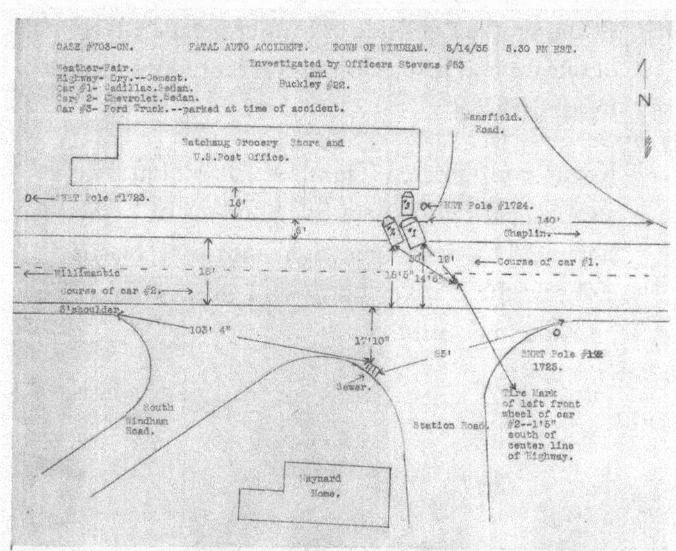

A map from the police report.

Thomas Killourey's Cadillac, left, and Ruby Blumenthal's Chevrolet, right, after the two cars hit head-on and came to rest. Visible near the Chevrolet, by the passenger side front bumper, is a woman's shoe. The combined force of the collision was like hitting a brick wall head-on at 85 mph.

The force of the impact physically separated both cars' chassis from their frames.

"That fellow ran right into me." How many times I read that one particular line and marveled at what those six words meant. My uncle Ruby was mere hours away from death, his body fatally broken and in indescribable pain. He saw the shattered lifeless bodies of his five relatives, including his son and his mother, and yet he spoke those words. My uncle needed to acknowledge the horrific crime of "that fellow" before he disappeared from the face of this earth.

While I felt a heartbreaking pride in the strength and determination of my dying uncle, few words exist to describe my rage as I read the description of the hours Thomas Killourey spent before the Accident. I managed, however, to compare those hours to the day spent by the occupants of the Blumenthal car. My relatives had driven from Providence to Mt. Sinai Hospital in Hartford, Connecticut, to cheer up the father of two of the children in that car. There was no police report of how they had spent those hours, but I never needed any police report to assure me there had to have been smiles and love and most probably relatively quiet voices as all six of them, the three young children as well as their uncle and grandmothers, told him stories of their past few days, as well as simply sitting beside his hospital bed, content merely to be in his presence. I also expected that the two grandmothers arrived carrying bundles of homemade items for the patient and the children. Stuffed cabbage, richly flavored soups, cookies, and brownies, as well as thick breads, perhaps still warm from their Providence ovens.

Leaving Dave late that afternoon could not have been easy for the visitors, but there had to be the promise of another visit, very soon. I could almost see Dave's gentle mother, Jennie Halpert, kissing him tenderly as she left the room, her face etched with worry about the health of her son. While their hugs would have been a bit less gentle, the three kids had to have been excited over the fact that they had been in a hospital and seen all kinds of fancy, noisy machines and friendly nurses. My grandmother Rose was probably efficiently ushering the children out of the room without their disturbing any of the equipment, while kissing her daughter and assuring Dave the kids were doing just fine. It is far too painful to try to imagine anything else about that visit, especially the farewell, which was final in every way possible.

For Killourey and the two occupants of his black Cadillac, every printed word about their activities before they ended the lives of those who walked out of Dave Halpert's hospital room is infuriating as well as agonizing to relate.

As the History of Offense report stated:

> Charles Worth and Howard corroborate Captain Thompson. Several witnesses were at the scene of the accident.
>
> Evelyn Kelley, 17, North Windham: Fast speed of Cadillac just before accident. Did not see accident but heard crash.
>
> Mrs. Bertha Fuller, 52, same as her daughter Evelyn Kelley, noting fast speed of the Cadillac just before accident. She did not see accident, but heard crash.
>
> Charles Tucker, 46, North Windham, saw accident, Chevrolet on right side of the highway, Cadillac on wrong side.

Officer Kenneth W. Stevens, Office James A. Buckley, Stafford Barracks: Officers who investigated this accident, who prepared a map and had photographs taken of accident, showing location of cars and tire marks on highway, and have in their possession, the bottle containing small amount of liquor.

On May 30th, 1935, the accused was arrested and charged with gross negligence with a motor vehicle so as to cause death. The arrest was made by officer Stevens, of the Stafford barracks, Killourey being held under $5000 bond, which was furnished, allowing him to be at liberty.

On June 26th, 1935, the accused was held criminally responsible, by Deputy Coroner Louis A. Woisard, of Danielson, for the deaths of the six persons killed in this accident. The Coroner found that the accused was operating his motor vehicle in a grossly negligent manner and while under the influence of intoxicating liquor.

June 29th, 1935-Willimantic Police Court. Accused through his attorney filed a demurrer. Demurrer overruled, accused bound over to Superior Court under $5000 bond which was furnished.

The accused has no previous record, but has the reputation of being a free user of intoxicants.

I emphasized that last sentence of the official report as proof that drinking while driving or at any other moment in his life was not unusual for Killourey.

Killourey's History of Offense record also includes the following personal histories of the deceased to indicate the amount of sorrow caused by Killourey's drunk driving. Reading and rereading each one, I had some small, very small, measure of satisfaction in knowing that these short statements are a permanent part of Killourey's criminal history. I wondered if he heard them repeated in a courtroom or read them himself. Of course, I had no idea; one could only hope. Unlike the victims, those brief descriptions were present in his courtroom.

<u>Mrs. Rose Blumenthal</u>: Age 62 years—mother of nine (9) children. Youngest child now 19 years of age. Two of them were living with her before her death. They are Hyman, age 19 years, and Bella [my mother], age 24 years. Her husband, Phillip, age 70 years, is still living in Providence at 7 Overhill Road. She was well known for personal charities and soliciting for organizations around Providence, R.I. Watched and cared for each child individually, and lived only for the good that she could do for others. Mourned by her husband, who has just reached the age of 70. They have never suffered any loss of this kind before.

<u>Mrs. Jennie Halpert</u>: Age 62 years. Mother of nine (9) children—She lived with two sons, whom she kept house for at 111 Eleventh St, Providence. She spent her entire life bringing up her children and taking care of them. She kept house for Edward O. Halpert and his brother Murray Halpert, at the above address; since her death this home has been broken up and the furniture disposed of. Is greatly mourned for by her family. Did a lot in the community for all organizations in and about Providence and was liked by all.

<u>Reuben Blumenthal</u>: Age 39 years. Married, wife living at 15 Taft Street Providence, R.I. One son Morton, who was also killed in this accident. He was in business in Pawtucket, in the liquor business. Since his death, his wife states that business has fallen considerably and it is hard for her to get along. He was well liked in the town of Pawtucket and in Providence, where he was active in the Jewish War Veterans. He was a World War Veteran. A good husband and father. His wife still mourns the loss of both husband and only son.

<u>Morton Blumenthal</u>: Age 12 years, son of Mr. and Mrs. Reuben Blumenthal. Attended the Junior High School, Pawtucket, R.I; was a bright boy in his studies and was well liked by all his playmates. Active in all school work. Never suffered ill health. Is the only son. His mother was an invalid for a period of one year after his birth. She was left in such a condition that it will endanger her life if she should attempt to bear children again. She has lost her only support—and has to hire two other persons to aid her in the business that formerly was conducted by her and her husband, before his death. Due to her inability to take care of the business, she has lost considerably.

<u>Barbara Ruth Halpert</u>: Age 10 years. Good health, never has been sick and was a bright young girl. Well liked in the community and always willing to help. Attended the Summit Avenue School, Providence, and is in the 5th grade.

This exquisite photo of Barbara, age two in 1927, was taken by her father, Dave Halpert, exactly eight years before Barbara was killed in the Accident. Note Dave's beautiful calligraphy.

Alan (Allen) Abot Halpert: Age Six years. Brother of Barbara, never had been sick, good bright young boy, attended the Summit Avenue School, Providence, in the 1st grade. Was well liked by others and always had a cheerful smile for everyone.

Due to the death of Rose Blumenthal, it has caused the family, Mr. and Mrs. David Halpert, who lost their two children, to break up their home and come to take care of Mr. Phillip Blumenthal who is reaching Old Age and cannot care for himself, and at this time is grief stricken by the loss of his wife and son, his two grandsons and granddaughter.

There was so little said about the three young children whose lives had barely begun. My aunt Etta and my uncle Dave, along with my mother and my aunt Jeanette, could have written pages and pages about each child, all three older cousins I never met. Nor was there much in these reports about the two grandmothers, one who would have been my *bubbe* (affectionate Yiddish term for grandmother), for each of them had led a quiet life, defined in every way by her love for her family. There was a bit more about my uncle Ruby, whose death and that of his son so destroyed the life of his wife, Jeanette, who was no longer a wife and mother or even a daughter-in-law.

As clearly stated in *Windham County Superior Court State v. Thomas H. Killourey*: "This case is one of the worst automobile accidents in the State this year. It occurred at North Windham, CT at about 5:30 p.m. May 14, 1935. One motor vehicle was operated by Thomas H. Killourey, the accused, of Willimantic, Connecticut; the other operated by Reuben S. Blumenthal, of Providence, Rhode Island. The six relatives, occupants of the Blumenthal car, died from the following injuries." Reading about each injury was pure torture, yet I felt it crucial that I did that, along with sharing it with others. It is the very least I can do for my relatives' suffering. It is an essential part of my shedding the light on the man who took their lives from those who loved them. To quote the writer, activist, and Holocaust survivor Elie Wiesel, who, of course, was talking about the millions of lives that were lost in the Holocaust, "To forget the dead would be akin to killing them a second time." Indeed, while there is no possible comparison to six deaths on a Connecticut highway to the atrocities in the concentration camps, I have no intention of killing my six relatives again, so I present the following details of the injuries suffered by each victim of the Accident:

Reuben S. Blumenthal — age 39, 15 Taft Avenue, Providence, RI. Fracture of skull and fracture of both legs and arms, died at Windham Community Memorial Hospital, shortly before midnight of the same day.

Morton Blumenthal — age 12, 15 Taft Avenue, Providence, RI, fractured skull and fracture of left leg. Died at the scene of the accident.

Mrs. Rose Blumenthal — age 62, 7 Overhill Road, Providence, RI. Fractured skull. Died at the scene of the accident.

Mrs. Jennie Blumenthal — age 62, 111 Eleventh Street, Providence, RI. Fractured skull. Died soon after admittance to Windham, Community Hospital, Willimantic.

Barbara Halpert — age 10, 460 Arnold Street, New Bedford, Mass. Fractured skull, severe lacerations of both knees. Died at the scene of the accident.

Allen Halpert — age 6, 460 Arnold Street, New Bedford, Mass. Fractured skull, base of brain, and broken neck. Died at the scene of the accident.

What painful, hideous deaths, unnecessary and unforgiveable!

There were, of course, injuries to the occupants of Killourey's car, all of whom were inebriated, which may possibly have lessened their pain:

Mr. Killourey — Contusion of the brain, concussion of the skull, compound fracture of the nose, fracture of the third and fourth ribs, right side; puncture of the lung, lacerations of both hands, and multiple contusions about the body. Discharged from Windham Community Memorial Hospital May 29, 1935.

Dennis Haggerty — lacerations on face and hands, abrasions on knee caps.

Joseph Osso — lacerations of face and hands, abrasions on both legs and shins.

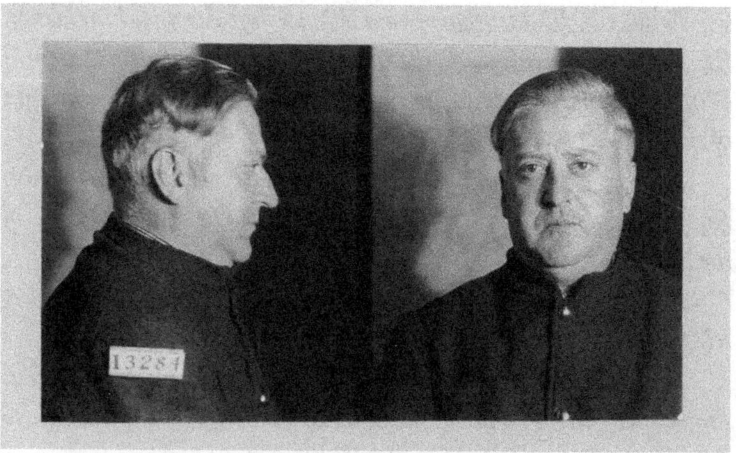

Thomas Killourey's mugshot. Inmate #13284.

They survived, eventually perfectly intact.

There were so many upsetting and infuriating incidents in the rest of Inmate #13284's 128-page prison file, but several angered me more than others. For example, following is a note written by Killourey, the recipient unknown: "I have made a promise to myself that I would never take another drink. I wouldn't go through this ordeal again for a million dollars."[1]

Indeed, Mr. Killourey's "ordeal" involved a fourteen-day stay in the same hospital where two of his victims died. As well as a seventeen-month stay in a Connecticut prison. He lost his driver's license, for a little while, anyhow, before it was restored. He lost his embalming license, too, but, that, too, was restored.

---

1 Note that there was no such thing as "vehicular homicide" in 1935. The only laws on the books were concerning operating a motor vehicle while intoxicated. There is still no national law, and three states do not have vehicular homicide statutes to this day.

What did not come back, despite Killourey's "ordeal," were my six relatives.

Another letter in #13284's prison file did not surprise me. This one was in his Connecticut State Prison Parole Department file. In describing the inmate's social attitude, it was written: "Admits guilt, but says he thought he was able to drive."

How could anyone who had consumed even half of the liquor imbibed by Killourey hours before he took the wheel of his car think "he was able to drive"?

On September 30, 1935, shortly after arriving at Connecticut State Prison, inmate #13284's psychiatric record offers yet another infuriating description of the Accident. In this report, "Killourey says that he had been drinking some beer prior to the accident. It occurred at a crossroads. Says the other car had pulled over to the left and was in his way when the accident occurred. Six people were killed."

"Drinking some beer"? "Had pulled over to the left"? "Was in his way"? The only truth reported in that statement was that "six people were killed," and by a very drunk driver.

As for inmate #13284's parole situation, two letters appeared in his prison file. The first was written on February 1, 1937, a little more than eighteen months after the Accident:

> To The State Board of Prisons
> Connecticut State Prison
> Wethersfield,Conn.
>
> Gentlemen:
>
> I am writing on behalf of Mr. Thomas Killourey, whom I understand is to appear before you Wednesday of this week.

> I have known Mr. Killourey ever since he was a boy, and I always found him to be honest, reliable, and very charitable, and well-liked by all who knew him. He is an undertaker, and up to the time of the unfortunate auto accident which sent him to prison, he was a highly respected business man conducting a business established by his father years ago.
>
> I feel that Mr. Killourey has paid his debt to society and is worthy of parole, and if paroled it will not be long before he will again become a respected member of this community.
>
> Sincerely yours,
> Thomas F. Grady
> Chief of Police

The words "unfortunate accident which sent him to prison" should have read: "Unfortunate accident which sent six innocent people to their deaths."

Following is the response to Grady's letter written three days later, on February 4, 1937:

> Mr. Thomas F. Grady
> Chief of Police,
> Willimantic, Conn.
>
> My dear Chief Grady:
>
> I received your letter yesterday morning with reference to the case of Thomas Killourey, who appeared before the Board of Parole yesterday.

> I am sure you will be pleased to know that Killourey was granted a pardon, and will probably be released upon the expiration of his minimum term, February 23rd.
>
> Thanking for your kind interest in this case, I am
>
> Very truly yours,
> Warden

It should also be worth noting that in Killourey's obituary, fifteen years later in 1952, the deceased was described as "a first cousin" of Police Chief Lieutenant John Killourey of Willimantic.

Another letter, this one less than a year later, on January 31, 1938, was written by Thomas H. Killourey to his parole office:

> Dear Sir
>
> I would like to make application for a discharge.
>
> Have been home since February 23, 1937 and have made every effort to live up to all off (sic) your regulations.
>
> Respectfully yours,
> Thomas H. Killourey

Not unexpectedly, a month later, Killourey received the following letter:

> Dear Sir:
>
> It is with a great deal of pleasure that we send you this final discharge and release from parole supervision.

It must be some satisfaction to you to know that you have kept your word that you gave to the Board of Parole, and merited the confidence they placed in you.

If you continue to do right, you will never forget it.

With best wishes for the future, I am

Very truly yours,
Warden

Thus, on March 2, 1938, a full nine months before the parole should have ended its minimum time of November 11, 1938, and less than three years since a drunken Killourey drove his huge Cadillac into my relatives' modest Chevrolet and killed all six of them, inmate #13284 had successfully paid his debt to society, served his eighteen-month term in jail and his year of parole, and was now a completely free man, with the instruction "continue to do right, you will never regret it."

While I never found any notice of subsequent crimes committed by the Killourey, I cannot help but wonder if the remaining years of his life were, in any way, affected by the events of May 14, 1935. Did he ever think of contacting the Blumenthal family to issue a sincere or, perhaps, an insincere regret over how his drunken actions on that day had affected their lives? Was there ever any discussion of a civil suit filed by the Blumenthal family against Killourey? Sadly, I believe the answers to both questions would be a resounding no.

Many years after the Accident I had an experience that showed me how deeply an event, at which time I had not yet been born, affected me. In April 1985, I was called to jury duty in a Salem, Massachusetts, courtroom. While I wasn't thrilled to be doing my civic duty, I was certainly not dreading it. As it turned out I was selected for the jury that would be formed that day and even chosen foreman of the jury. Feeling a bit proud of that distinction, I marched into the courtroom with the other eleven members of the jury, plus the several substitutes. We were seated when the judge explained that the case involved an eighteen-year-old male, who had been arrested a few months earlier, driving while intoxicated. When I glanced at the first row of the courtroom and saw a rather pleasant looking teenager seated between his nicely dressed parents and his lawyer, something snapped inside me. All I wanted was to approach that young man and shout into his face, "Do you have any idea what you might have done that evening when you drove while drunk? You could have killed an innocent family of six, including three children, because you went to a party and drank way too much beer. You might have ended up with a broken arm or some stitches in your face and spent a few years in prison, and your parents could have lost a lot of money in civil suits brought by the families of those six people who died in the accident. And you would have to go through the rest of your life knowing you killed six people. Unless, of course, you were not only stupid but incredibly heartless and insensitive and could just shrug off what you did and go back to your everyday living."

By some miracle, I did not utter any of those words, but as tears filled my eyes, I softly asked the judge if I could speak to him for a moment before the opening arguments were heard. He kindly led me into his anteroom where, unsuccessfully holding back tears, I told him I did not think I could be a fair and unbiased juror for this case. When he asked me why, I responded,

"My grandmother, my uncle, and three of my young cousins were killed by a drunk driver."

"I am so sorry for the pain your family must be suffering," the judge gently responded. "When did this happen?"

I waited just a second before I answered, "Fifty years ago, almost to the day." The judge appeared a bit surprised but quickly regained his composure, thanked me for my service, and excused me from the case.

After I walked the short distance from the courthouse to my car, I waited a long time before I felt composed enough to drive home. I understood only too well that there would always be drunk drivers on the road, and what I had done had certainly not prevented any accidents. Perhaps had I stayed on the jury and did all I could to make sure that young man received the strongest sentence possible I might have prevented him from getting behind the wheel of a car for some time, but I would have been punishing him for Thomas Killourey's crime and obvious lack of sensitivity. How fair would that have been? Still, I suffered a fair amount of guilt for my action that still remains with me today. I wish I could have somehow gotten my message and my story to that defendant. Perhaps the story I am writing today might have the effect of reaching one such kid who stops drinking long before he gets behind the wheel of his car. One can only hope.

Not surprisingly, Killourey attempted to have his automobile license restored mere weeks after his release from prison in February 1937. When this application for his license renewal was refused by his parole agent, he was informed, "This may not seem fair to you, but it is the law; it is one of the consequences of your having been here [prison]. Please let me know if there is anything further that we can do."

The following letter was written by one of Killourey's acquaintances, William J. Fitzgerald, a US representative from Connecticut's Second Congressional District, to another of Killourey's acquaintances, Alton T. Minor, the mayor of New London, Connecticut, in 1934. This letter, sent less than nine months after Killourey's parole, talking about "this man slipping back into old habits," makes one wonder if the former inmate #13284 had actually mended his bad habits.

At the congressman's request, if the mayor were to hear any unkind words about his and Fitzgerald's mutual friend, he would summon the "lovely" Mrs. Killourey to his office so she could explain that these "vicious rumors" about her husband were simply a "frame-up" from an undertaker competitor. Personally, although I was a bit prejudiced, I tended to believe the rumors, but I would not be surprised if some campaign donations might have been spent trying to get the congressman, as well as the mayor, to ignore such gossip.

Every time I read William's letter, I found myself muttering nasty words about "the misery and suffering" that might have been brought upon Killourey's "lovely wife and family" if he had been found "slipping back into his old habits." I never knew if that happened for more than eighty years since the Accident; I sadly discovered that all those directly involved are long gone, including any direct relatives of Killourey.

Indeed, the fact that helped me stop dwelling on what I would never know was the knowledge that the descendants of the Blumenthal and Halpert families still walked the earth. Undeniably, we still carried the scars of what happened on May 14, 1935, because one man decided to drink too much and get behind the wheel. Far more importantly, we carried the memories of those we would never stop loving, while at the same time, feeling immense gratitude for every Halpert and Blumenthal who would continue to be a vital part of our lives. Our little clan was still alive and growing. How lucky were we?

My story of Killourey was finished. According to the legal system, he paid for his crime, despite the fact that even at the time the penance seemed lacking. it. In the present, of course, the punishment for a Connecticut drunk driver whose intoxication took the lives of six people is far greater than eighteen months. It is considered a class C felony, manslaughter in the second degree with a motor vehicle, with a possible sentence from one to ten years in prison, up to $10,000 in fines, or a combination of both. A conviction would also result in a mandatory one-year driver's license suspension and the requirement that an ignition interlock breathalyzer device be installed on the vehicle for at least two years following the reinstatement of driving privileges.

Yet, depicting the actions of the driver of the car who killed my relatives, try as I might, I could not ignore the distressing fact that his behavior could rightly be traced to the actions and livelihood of the relatives of the victims of the Accident. Blaming Killourey was far too easy, for he drank and drove and was guilty of vehicular homicide. Yet, the root of his crime was unquestionably the alcohol with which he recklessly guzzled on May 14, 1935.

There was no sense denying the painful connection of my family to Thomas H. Killourey's unforgivable crime. For a vital and negative part of my family's history was that we were bootleggers and liquor store owners who manufactured and sold the booze that Killourey imbibed the day he killed my relatives. Prohibition, begun in 1920, thanks to the Eighteenth

Amendment, had ended in 1933, two years before the Accident, and we Blumenthals had surely broken the law ourselves. But this is an important and undeniable story to be explained later.

CHAPTER FOUR
Citizen Osso

While some questions about the Accident haunted me, it was Joseph Osso whose name held a special significance to me. After all, if Killourey had not driven his big, black Cadillac to the Putnam Court on the morning of May 14, 1935, in order to stand as a witness for Osso's petition for US citizenship, my relatives would not have died later that afternoon. Of course, if Killourey had not drunk himself into an altered state that entire day the crash probably would not have happened. But in my obsession about the specifics of that fatal crash, however, it was Joseph Osso who stood as another center of interest.

Who was Joseph Osso? What I was able to unearth about this crucial character in my family's story was that, in 1917, according to the military census of that year, Osso, an immigrant from what is now Lebanon[2] then aged around twenty-three, was a weaver and a carpenter, was five feet five inches tall, weighed 140 pounds, was relatively handsome and single, and had six people dependent on him for support. He had entered the United States at New York City from Cherbourg, France, five years earlier on June 30, 1912, at the age of eighteen on the SS *Philadelphia* under the name Joseph Kawam.

Indeed, life had to have been difficult for Osso when he immigrated to the States, perhaps knowing little English. He had to support his mother and three sisters. Sources related that the majority of Syrian and Lebanese immigrants came here between 1890 and 1920, with an interruption during World War I, when the French and British enforced a severe sea blockade off the coast of Lebanon, then part of the Ottoman Empire. Osso was fortunate to have left Damascus in 1912. There was another short-lived spike in immigration between 1920 and 1923, when control of the region passed into French hands after the carving up of the Ottoman Empire by the League of Nations. In 1924, the passage of restrictive immigration laws in the United States effectively reduced that second wave to a trickle.

According to Osso's 1917 military draft card, he never performed any military service in his native country of Syria and would be excused from doing so in his new homeland. After all, as his draft card further explained, he wrenched his ankle once, could not ride a horse or handle a team (of horses, I imagined,

[2] It gets a little complicated when untangling Joseph Osso's nationality as listed on various pieces of paperwork, mostly having to do with the League of Nations' partition of the Ottoman Empire after World War I. Osso, born in Damascus, Syria, was a Syrian national by today's standards. He came to the US from Ottoman-held territory in 1912 by way of France, but by 1935, territories that make up present-day Syria and Lebanon were controlled by France before becoming independent nations.

as opposed to a baseball or football team), drive an automobile, ride a bicycle, operate a wireless, or handle a boat; he had no experience with high-speed marine gasoline engines and was not a good swimmer. No one in the US military, not even in 1917 when the US entered World War I, chose him for their team.

In the 1940 US census, Joseph Osso (state as being born Joseph Kawam, in Syria in 1894) would have been around forty-six years old, making him forty-one on May 14, 1935. In that 1940 Census report, his citizenship was listed as "alien," so he had obviously been unable to gain US citizenship, which was the reason he'd traveled to Putnam, Connecticut, on May 14, 1935. In some way, according to my far-from-reasonable reasoning, his denial of citizenship played a vital part in that fatal crash.

According to the 1920 US Census, Joseph Osso had a wife, Mary (Hellpe) Osso, who had arrived in the States from Syria in 1908 at the age of seven. Mary, born in 1901, was seven years younger than Joseph. Joseph and Mary married on August 29, 1918, when Mary was seventeen, and soon had two children: Alice, born in 1919, and Louis, born in 1920. In 1920, Joseph was a candy maker. His draft registration a year later showed him living at 54 Prospect Street in Willimantic, the accompanying photo showing him with black hair, dark eyes (brown), and slender build. He supported his mother and three sisters under age thirteen in addition to his wife and two children. That certainly seemed like a lot of responsibility for one man.

I had no doubt that Joseph Osso was hardworking and did everything he could to support all his family members. Every report I found about him depicted a man who often worked at more than one job at a time and who wanted, more than anything, to become a US citizen. Even I had to accept the fact that accusing him of being responsible for the fatal Blumenthal crash made no sense. I couldn't hold anything against him, except that I wished he had asked anyone besides Thomas Killourey to drive him to the Putnam Courthouse.

On April 13, 1929, Joseph Osso made his first official declaration of his attempt to become a US citizen.

By 1935, things had changed drastically in Joseph's personal life. Joseph, now thirty-five and working as a storekeeper, was divorced. His ex-wife, Mary, according to his petition for citizenship, "now resides at Norwich State Asylum." The hospital, established in 1904, had a population of 2,422 in 1930, climbing to 2,918 by 1939. Many negative stories about the Norwich State Asylum were reported, including a hot water heater explosion in 1919 that killed two employees, another employee killed trying to cross the road, a nurse killing herself at her home, and multiple patients dying during their sentences or while undergoing treatment. Heaven only knows what happened to Mary Hellpe Osso to put her in the asylum, or what happened to her while she was there.

One of Joseph's census reports shows that, before the time of the Accident in 1935, he had had a housekeeper, later identified as Phoebe Chapman, to help with the two children, most likely because Mary was in the asylum at that time. Life could not have been easy for Joseph at that time, and obviously he had hoped that becoming a US citizen would help him as well as his family.

ORIGINAL
(To be retained by clerk)

UNITED STATES OF AMERICA

PETITION FOR CITIZENSHIP

No. 1894

To the Honorable the Superior *Court of* Windham County *at* Windham

The petition of Joseph Kawam Windham, Conn hereby filed, respectfully shows:

(1) My place of residence is 81 Jackson St., Willimantic. (2) My occupation is store proprietor

(3) I was born in Damascus Syria on Jan.3, 1894 My race is Syrian

(4) I declared my intention to become a citizen of the United States on Apr.13, 1929 in the Superior Court of Windham County at Willimantic, Conn.

(5) I am Divorced. The name of my former wife Mary Hellpe we were married on Aug.29, 1918 at Pawtucket R.I.; She was born at Damascus Syria on July 1, 1901; entered the United States at New York on Aug. 10, 1908 for permanent residence therein, and now resides at Norwich State Hospital (Asylum) I have 2 children, and the name, date, and place of birth, and place of residence of each of said children are as follows:

Alice born May 15, 1919 born Willimantic, Conn., resides Willimantic, Conn.

Louis born Dec.17, 1920 At Willimantic, Conn., resides Willimantic, Conn.

(6) My last foreign residence was Damascons Syria I emigrated to the United States of America from Cherbourg France My lawful entry for permanent residence in the United States was at New York, N.Y., under the name of Joseph Kawam on June 30, 1912, on the vessel Philadelphia as shown by the certificate of my arrival attached hereto.

(7) I am not a disbeliever in or opposed to organized government or a member of or affiliated with any organization or body of persons teaching disbelief in or opposed to organized government. I am not a polygamist nor a believer in the practice of polygamy. I am attached to the principles of the Constitution of the United States and well disposed to the good order and happiness of the United States. It is my intention to become a citizen of the United States and to renounce absolutely and forever all allegiance and fidelity to any foreign prince, potentate, state, or sovereignty, and particularly to

The Present Sovereignty in Syria and the Lebanon

of whom (which) at this time I am a subject (or citizen), and it is my intention to reside permanently in the United States. (8) I am able to speak the English language. (9) I have resided continuously in the United States of America for the term of five years at least immediately preceding the date of this petition, to wit, since June 30, 1912 and in the County of Windham this State, continuously next preceding the date of this petition, since August 1913, being a residence within said county of at least six months next preceding the date of this petition.

(10) I have not heretofore made petition for citizenship, on at

Attached hereto and made a part of this, my petition for citizenship, are my declaration of intention to become a citizen of the United States, certificate from the Department of Labor of my said arrival, and the affidavits of the two verifying witnesses required by law.

Wherefore, I, your petitioner, pray that I may be admitted a citizen of the United States of America.

I, your aforesaid petitioner being duly sworn, depose and say that I have read this petition and know the contents thereof; that the same is true of my own knowledge except as to matters herein stated to be alleged upon information and belief, and that as to those matters I believe it to be true; and that this petition is signed by me with my full, true name.

(Complete and true signature of petitioner)

AFFIDAVITS OF WITNESSES

Dennis F. Haggerty, occupation letter carrier residing at Willimantic, Conn., and Thomas H. Killourey, occupation undertaker residing at Willimantic, Conn. each being severally, duly, and respectively sworn, deposes and says that he is a citizen of the United States of America; that he has personally known and has been acquainted in the United States with Joseph Kawam, the petitioner above mentioned, since 1920 and that to his personal knowledge the petitioner has resided in the United States continuously preceding the date of filing this petition, of which this affidavit is a part, to wit, since the date last mentioned, and at Willimantic, in the County of Windham this State, in which the above-entitled petition is made, continuously since 1920, and that he has personal knowledge that the petitioner is and during all such periods has been a person of good moral character, attached to the principles of the Constitution of the United States, and well disposed to the good order and happiness of the United States, and that in his opinion the petitioner is in every way qualified to be admitted a citizen of the United States.

Dennis F. Haggerty (Signature of witness) (Signature of witness)

Subscribed and sworn to before me by the above-named petitioner and witnesses in the office of the Clerk of said Court at Windham Conn. this 31st day of January, Anno Domini 1935. I hereby certify that certificate of arrival No. 1 142003 from the Department of Labor, showing the lawful entry for permanent residence of the petitioner above named, together with declaration of intention No. 2703 of such petitioner, has been by me filed with, attached to, and made a part of this petition on this date.

Curtis Dean
Clerk. (SEAL)

By Asst. Clerk.

No. 41245

Form 2204–L–A
U. S. DEPARTMENT OF LABOR
IMMIGRATION AND NATURALIZATION SERVICE

Thomas Killourey was driving his Cadillac into Willimantic, Connecticut, because he'd agreed to appear as a character witness for the citizenship petition of Joseph Osso. Mr. Osso died in 1954 and never did become a US citizen. Perhaps showing up drunk before the judge was not such a good idea.

The 1930 census reveals that Joseph's daughter Alice was ten and a "boarder" on 38 Jackson Street in Willimantic, Windham, Connecticut. She was not in school at that time but knew how to read and write. Ten years later, in the 1940 US census, Alice was twenty, single, and living on 4A Lauren Hill Road in Norwich or New London, Connecticut. She had completed her third year of high school but had not graduated, and worked fifty-four hours in the week prior to the census and, most startlingly, worked as an attendant at the Norwich State Hospital for the Insane. While her mother was an inmate there, it is unlikely that Mary was a resident at the asylum when her daughter worked there as an attendant. Alice had another job, working as a twister, meaning she "twisted" yarns or threads in a textile mill. Despite my heavy sleuthing into her family's affairs, however, I had no way of knowing where or exactly when Alice did her "twisting."

By July 31, 1941, six years after the crash, in another declaration of intent to apply for citizenship, Joseph Osso weighed 190 pounds. His ex-wife, Mary, had recently passed away. He had tattoos on his right arm, and his two children, Alice and Louis, were twenty-two and twenty-one. Joseph certainly had not had an easy time, living without his wife when their children had been younger.

As I continued my research, however, Alice's life began to appear quite interesting. For instance, according to her 1936–2007 United States Social Security Applications and Claim Index, in 1976 Alice had been listed as Alice Gordon. By 1981 she was listed as Alice M. Head, living in Brooklyn, New York. On May 15, 1998, at age seventy-nine, Alice married Freddie H. Head, age seventy, who was a US Navy Vietnam War veteran. Freddie died a year after their marriage in 1999, and Alice, who died five years later in 2004, at age eighty-five, was buried next to him in Bourne, Massachusetts. Other marriages and husbands might well have existed before Freddie since Alice had also been listed as Alice Gordon. To complicate and complete my search into Alice Osso's life, a document from Ancestry.com declares that she had four children: Marilyn Coons, Cynthia Bowns, Barbara Jean Myrick, and Edwin Gordon. If any of these children are still alive, I wish them well, but my interest into their mother's life officially ended.

As for Alice's brother, Louis, born in Providence, Rhode Island, a year after Alice in 1920, I learned that he had enlisted in the army on October 30, 1942, in Hartford, Connecticut, becoming a private and serving as a warrant officer during World War II. His last residence before he died in 1991 was in Tolland, Connecticut. I have no idea whether he married and had a family, but I know that he lived for seventy-one years.

In a most ironic fact, it is highly possible that Joseph Osso was indeed shopping for a present for Alice, who turned sixteen on May 15, 1935, a day after the crash. Joseph could have made it home in time for a birthday celebration even though he ended up with "lacerations of face and hands, abrasions on both legs and shins." Except for his injuries suffered in the crash, plus the fact that he did not receive US citizenship, it might have been a fun-filled afternoon. If Joseph had been granted citizenship that day, perhaps he would have partied a bit longer in Putnam and not headed home to Willimantic at the same time Ruby Blumenthal was heading back to Providence, and my relatives would have lived.

An obituary in the *Willimantic Chronicle* on April 10, 1940, showed that "Mary Osso, 40, wife of Joseph Osso and former resident, died on April 9, in Norwich, of an extended illness. Besides her husband, she leaves a daughter Miss Alice Osso of

Norwich and a son Louis Osso of this city. She also leaves a sister Nellie Crom of Brooklyn, two brothers, Habid of Pawtucket, George Osso of Brooklyn, nephews and nieces." The one thing the obituary did not reveal was whether Mary died while still a resident of Norwich State Hospital, although it seems likely.

I have two final pieces of information about this pivotal man in my relatives' deaths. First, as of the 1950 census, Osso is listed as not being a naturalized citizen. The second is that Joseph Osso died at the age of sixty, on June 4, 1954. Coincidentally, Thomas Killourey, Osso's 1935 driver, also died at sixty at Windham Community Memorial Hospital two years earlier, in August 1952. Osso's funeral arrangements were handled, not unsurprisingly, considering where he lived and his relationship with Killourey, by Joseph Killourey Brothers, Inc. According to all accounts I have researched, he was still not a US citizen.

Thus ended, although not likely for the final time, my obsession with the obscure Joseph Osso and his vital, yet tangential role in the death of my six relatives.

CHAPTER FIVE
Blumenthals: Moving On

My Dear Mother Belle

The Blumenthal family had to move ahead after the Accident; they had no choice. Disbelief, denial, and rage were not options. Interestingly, this was halfway through the Great Depression, decades before Elisabeth Kübler-Ross had written about the five stages of grief. Life was not particularly easy for most people in 1935. Obviously, some members would be more grievously affected than others. For the most part, as a group, the family was solid and quite remarkable, not unlike their ancestors in Latvia. Somehow, some way, they conjured up the strength to live on.

For my mother, Belle, the horror of May 14, 1935, was intensified with her own personal heartbreaking crisis.

When I was growing up, I thought I knew my mother well. I always thought she was pretty, outgoing, fashionable, and my greatest cheerleader, wanting only the best for me and proud of any of my accomplishments. After my first book was published, she told me that she had a met a woman in our community who didn't know who I was. She'd been aghast and insisted the woman must live, in my mother's words, "in a closet without windows." There were times, of course, when I was certain she would drive me out of my mind, especially when she compared me to my cousin Gail, from my father's side, as opposed to the Blumenthal cousins whom I'd always adored and to whom I would love to be compared in any way possible. I even wrote a column for the *Boston Globe* titled "How Is It Humanly Possible for a 32-Year-Old Woman to Live 1½ Miles From Her 60-Year-Old Mother and Survive?" When the article was published before I had a chance to tone down some of the rather nasty examples I'd used, the timing could not have been worse for me. My husband and I had left for Italy the day before the article appeared, leaving my mother in charge of our two young sons. The day the story ran in the *Globe,* she sent me a telegram in Italy stating: "Darling, your adorable story appeared in this morning's *Globe.* Stay in Italy, children and furniture to follow." Yes, indeed, my mother had a terrific sense of humor and survived the family saga more determined than ever to keep on with her impossible task of trying to make me as perfect as the impeccable Gail.

As it turned out, there was a huge hidden chunk of my charming mother's life that was far from "impeccable." How I wish I had known all the details of my mother's life before I was born when she were still alive. Indeed, I never heard about my mother's secret until I was well into my forties. Coincidentally, it came to my attention in 1980 when my sister, Toby, and I were helping our parents clean out the basement of their home near the ocean in preparation for a move to a smaller condo. Among my mother's hundreds of family photos, each one carefully marked with a date and explanation in her neat handwriting, I found an old photo of my mother in a white wedding dress. There were no handwritten words on the photo. Most remarkably, the image of what I assumed to be the groom beside her had been carefully cut out from the photo. It was typical of my mother not to discard a photo in which she had photographed well. Indeed, she looked glowing and gorgeous in the groomless wedding photo.

I knew my parents had been married in a small service in a rabbi's study on December 25, 1938. My mother told me that times had been hard then, and she and my father did not want to miss a day of work for the wedding; thus, they chose Christmas Day to ensure no lost paycheck. I saw those photos, with my handsome father in a dark suit and my mother looking fashionable and happy in a lovely ankle-length dress. Yet, as my mother finally explained that day, forty years after that event, her first marriage had been a disaster, and two years after her divorce, she had met and married my father. That was all she told me and Toby, and so I left the subject alone, believing that first marriage had simply been a mistake.

In another old family photograph that I later discovered, I learned that my mother's first husband's name was Herman Kaufman and that he was very tall with thick hair cut in a sort of boxy look piled rather messily onto the top of his head. There was something weird about him, maybe the way he lurked above my mother, easily the tallest man in the photo, or the slight smirk on his face. Or maybe it was my own feelings lurking inside my mind, a vague sense of mistrust for this man, who was not my father, married to my mother. When I asked my mother for details about this man, she told me she had never seen him after the divorce and had thought he moved far away. But when she had been working in an upscale Providence dress shop a few years later, another employee, who was her close friend, told her that a well-dressed woman who introduced herself as Mrs. Herman Kaufman had just walked into the store. My mother, shocked by this news, had been working in the back room of the shop at the time, and exited quickly through a rear door, managing never to see this woman. When she told me this story she hadn't seemed all that upset, but that was all she ever revealed about Herman and their marriage. As I finally learned through painstaking research of court records, it had been far worse than a mistake, but rather a deep, dark, ugly secret kept by all members of the Blumenthal family.

Later on, when I related the story about my mother in the clothing shop to my cousin Mel, he was surprised that the Aunt Belle he remembered as the most feisty of the four Blumenthal sisters had just snuck out. "Quite unlike Belle," he said. "I would have thought she would have spilled the beans to the woman about her husband."

And "the beans" indeed, when I finally learned them, would not have easily been spilled in a clothing store. Anxious to learn as much as I could about my mother's first marriage, I questioned my other cousins to find out if they had ever heard any details about the obviously painful event. I learned quickly that they knew as little as I did. My cousin Fred, who was probably my mother's favorite and closest nephew, told me, "All I remember was that he was not a nice guy."

My cousin Mel added, "There was no discussion about him. He was cut out of most family photos. I am surprised the Bootleg Boys (his joking yet correct nickname for a few of our uncles) didn't kneecap him or worse."

As I discovered, however, finally unraveling the "deep, dark, family secret," Herman "Harry" Kaufman was far worse than "not a nice guy." And kneecapping him would not have been a bad idea. He was, actually, as my mother agonizingly discovered, a sexually disturbed man. The horror and shame that his behavior inflicted on my mother in 1935 had to have been almost unbearable, especially because her nightmare marriage and divorce happened during the same time the family was suffering the agony of the Accident. With her brother Lew and adored brother-in-law, Jack Brown, her sister Marion's husband, at her side, my mother managed to sue Kaufman for divorce, bravely relating the agony of her year-long marriage in a divorce court. Her obviously painful testimony included this statement about her husband: "On the day he left, he sent me a letter by Western Union in which he stated that he wasn't fit to live with decent people." From what I learned from her divorce record, that was an understatement.

While I understood how my mother never wanted to open the ugly wound caused by this marriage, I could not help but wish she had at some time in her life revealed it to me. Holding such a humiliating secret for the rest of her life could not have been without its consequences. It was a life-alternating event. Keeping it in the confines of her mind, watching her two daughters date and eventually marry men, she had to have worried about our choices. Then again, revealing the details of her hideous first marriage to Toby and me might have been too much for her. She'd suffered through the Accident, which was rarely, if ever, discussed, though it obviously affected her every time she drove a car. Yet, she most probably could never summon the inner strength it would have taken to talk about the man who humiliated her beyond description. In court, my mother revealed her humiliation, yet she recovered from the damages exacted by Kaufman's aberrant behavior. How fortunate my sister, Toby, and I were that she did.

When I discovered and read the following deposition presented nearly ninety years ago in a Providence courtroom, when bravery such as my mother's in revealing in a courtroom the truth about a sexually abnormal man was a gigantic act of courage, I wanted to say only, "Bravo, Mother. I could not be prouder of you." Although it never would have happened, that is the story I wish I had written for the *Boston Globe*. The fact that my mother needed two male family members to confirm her words in order to be believed by a judge merely increases my admiration for my mother's bravery.

Deposition of Belle R. Kaufman. Sworn.

Q. What is your address?

A. 7 Overhill Road, Providence, Rhode Island.

Q. How long have you lived in Rhode Island?

A. All my life.

Q. How old are you?

A. Twenty-four.

Q. You were married on the 28th day of October, 1934 in the City of Providence to Harry Kaufman?

A. Yes.

Q. You were married by Rev. Smith?

A. Yes.

Q. You have been residing in the City of Providence at 7 Overhill Road since the time of your marriage?

A. Yes.

Q. How has your husband been behaving since the time of your marriage?

A. Not very good.

Q. What do you mean by that?

A. Six weeks after we were married, he was arrested for making an assault upon the body of one Beatrice Toner in the Town of Lincoln. It was on December 7th, 1934. While he was operating an automobile in Lincoln, he "picked up" this Beatrice Toner and then indecently assaulted her. A warrant was sworn out against him by James Axon under the name of "Harry Kaufman" and he was arrested December 14th, 1934 at which time he was placed on probation. He admitted to me that he picked her up and that he did make a simple assault upon her; he promised me then that he would never do it again.

Q. Did he behave from then on?

A. For a couple of weeks.

Q. What happened after that?

A. Then he started to attack various female members of the family....attacking them in an indecent manner. About the 18th day of May, 1935 while I was in mourning with my family over the recent death of my mother, he indecently attacked a female member of the family.

Belle R. Kaufman

Officer's Fees on Citation,

Deposition of Jacob Brown. Sworn.

Q. What is your address?

A. 84 Ninth Street, Providence, Rhode Island.

Q. How long have you been a resident of Rhode Island?

A. All my life...I'm thirty-one years old.

Q. Are you related to the petitioner, Belle R. Kaufman?

A. Yes, a brother-in-law of Mrs. Kaufman.

Q. Since the date of the petitioner's marriage in October, 1934 to Harry Kaufman, the respondent, has she always behaved as a married woman should?

A. Yes.

Q. Of your own knowledge, do you know the respondent's behavior during their marriage?

A. Yes, it was very bad.

Q. What do you mean by that?

A. Well, they were only married a short while when he was arrested, December 14th, 1934, on a warrant sworn out by James Axon for assault on a girl by the name of Toner in Lincoln; he had "picked" her up while he was driving around that section and assaulted her.

Q. Do you know of any other bad behavior of the respondent?

A. Yes, while we were morning the death of my mother-in-law, on May 18th, 1935, he indecently attacked a woman of the family; he had attacked other members, women members, of the family from time to time.

Q. To your knowledge was the respondent guilty of any other behavior of this sort?

A. The day before he left his wife, he indecently attacked a woman member of the family, that was on July 11, 1935. Then a woman by the name of "Butterworth" of Warwick, Rhode Island turned a case against him over to her lawyer because of an indecent attack upon her, some sort of a settlement was made of this.

Q. To your knowledge, has the petitioner resided in Rhode Island for two years prior to the filing of her petition for divorce?

A. Yes, all her life.

Jacob Brown

Officer's Fees on Citation,

Deposition of Lewis J. Blumenthal. Sworn.

Q. What is your address?

A. 32 Ninth Street, Providence, Rhode Island.

Q. How long have you been a resident of Rhode Island?

A. All my life, thirty-six years old.

Q. You are related to the petitioner, Belle R. Kaufman?

A. Yes, a brother of the petitioner.

Q. The petitioner was married in October of 1934 to Harry Kaufman, the respondent, by Rev. Smith?

A. Yes.

Q. Since the date of the marriage of the petitioner has she always behaved as a married woman should?

A. Yes.

Q. How has the respondent behaved during the period of his marriage to the petitioner?

A. Very badly.

Q. What do you mean by that?

A. Shortly after they were married, about six weeks, a warrant was issued against him because of assault upon the body of one Beatrice Toner in the Town of Lincoln. It seems that while he was driving an automobile in Lincoln, he "picked up" this girl and then assaulted her. He was arrested December 14th, 1934 on this warrant sworn out against him by James Axon.

Q. Do you know of any other bad behavior on the part of the respondent?

A. For a while...after that he started to attack various women in the family. On May 18th, 1935, during the time my family were mourning the recent death of our mother, he indecently attacked one of the women of the family.

Q. To your knowledge, what other bad behavior has the respondent been guilty of?

A. Then he indecently attacked a woman member of the family on July 11, 1935, the day before he left. Then before that he had indecently attacked a woman by the name of "Butterworth" of Warwick, Rhode Island and after she turned the case over to her lawyer some sort of settlement was made.

Q. To your knowledge, the petitioner has resided in Rhode Island for two years prior to the filing of her petition for divorce?

A. Yes, all her life.

Lewis J Blumenthal

Officer's Fees on Citation,

State of Rhode Island and Providence Plantations.

Providence, sc.

To the Honorable Superior Court, next to be holden at Providence, within the County of Providence, on the first Monday of September *A. D. 19* 35

Respectfully Represents, Belle Ruth Kaufman

of Providence *in the County of* Providence *that* s*he resides in said County, and has been a domiciled inhabitant of said State and has resided therein for more than two years next before the preferring of this petition and is now a domiciled inhabitant of said State; that* s*he was married to* Hyman Kaufman alias Harry Kaufman *h*er *present* husband *on the* 25th *day of* October *A. D. 1*934*, and hath ever since on h*er *part demeaned h*er*self as a faithful* wife *and performed all the obligations of the marriage covenant; but that the said* Hyman Kaufman alias *hath violated the same in this that* *he hath* been guilty of extreme cruelty toward your petitioner and gross misbehavior and wickedness repugnant to and in violation of the marriage covenant, to wit, that he hath conducted himself improperly with women

*Wherefore your petitioner prays that a decree of this Court may be made divorcing h*er *from the bond of marriage, and from the said* Hyman Kaufman; and that she be allowed to resume her maiden name, Belle Ruth Blumenthal.

Belle Ruth Kaufman

Subscribed and sworn to before me at Pawtucket *in the County of* Providence *in said State of Rhode Island and Providence Plantations, this* 25th *day of* July *A. D. 19* 35.

Morris Resnick
Notary Public
~~Justice of the Peace.~~

I, Belle Ruth Kaufman *the petitioner above named, depose and say that the respondent* Hyman Kaufman alias Harry Kaufman *is without this State at* New York *in the State of* New York *and to the best of my information and belief may now be found at said* New York

~~*I, ... the petitioner above named, depose and say that the respondent ...., is without this State, and that I have no information or belief as to the resident of the respondent or where may be found. I last heard of .... on or about the .... day of .... A. D. 1 .... at which time .... was at ...., in the State of ....*~~

~~*I have not been able to ascertain either the address or residence of said .... after reasonable and due inquiry and search for six months I have made the following effort to find the said ....*~~

Belle Ruth Kaufman

Subscribed and sworn to before me, at Pawtucket *in the County of* Providence *in said State of Rhode Island and Providence Plantations, this* 25th *day of* July *A. D. 19* 35.

Morris Resnick
Notary Public

COMPLAINT AND WARRANT.

To ~~ROSCOE M. DEXTER~~ Chas F. Risk, Esquire, Justice, SAMSON NATHANSON, Esquire, Clerk of the District Court of the Eleventh Judicial District in the County of Providence, in the State of Rhode Island and Providence Plantations.

James Axon .... Chief of Police, of ~~Central Falls~~, Lincoln, ~~Cumberland~~, in said county, on oath complains, in the name and behalf of the State, that at said ~~Central Falls~~, Lincoln, ~~Cumberland~~, in said county, on the 7 day of December, A. D. 1934, with force and arms,

Harry Kaufman alias John Doe

of ~~said Central Falls, Lincoln, Cumberland~~ Providence, in said county, laborer,

did make a violent assault upon the body of Beatrice Toner and ~~him~~ he did beat wound and ill-treat,

~~did feloniously steal, take and carry away from the possession of~~

~~being his property,~~

~~all of the value of $~~

wantonly and maliciously injure and deface a building not his own, and break the glass therein, the property of

to the damage of said building $

ride and drive faster than a common travelling pace, in one of the streets of said Central Falls, Lincoln, Cumberland, to wit:

not being licensed as required by Chapter 191 of the General Laws of Rhode Island as a Hawker and Peddler; did sell and offer for sale in said City of Central Falls, town of Lincoln, Cumberland certain goods, wares and merchandise, to wit:

~~said goods, wares and merchandise not being articles manufactured by his own hands,~~

against the Statute and the peace and dignity of the State.

Wherefore he prays advice, and that process may issue, and that the said Respondent may be apprehended and held to answer to this complaint, and be further dealt with relative to the same according to law.

Dated at Central Falls, this 14 day of December A. D. 1934

James Axon – Chief of Police Lincoln

PROVIDENCE, SC.—In Central Falls, this 14 day of December A. D. 1934, personally came James Axon subscriber to the above complaint, and made oath to the truth of the same, and at the same time and place, himself as principal and as surety, and were each recognized according to law, in the sum of fifty dollars, to prosecute said complaint with effect, or in default thereof to pay all lawful costs which may accrue thereon, to the State.

Before me,

Samson Nathanson

~~Justice~~, Clerk of the District Court of the Eleventh Judicial District.

Court Fees, 1.50	
Mittimus,	
Recognizance,	
Continuance, 1.00	
On Warrant, 1.70	
Aid,	
Com., and Travel,	
Return to Court,	
On Summons,	
Witnesses' Fees,	
Interpreter,	
$4.20	
Paid	

STATE OF RHODE ISLAND AND PROVIDENCE PLANTATIONS.

PROVIDENCE, SC.—*To the Sheriff, his Deputy, or to either of the Town Sergeants or Constables in the County of Providence.*

L.S.

GREETING:—Complaint having been made to me on oath, as above written, you are therefore hereby required in the name of said State, forthwith to apprehend the body of the said Respondent above named (if he may be found in your precinct), and him have before the District Court of the Eleventh Judicial District, or some other lawful authority, to be dealt with relative to the premises, as to law and justice shall appertain. And for so doing this shall be your warrant. Hereof fail not.

Given under my hand and seal, at Central Falls, in said County, this 14 *day of* December *in the year A. D.* 1934

Samson Nathanson

~~Justice~~, *Clerk of the District Court of the Eleventh Judicial District.*

Depositions of Belle Kaufman, Jacob Brown, Lewis Blumenthal, State of Rhode Island Divorce papers, Complaint and Warrant

The words against her husband in my mother's petition for divorce were searing, accusing him of being "guilty of extreme cruelty...and gross misbehavior and wickedness repugnant to and in violation of the marriage covenant...that he hath conducted himself improperly with women." No wonder she would have found it painful to discuss this aberrant behavior with her daughters.

When I revealed the new, ugly, and painful information about my mother's divorce to my cousin Fred, who had always maintained deep personal ties with my mother and had actually been her last visitor when she died in 1998, he was, in a rare moment, speechless. "How did your mother ever meet this bum?" he asked. "How did he get by the rest of the family?"

I had no answer to his questions. On October 29, 1934, when my mother and Harry were married, there were no obvious extenuating circumstances in the Blumenthal family to be considered as reasons for why the negative issues surrounding Kaufman could have escaped notice from my mother's four brothers and two brothers-in-law. Needless to say, the tragedy that hit the family a mere seven months later had not happened, and it was surely time for the twenty-four-year-old Belle to begin a married life. As was typical for any of Rose and Phillip Blumenthal's eight children, the newly married couple could remain at 7 Overhill Road for a short time until they moved into a place of their own. What I found so jarring about this practice is the fact that 7 Overhill Road was so small, with barely enough bedrooms for the unmarried children, never mind the addition of a new sister-in-law or brother-in-law. Upstairs there were three tiny bedrooms, but as my older cousins explained to me, the newly married couple was most probably given the master bedroom. Truthfully, I never imagined my arrogant aunt

Edythe ever condescending to spending her wedding night with my uncle Barney at 7 Overhill Road, an opinion shared by several of my cousins. But some "facts" simply have to be accepted as family lore.

According to my cousin Dick Halpert, Etta's son who grew up in the house, the master bedroom was not any bigger than the other two small bedrooms, and the only way to get into it was to walk through one of the other bedrooms. Privacy was definitely not possible. In addition, when my mother married Harry, Esta and Hy were still unmarried and living at home with their parents. Seven Overhill Road was, indeed, a full house.

Still, had my mother and her new husband spent their first few married nights anywhere beside 7 Overhill Road, their marriage just might have lasted a bit longer. Yet, there was no way Kaufman would have been able to hide his problems regarding other women from his wife for very long. On December 7, 1934, six weeks after he married my mother, Kaufman was arrested for "making a violent assault upon the body of Beatrice Toner…in which he did beat, wound and ill-treat" her.

According to an article in the *Pawtucket Times* on December 14, 1934, Kaufman, twenty-two, of Chester Avenue, Providence, was "arraigned on a charge of assault on Beatrice Toner, of Lincoln…and pleaded guilty and was placed on probation by Clerk Nathanson. Kaufman is alleged by state police to have picked up the girl in his truck on Louisquisset Turnpike.[3] The girl jumped from the machine, she told police, when the driver made improper advances. She took the registration number of the truck and turned it over to the state police. Kaufman's arrest followed."

---

[3] Current Rhode Island Routes 146 and 246.

Again, the idea that forty days after he married my mother Kaufman "made improper advances" to a girl he picked up in his truck is mind blowing. Poor Beatrice Toner most likely wasn't the first (and definitely not the last) woman this man assaulted. I also did not know exactly when my mother learned of this assault, but seeing it published in a local newspaper while she was still married to Harry had to have been mortifying for my mother and her entire family.

Apparently, however, my mother remained married another seven months until, on July 11, 1935, her husband "attacked women members of my family." By that date my mother's world had changed, for she had lost her mother, brother, niece, and two nephews two months earlier. How on earth, I had to wonder, while in the deepest mourning and living with her heartbroken and newly widowed father, did Belle Blumenthal Kaufman find the strength to deal with the hideous behavior of the man to whom she was still married?

As my uncle Jack, my aunt Marion's husband, stated in his deposition, "Well, they were only married for a short while when he was arrested, on December 14, 1934, for a warrant sworn out by James Axon for assault on a girl by the name of Toner in Lincoln; he had 'picked' her up while he was driving around that section and assaulted her."

Jack also included in his depiction, "While we were mourning the death of my mother-in-law on May 18, 1935, he indecently attacked a woman of the family; he had attacked other members of the family, women members of the family from time to time. The day before he left his wife, he indecently attacked a woman member of the family, that was on July 11, 1935. Then a woman by the name of 'Butterworth' of Warwick, Rhode Island turned a case against him to her lawyer because of an indecent attack upon her, and some sort of a settlement was made."

Reading my uncle Jack's deposition continued to boggle my mind. What on earth was Kaufman doing? What was wrong with him? The image of my mother's aberrant husband slinking throughout the Blumenthal house, inappropriately touching any girl or woman, was revolting; or, as my uncle put it, "indecently attacking women members of the family" during the family's devastating mourning period was repulsive. Of course, I had no idea exactly what they all meant by these "indecent attacks," but I doubted that any of them was merely a kiss on the cheek.

I was, however, certain that the Blumenthal family strictly observed the seven days of shiva, the Jewish period of mourning, necessary to honor the memories of the five Blumenthal members so recently lost. Every day of that shiva week, the house at 7 Overhill Road had to be filled with family and friends who came to offer their sympathies, to deliver kosher food, to hold daily morning and evening minyans (which offered prayers for the dead), creating its own confusion and chaos. Mirrors in the house would be covered, as well. Through all this anguish and heartache was my mother's husband, Harry Kaufman, ill with his own sexual drives, unable to resist attacking a woman.

It took my mother eleven months before she had finally had enough, and in September 1935, with her brother Lewie and brother-in-law Jack Brown at her side, she managed to do what needed to be done and headed to court to divorce Kaufman. She also began the proceedings required for an Orthodox Jewish girl to obtain a Get, the document necessary under strict Jewish law to free her from her marriage and allow her to marry again, which, less than two years later, she did.

Thankfully, this time, she married a good man, Maurice "Moe" Klasky, whom she met at Old Orchard Beach in Maine. When they married in1938, Belle left Providence and hopefully the memories of her hideous first marriage behind her. Leaving her sisters, brothers, and father behind could not have been easy for her. I could only hope her new home brought her some therapeutic help. She'd been through so much with the Accident and Kaufman, perhaps a fresh start in a new place was just what she needed. Belle and Moe Klasky settled in his hometown of Malden, a city six miles north of Boston, where his parents, four sisters, and two brothers lived, and where Belle had no trouble keeping her secret shame from their two children and, most likely, the rest of their world. Had she not held on to the groomless wedding picture from 1934 in which she looked so lovely I would never have found out about Harry Kaufman.

Apparently, before my mother found and married my father, Dave Halpert had been one of her strongest allies during that difficult Kaufman time. His two children, Barbara and Allen, were the only ones who seemed able to elevate Belle's deep distress. "I don't think I could have survived that dark time without Etta and Dave and those precious children," she told me after I discovered the existence, though not the sordid details, of her first marriage. I could only imagine how deeply she, too, suffered from their loss in the Accident. Still, the divorce of an Orthodox Jewish woman in the 1930s was never anything but a humiliation. Perhaps because the Accident had changed the Blumenthal world so soon before my mother's divorce, it would be challenging to compare it to any other calamity. Even murder.

CHAPTER SIX
Losing Ruby

What exactly did Thomas Killourey take from the Blumenthal family besides its mother and three of its children under the age of twelve?

The loss of Ruby, the oldest Blumenthal child, the only one of Rose (Teibe) and Phillip's first three children to survive beyond ten years of age, was especially crushing to the entire Blumenthal family. Needless to say, the loss of Rose herself and her three grandchildren was an indescribable tragedy that reverberated like a never-ending tornado throughout the whole family. Yet there was something about losing the thirty-nine-year-old Ruby that was shattering in its own unique manner. All I ever directly knew about my uncle Ruby were his unblemished eyeglasses. While I could never satisfy my thirst to know more about Ruby, I am grateful for every small piece of knowledge I did discern. From photos, I could see that Ruby was solidly built with dark hair and dark eyes, which were often covered with the glasses I did get to hold. His face was long and thin, yielding a soft and slight yet still-winning smile. His ears protruded, but there was no doubt he was a handsome Blumenthal man.

The family stories about my uncle Ruby abounded. After the Accident, however, only a brief sentence appeared in the *Providence Journal* and several other out-of-town newspapers, to note his age and the fact that he was the driver of one of the cars involved in the crash, the sole occupant of that crushed car who lived for a few hours, long enough time to somehow, despite his unrelenting pain, identify the other passengers in his car.

No matter how many times I read that brief passage from the *Providence Journal,* I needed to stop and consider it more fully. I tried to imagine exactly what it is describing. This is what I saw: A thirty-nine-year-old man, possibly trapped inside a wrecked car, his fractured leg most likely making it impossible for him to stand, his two broken arms hanging uselessly at his sides, his head aching in pain and confusion as a result of his fractured skull. Perhaps there was blood on his pants or shirt; perhaps not. His eyes had to be dimmed by shock at what his body and mind had just experienced. I will never know if his eyeglasses were given to the family by the hospital after he died or if they had fallen off his face during the crash and he was left with blurry vision for the few hours that he lived afterwards. All that the eyes, with or without his glasses, could possibly see was a scene of carnage. I wondered if it was a silent scene he surveyed, although it is more than possible that the three living occupants of the Cadillac that caused the accident were moaning, screaming, or crying. The three would be healed, however, and would either walk away from the scene or recover shortly thereafter. No doubt there were onlookers and bystanders who came out of the general store/post office. Perhaps other cars slowed down to rubberneck the scene. Police and ambulances would have been on their way, sirens blaring. Steam would have been escaping from smashed radiators, water sizzling on hot engine blocks. Yet, in the immediate aftermath, all Ruby could see for certain was that his five passengers were already dead or perhaps one was minutes away from death. Not a moan could be heard from their dying lips.

Ruby was alive, though barely. Through his agony, both in his body and in his heart, he, the only Blumenthal survivor of the destruction surrounding him, found the strength to identify the occupants of the car he was driving. As the *Providence Journal* stated, "He was able to partly identify those who had been riding with him to Dr. C.E. Simonds, the medical examiner." I will always wonder exactly what he said. What words did he use to tell Dr. Simonds that his son was dead, as was his mother and his niece and nephew, along with the mother of his ill brother-in-law? How he could speak at all was miraculous to me. But he spoke those words so that the bodies of those he knew and loved, whose lives had been entrusted to him when he sat behind the wheel of his brother's-in-law car, were not just dead bodies, but rather people who were loved and whose lives had been snuffed out in a matter of seconds. With whatever breath Ruby could find, he gave the authorities their names. He had to understand that they were gone, that none of them would ever speak a word again. It was crucial, however, that the medical examiner beside him now knew who they were. That in his own agony, he was able to offer them that tiny gift of recognition in death. In that moment, my uncle Ruby, the innocent driver of a car destroyed by a drunk, was a hero. In my mind, he always will be. There had never been the slightest chance that he could have saved those lives when the car he drove, the one in which they died, was destroyed by an enormous, out-of-control Cadillac; but they were not nameless, not for a single moment.

This summary of Ruby appeared in Thomas Killourey's prison records, which included descriptions of his victims: "Reuben Blumenthal: Age 39 years. Married, wife living at 15 Taft Street Providence, R.I. One son Morton, who was also killed in this accident. He was in business in Pawtucket, in the liquor business. Since his death, his wife states that business has fallen considerably and it is hard for her to get along. He was well liked in the town of Pawtucket and in Providence, where he was active in the Jewish War Veterans. He was a World War Veteran. A good husband and father. His wife still mourns the loss of both husband and only son."

I learned that Reuben had more than one nickname or alias besides Ruby: Herbert, Sam, and Austin were just a few. While it was not unusual for people to have more than one nickname, I have wondered why my uncle needed three. Could that have anything to do with the fact that he and Jeanette lived in an upscale area of Providence and he wanted a name more sophisticated than Ruby? Or were these aliases related to his role in bootlegging, which had been, as I will explain more fully in a following chapter, a family business in several ways?

I learned that Uncle Ruby had a lovely voice and sang in a chorus of the Hebrew Criterion Society in Providence, that he worked in a drugstore, and that he had most probably attended the College of Pharmacy in Providence. I knew that Ruby had married Jeanette Zura, a vivacious and outgoing woman from Providence, in 1921; that there was a strong chance that Ruby was equally sociable and fun; and that their only child, Morty, was born two years after their marriage. Had Thomas H. Killourey not ended my uncle's life at age thirty-nine, I wondered what Ruby's future might have been. Would he and Morty have taken some fun road trips together? Would they have spent more summers at the family Halpert cottage in Barrington, Rhode Island, with the rest of the Blumenthal family? Would Jeanette and Ruby have stood beneath a chuppah (marriage canopy) when Morty married? Or at the bris or baby naming of a grandchild or two? While I'd learned far too many (mostly unsavory) details of his killer's life, who died at age sixty, the future of my uncle Ruby, who died at age thirty-nine, was still mostly a blank.

Sometime after the Accident, my heartbroken aunt Jeanette remarried. Her second husband, Dave Schaeffer, was a warm, gentle widower, with an adult daughter named Bernice. Before Dave's wife died, she and Dave and Jeanette and Ruby had been good friends. Dave and Jeanette continued to live in the home at 15 Taft Avenue in Providence, where Ruby and Jeanette had raised Morty for nearly thirteen years. Jeanette remained an integral part of the Blumenthal family, and Dave was warmly welcomed by all of them. Ruby's sister, my aunt Etta, and Jeanette were especially close, speaking nearly every day, and they remained both dear friends and sisters-in-law. A skilled milliner (hatmaker), Jeanette worked in a women's shop in downtown Providence.

My memories of my aunt Jeanette were of a dark-haired, elegant woman who elicited indescribable joy from me with the packages she frequently sent me from Providence, each one filled with gorgeous clothes she created for my dolls. I must have been around six when the first of those packages arrived, but I never forgot the thrill when I unwrapped a beautiful coat or stunning dress that perfectly fit at least one of my dolls. I'm not sure when I lost interest in my dolls, but I knew that for as long as I adored them, I treasured each and every perfectly sewn article of their Providence wardrobes. None of my friends ever had such gems for their dolls. The tiny hats Jeanette also created for my dolls were even more prized. More than once, she fashioned a miniature dress for one of my dolls along with a matching dress in exactly my size. How lucky could a little girl be? Most of my friends stopped caring about their dolls a long time before I followed suit. Then again, they never had an aunt who made their dolls look so beautiful. I was sad when I learned that my aunt did not have any little girls of her own, but I was so happy that she knew how much I loved my dolls. Even before I could write them myself, my mother and I always sent her thank-you notes. How this generous and thoughtful woman found the courage to overcome the loss of her son and her husband without ever losing her kind spirit will never fail to astonish me.

Perhaps because he died so tragically at age thirty-nine, Uncle Ruby would forever be remembered as almost saintlike (if there can be a Jewish saint!). Most of all, my family's memory of him would be of a man devoted to his family, especially to his only child, Morty, who was always by his side, as he was in the car on that May day in 1935. Negative stories and attributes related to Ruby had to have existed, but the horror of his death inevitably wiped them away.

Still, more unanswered questions about Reuben Blumenthal's thirty-nine years of life before the Accident lingered. Described in his obituary as a "druggist and World War veteran," he had been an officer in the Rhode Island Post of the Jewish War Veterans. Indeed, outside the Providence funeral home where he and the other five victims of the car crash were eulogized, his Rhode Island Post of the Jewish War Veterans group stood guard. They also escorted the cortege to the Lincoln Park Cemetery in Warwick, Rhode Island, where a rifle squad fired a volley over his grave in front of the 1,500 mourners in attendance. In a Providence newspaper article on August 20, 1914, three weeks before the start of World War I, Reuben Blumenthal had been described as a private in the Seventeenth Company with an excellent shooting record at the Rumford Range, which was one of the first Navy ranges to offer training with rifles and machine guns. As part of the Rhode Island National Guard, my uncle's unit must have been involved in a riflery competition. At that time, he was just eighteen, unmarried, and living with the rest of the Blumenthal family on 7 Overhill Road. He might have joined the National Guard to make a little extra money, and I had no idea whether he considered himself lucky or unlucky that he wasn't called up for active duty during the war.

While Ruby remained in Rhode Island during World War I, his youngest brother, my uncle Hy, served in an artillery unit in General Patton's Third Army in Europe during World War II. Hy was an especially handsome and energetic man, the adored baby of the Blumenthal family, nineteen years younger than Ruby, who was the oldest. Needless to say, the entire family worried about Hy every day he was in Europe. Aunt Etta, the oldest of the four Blumenthal daughters, used to check the newspaper every day for those three long years while her baby brother, fourteen years younger than she, served his country, nervously checking the list and photos of lost Providence servicemen. Ironically, while my brave uncle Hy arrived home from the European Theater safe and sound, within a week of his return to Providence, he fell and broke his leg. My aunt Etta lovingly cared for him at 7 Overhill Road, no doubt cooking and baking every one of his favorite foods during his recuperation.

My handsome Uncle Hy during WWII.

I imagined that my two uncles, the oldest and the youngest, were not particularly close as they grew up nineteen years apart. Uncle Hy was twenty, unmarried, and still living with his parents at 7 Overhill Road when he lost his oldest brother. How painful could that have been for him?

I am certain that if Ruby had been alive in September 1935, he would have joined his brother Lewie and his brother-in-law Jack Brown in the courtroom to assist his sister, fourteen years younger than he, and to help her fight for her Get.

CHAPTER SEVEN
Seven Overhill Road

While every member of the family adored Etta and knew she loved each and every one of us, we understood that the great love of her life was her husband, Dave Halpert. Dave wasn't just an in-law in the Blumenthal family. The love he shared for his wife's family matched hers.

Dave Halpert had bought a cottage close to the beach in Barrington, Rhode Island. This 1948 photo shows my aunt Etta (in sunglasses) and my father, standing at the back.

While I never got to meet this extraordinary man, I did get to hear and understand my mother's infinite love for him. One of the most difficult parts of my mother's move to Malden was leaving behind her cherished brother-in-law Dave Halpert. Dave lived at 7 Overhill Road for eight years beyond the Accident. His talent as an artist and as a decorator kept his services in great demand at the Mill's End, the home furnishing store in Providence that he and Etta ran. He had been in Connecticut before the Accident to check out another home furnishings store they might have either bought or managed, which was how he ended up in a hospital in Hartford rather than in Rhode Island.

Yet, after the Accident and moving back to Providence, Etta and Dave joined my brokenhearted sixty-five-year-old grandfather, Phillip Blumenthal, at 7 Overhill Road. After burying his wife, son, three grandchildren, and his son's mother-in-law, the patriarch of the Blumenthal family had somehow found the courage to remain strong, firmly connected to his Jewish faith, and devoted to the family that was still the center of his every day. For many years, he had been well-known for joking that any prospective husband of his daughters who did not play pinochle was not welcome in his house.

A tall, elegant man, called Pops by his children and Grandpa by his grandchildren, his days as a tailor made obvious by his neat and crisp clothes, Phillip appeared happiest when he was with one of those grandchildren, most of whom lived nearby and frequently visited 7 Overhill Road. These grandchildren, my fortunate cousins, hold on to memories of sitting on his lap in his rocking chair, as he spoke softly and gently to them, his large white mustache tickling their faces, eliciting a feeling of calm that warmed them all. My cousin Toby Brown Smolokoff, who was one of his granddaughters lucky enough to meet him, was born one day and one year after the Accident. She remembered resting happily on Phillip's leg. "Then he would lift his leg up and down and say, 'La, la, poops!'" she related. "Sad that this is my only memory. I was so very young." Toby also remembered hearing more than once that the entire family breathed a sigh of relief when she was born on May 15, 1936, rather than on May 14, the day of the Accident.

At 7 Overhill Road, new joy and new life once again filled my grandfather's heart when Etta and Dave miraculously created a new family. In 1937, two years after the Accident, Etta gave birth to my cousin Dick; five years later, in 1942, my cousin Bob arrived. When Phillip died of cancer at age seventy-three, on March 15, 1943, thirteen months after Bob was born, the grandfather I never met left yet another giant hole that could never be filled in our Blumenthal family. And then again there was my cousin Ronnie, born five months after the Accident, who was age seven when our grandfather died. Ronnie was the namesake of Phillip's first-born son, Ruby, making him all the more precious to our grandfather. This grandson was living proof that life and love could return even after tragedy took away six beloved members of a family. It was as if every aunt and uncle, along with my grandfather, wanted to touch and hug this precious gift, just to prove that he was indeed real.

Even after her father died, my mother never lost the strong pull of Providence. Or her adoration for her eldest sister Etta. I remember one particular story my mother told me about Etta's wedding day, at 7 Overhill Road in 1923. My mother and her younger sister Esta were twelve and ten at the time. "Yet Etta refused to get herself ready and dressed until she was certain that Esta and I were perfectly adorned in the two beautiful matching dresses she had made for us," my mother told me, smiling warmly as she remembered that day so many years ago. "No matter what our mother said to her, Etta would not put on her own dress or fix her hair until Esta and I were all set. She could have cared less what she looked like, but she needed to be certain the two of us were happy and looking perfect in our new dresses."

Indeed, some of my earliest memories are the Sundays I spent in our car, my father driving his two daughters and his wife the two hours from Malden, Massachusetts, to Providence, Rhode Island, to see his wife's family. Six days a week, she was in Malden, within reach of his own large family. But Sundays belonged to the Blumenthal family. While I was always carsick during the ride, I was certain my mother never relaxed one minute during those two hours, her right foot on an imaginary brake, especially as we drove on the highway, always remembering May 14, 1935. No matter how nervous she had been or how nauseated I was, both of us felt perfectly healthy and excited the second we arrived at 7 Overhill Road.

While the chairs at my aunt Etta's Sunday table, laden with her delicious cooking, were always filled, sadly, the empty seats never went unnoticed. Only a few of my older cousins, Irma and Elaine Blumenthal, the daughters of my uncle Lewie, who was born in 1900 and the fourth of the original eleven Blumenthal children, had a chance to know our grandmother, Uncle Ruby, and our three first cousins, Barbara, Morty, and Allen. My Uncle Lewie and his wife, Sally, and their two daughters lived around the corner from 7 Overhill Road. It was to her brother Lewie's house that my hysterical mother ran seconds after she received the devastating phone call from the state police on May 14, 1935. Because Elaine and Barbara were both born in 1925 and their younger siblings, Irma and Allen, born in 1930 and 1929, were just one year apart, the four of them were very close. While

I had been in the company of my two older cousins Elaine and Irma countless times at family gatherings, I never once thought of asking them about the two cousins they had lost in the Accident. Elaine and husband Eddie's five children, Hershey, Mark, Alan, Paul, and Scott, felt more like my cousins. I was always amazed at the size of Elaine and Eddie's family, especially the fact that Hershey had four active and fun-filled younger brothers. Perhaps, after seeing firsthand such horrendous loss in her extended family, Elaine might have felt the need to fill some of those empty places. Yet, heartbreak enveloped the Blumenthal family again when Hershey, a tall, pretty, dark-haired woman, died of lung cancer in 1981 at the age of thirty shortly after she was married.

Ronnie Blumenthal, born in 1935, was closer in age to three of our male cousins, Freddie (1934), Mel (1936), and Dick (1937), all born to the three sisters, Marion, Esta, and Etta, respectively, within three years of one another. But he would always be the golden one, born less than five brief months after the Accident.

Ronnie's father, my uncle Barney, shared my mother's feelings about returning to Overhill Road on Sundays. Though Etta showered her soothing love on all of her Blumenthal siblings, along with every one of her nieces and nephews, it was obvious she had a unique place in her heart for her five-years-younger-brother Barney. A special excitement accompanied Barney's arrival each Sunday. Smiles and hugs were everywhere when Barney walked in, happily minus his unpleasant wife, Edythe, but always with an adorable, smiling Ronnie. Since the other two brothers, Louie and Hy, produced four girls with their wives and Morty was lost in the Accident, this little boy was the only male heir to the actual Blumenthal name.

My affluent uncle Barney owned and operated a liquor store in Boston.

The facts that Barney's sister Etta was also a superb cook and his wife, Edythe, didn't own a skillet, made it easy to understand Barney's faithful trips from Brookline to Providence on Sundays, the only day, thanks to the blue laws in Massachusetts, when his liquor store was closed. No one could compete with my aunt Etta's cooking. And Aunt Edythe certainly never tried.

Barney also made trips to Overhill Road to visit his widowed father, Phillip. But there were always other reasons for the Sunday drive—Etta's delicious baked beans and sweet-and-sour meatballs, to name just a few of the delicacies she prepared. In truth, no matter what day of the week Barney arrived at Overhill Road, his sister had something special to feed him. Undoubtedly, Barney brought home some of the stuffed cabbage to put into his empty refrigerator back in Brookline. There was no way Aunt

Edythe would ever prepare this recipe herself. I know I digress, but family get-togethers always seem to have food involved and it's the food that triggers the memories.

On Sundays, however, once the table was cleared of the empty plates that were previously overfilled with food, Barney would settle down to play pinochle with his brothers and brothers-in-law while Ronnie, whose plate was always filled twice by his aunts who were convinced, despite their nephew's chunky body, that his mother never fed him, headed to the downstairs playroom with his cousins. Before he disappeared, lipstick marks would have covered his round cheeks, more remnants of the affection of aunts, especially Etta. His thick, blond curls would have been tenderly tousled. After all, he was their brother's namesake, the small seed already planted that sprang to life less than five months later. In fact, he looked nothing like his dark-haired, olive-skinned, dark-eyed, slim uncle Ruby. Instead, Ronnie was fair, blond, and blue eyed, and huskily built. None of that mattered. Ronnie was Ruby's nephew, the family darling, its miraculous phoenix born from the ashes of the car crash.

My uncle Dave had personally redone the basement at 7 Overhill Road, turning it into a spacious kids' playroom, a place where he also kept his artist's tools. While Dick and his cousins Mel, Fred, and Ronnie played fun games down there, Dave also spent many hours in the basement, creating watercolor paintings, ink sketches, calligraphy projects, and fascinating pictures. On Sundays, however, the space belonged to the cousins. Family friends in Boston who owned a photography store had given seven-year-old Dick a photographic enlarger, which he adored. The fact that Dick eventually followed his father's footsteps into the Rhode Island School of Design and became a successful architect could perhaps be traced back to those basement experiments with photographs. One particular Sunday, before the advent of the Polaroid camera, he managed to take a roll of photos of the family members and develop them in a few hours. When he was later given a projector, he happily entertained his cousins with short silent children's movies.

Many years later, the same cousins who had spent Sundays at Aunt Etta's, more than a dozen of us, analyzed Ronnie's parents, trying to see if the key to the mystery that turned our much loved cousin into a convicted murderer lay there. If we had to throw blame on anyone for screwing up Ronnie, it would have to have been the Blumenthal absent from Providence Sundays, our aunt Edythe, the entitled, socially conscious lady from a well-off Boston family. She was infinitely less likable than Uncle Barney. Twenty-four when her only son was born in 1935, she was five years younger than Barney. No one could deny how she doted on Ronnie, who grew into her tall, muscular, blond, blue-eyed boy, more handsome than his father, more like the Franks, Edythe's side of the family. She never exhibited any type of maternal warmth to any of her Blumenthal nieces or nephews. While we might have called Aunt Edythe "a bit snooty" and the key word for Ronnie was always "spoiled," that didn't change his Rhode Island cousins' affection for him.

Of course, there were other family gatherings at 7 Overhill Road before I had been born. My cousin Fred, who was eight months old at the time of the crash and nine years old when Grandpa died, remembers another happy family together, though not on a Sunday, at 7 Overhill Road. This one was on Christmas Day in 1943 in the same basement where the cousins entertained one another every Sunday. The idea of a Jewish family, especially an Orthodox Jewish family, celebrating Christmas was a bit strange, but I was sure any day off from work was worth celebrating. Perhaps it was even a five-year anniversary party for my parents. Grandpa Phillip had died nine months earlier, and, despite the rest of the Blumenthal family who were all there, Fred remembered the house feeling a bit empty.

Fred also recalled other days in the house when the kids were being told to be quiet because Uncle Dave was resting. While he had recovered from his initial heart attack in 1935 and was successful at his job at the Providence drapery shop, my uncle was still fragile, far from strong and healthy. Five months after the 1943 Christmas party, Dave suffered his second heart attack, this time fatal. His death was a heartbreaking event in every family member's life but most especially for his two young sons, seven-year-old Dick and fifteen-month-old Bobby.

"I was never really told he had died," Dick recollected. "I just remember that he was sick and one day some men came and put him on a stretcher and took him down the stairs to the hospital. He never came home and died in the hospital. But I was just told that he had gone to heaven. I was never taken to the funeral."

Everyone had known Dave was in precarious health, but they all believed he was a miracle as were his two sons and that he would remain with them, a testament to the power of love after the destruction of his family. My mother was five months pregnant with me when Dave died, and while she named me Phyllis after her gentle father, my middle name is Davida, after the brother-in-law she loved like a brother. Both these names are treasures to me.

Coincidentally, two of my aunts were also pregnant at that time. My aunt Marion named her son Phillip David, born a month after her father died. A few years later, my aunt Esta named her son David Robert, after her brother-in-law Dave and her mother. Both my aunt Marion and my mother had named their daughters Toby, for their mother, Rose, a.k.a. Teibe. Undoubtedly, Ronnie had spent time with both his grandpa Phillip and his uncle Dave. I have no doubt both of them would have cherished their grandson and nephew.

When first her two children and then Dave died, my aunt Etta once again suffered indescribable loss. Through all the devastations, she never lost even a small bit of her quiet strength and abiding love for her young sons, her second family, or for her nieces, nephews, sisters, and brothers. She was something else, my aunt Etta. And her devotion to her golden-haired nephew Ronnie, the namesake of her brother Ruby, never faltered.

CHAPTER EIGHT
Etta Blumenthal Halpert Adelman

Thirty-three at the time of the Accident, my aunt Etta lived for another thirty years after losing Dave, continuing to welcome her extended family every Sunday, finding great joy in each of us, especially in her two new sons raised with absolute love. One of the greatest joys came at the end of her life: the blessed arrival of her grandson, David Zalman Halpert, in 1970. His parents, Bob and Naomi Halpert, had settled just a few doors away from 7 Overhill Road, and for the final three years of Etta's life no day ever went by without her hugging and marveling at this precious gift. For Bob, who had been so very young when his father, David, died, bestowing this gift on his mother was uniquely important.

I always marveled at the affection between Bob's wife, Naomi, and my aunt. Of course, Etta would have welcomed any girl whom Bob loved, but there was something special about the relationship between Etta and Naomi. In a strange way it reminded me of the biblical story of Ruth and Naomi. Of course, in that story, unlike the one between Etta and Naomi,

Naomi is the mother-in-law and her son's wife is Ruth. Yet, I was certain the words "wherever you go, I will go" could be spoken by either my aunt Etta or Naomi. Of course, there had never been any doubt that Naomi would want to live no more than a few doors away from her mother-in-law. While Etta had unquestionably adored Dick's first wife, Dotty, that couple had lived in New York so daily contact could never have happened. Naomi was, in so many ways, the daughter Etta had lost, and although Naomi was devoted to her own mother, Faye Finkel, her bond with Etta was equally strong, as well as palpable when the two of them were together. I loved Naomi for many reasons: because she loved my cousin Bobby as much as he loved her, because she was kind and an excellent nurse, and lastly because she was just plain fun to be around. Mostly I loved her because she made my aunt Etta happy.

In March 2020, many years after Aunt Etta had died, shortly after he turned fifty, David Zalman Halpert, the extraordinary gift Bob and Naomi had given to my aunt, died unexpectedly from sepsis, shattering the hearts of Bob and Naomi Halpert and the rest of our family. It seemed so unfair, one more tragedy bestowed upon the Blumenthal family. It was the only day in my life when I was grateful that Aunt Etta was no longer alive.

In 1947, many years before David Z. Halpert was born, four years after my uncle Dave died, Etta married an old family friend and widower, Eli Adelman, the father of a twenty-year-old daughter who was on her own by then. Eli's wife, Sarah Adelman, who died the same year as Dave, had been a close friend of Etta's. Eli and Sarah had lived near Dave and Etta, but after Eli and Etta married, he moved into 7 Overhill Road.

Etta's second husband, Eli Adelman, is mowing the lawn at the Barrington house. My cousin Bobby Halpert and I look on.

I remember Eli as a quiet man who loved books and was usually sitting by himself and reading when the noisy Blumenthal clan arrived on Sundays. He was friendly and would chat with each visitor for a few minutes before retreating back to his books. Dick, who was ten when his mother married Eli, is honest in his description of his stepfather. "Eli tried very hard to be a good father," he said. "And when he married my mother, we were a family again. Eli would take me to my Boy Scout events, and we always got along well. But he just wasn't a businessman, and he was prone to depression. Though he didn't really yell often, there were times he did."

Dick also described his mother as being understandably overprotective of him and Bobby. After the trauma of losing two children, there was no way she would take any chances with these two priceless sons. "When I was in junior high school, a truck ran into me when I was riding my bike home," Dick said. "The bike was completely smashed, but somehow, I was not injured. I never told my mother the truth about what had happened to my bike. If I had, she would never again have let me on a bike, or even out of the house." Yet one of Dick's most vivid memories of his mother was of her sitting in her favorite chair, knitting needles always in her hand. "She was always knitting beautiful things. Large multicolored afghans, tiny sweaters, and hats for infants."

My sons were the lucky recipients of so many of those exquisite sweaters, and I will never discard the pink and blue afghan that is spread at the bottom of my bed or the delicate, white, embroidered tablecloth covering the round table in my living room. While Etta tried more than once to teach me how to knit, as a lefty I could never quite get the hang of it. I did complete sweaters for each of my three grandchildren, but I cannot imagine that my daughters-in-law felt even a tiny bit of the pride I felt dressing my sons in my aunt Etta's knitted masterpieces. When I left one of my "creations" on an airplane, I was certain both of my daughters-in-law sighed with relief. I have the recipe for Aunt Etta's delicious strudel, made with strawberry jam, nuts, and raisins, with a wonderful fluffy crust, but when I really wanted to taste Aunt Etta's strudel, I asked my cousin Bobby to make me some. My original recipe card was so stained with oil and jam that I recently rewrote it. It didn't really matter that it was hard to read since I pretty much know it by heart. Every time I make it, I'm determined that this batch will resemble my aunt Etta's or my cousin Bobby's, but, to be honest, it never comes close. Maybe because I end up eating so much of the jam and nut and raisin combination. Or maybe because I know that Aunt Etta's strudel was filled with so much love that nothing can ever equal its taste. But, still, I try.

My cousins Dick and Bob thrived under their mother's close watch, yet, sadly, Etta's second husband's professional life did not. Shortly after Eli married my aunt, he lost his job at a jewelry manufacturing company. He tried his hand at opening a deli, but that did not succeed. He worked with Etta at the Mill End shop, but eventually that closed. When that happened, my aunt found a job she adored as a volunteer at the nearby Miriam Hospital. How she loved putting on her pink hospital smock and working in the gift shop or bringing flowers and cheer to the patients. Year after year, she won an award as the hospital's most outstanding volunteer. I could not think of a more perfect person to bring a smile to a hospital patient's face. She was forever grateful to the Mount Sinai hospital in Hartford, Connecticut, which restored Dave's health after his initial heart attack. She was well aware of the fact that Mount Sinai was founded in 1923 as a facility for Jewish doctors who were not allowed to work at other hospitals in the area because of the casual anti-Semitism that was pervasive in American life at the time.

When the New England hospital where my husband worked as a pulmonologist had a large expansion in 1975, Jack and I decided to dedicate a new room to my aunt, who had been such an angel at the Miriam Hospital in Providence. When the new expansion was celebrated, my aunt was no longer with us, but a large contingency of my cousins, aunts, and uncles arrived at the hospital for the event. What joy to see the plaque with the words, "In Honor of Etta Blumenthal Halpert Adelman, whose kindness as a hospital volunteer will never be surpassed or forgotten." My mother, as well as Etta's sons, Dick and Bob, never stopped smiling with pride, despite their tears of joy.

Throughout their twenty-six-year marriage, my aunt also took very good care of Eli, never complaining about his business problems, preparing his favorite foods, showing him affection and concern. That was simply the type of person she was. Eli died in 1984, living eleven years after Etta was gone. He remained in that house after her death, finally finding a job that pleased him, as a guard at the Brown University Library. For a friendly man who loved books, this was, indeed, the perfect job for him.

For the eleven years that Eli lived as a widower at 7 Overhill Road, he continued to be well taken care of. Bob's wife, Naomi, so much like Etta in so many fine ways, made sure that Eli's refrigerator was well stocked and that all his other needs were handled. Most nights, Naomi, a sensitive and skilled nurse, would bring over a dinner she had prepared for him, making sure that he was in good health. And Bob and Naomi made sure that little David Halpert was a part of Eli's life as well. Etta's children would never allow their mother's second husband to be neglected in any manner.

After Eli died, Dick remembered clearing out his now-empty childhood home at 7 Overhill Road to prepare it for the real estate agents. He found a tricycle in the attic, which he is certain belonged to Allen, the older brother he never met. He also found a hope chest filled with blankets, but, sadly, nothing that might have belonged to his sister Barbara.

While 7 Overhill Road had remained the center of the Blumenthal family until Eli's death in 1984, the Halpert cottage yards away from the beach in Barrington, Rhode Island, was another prized meeting spot for our family. Many years before his death, Dave Halpert bought the 1200-square-foot house, a mere eight miles from Providence, as a surprise for Etta. The Barrington cottage seemed to have so many bedrooms and cots everywhere that it originally appeared like a mansion to me. When I saw it as an adult, however, I was shocked to see how small it was. Its size never mattered to any of my relatives who eagerly spent days there, enjoying the beach and one another, and somehow finding more than enough room to spend a night or two with Dave and Etta and later with Eli, Etta, Dick, and Bobby.

Photos of my cousin Ronnie at Barrington, an endearing little blond boy, huge smiles on his chubby face, filled the family albums. Even my aunt Edythe appeared to have made a visit there, albeit before her blond days.

Ronnie in overalls, his mother, Edythe, in the middle, my mother, Belle, hiding behind my sister Toby.

All the photos and my memories, along with those of my cousins, denoted a relaxed, easy spot where there was room for anybody who wanted to escape the heat in Providence or Boston on a blistering summer day or night—in a time before air-conditioning was everywhere.

No matter where Etta was, I was deeply blessed to have her in my life for so many years. She was, without question, one of the most favorite people in my life, and over fifty years after her death, I still miss her dearly. The yellow house on 7 Overhill Road was long gone from our family's lives, and the door to the Barrington cottage was permanently closed to all of us, but, along with her lovingly knitted sweaters and blankets, Aunt Etta was and always will be with us.

I always regretted that I was not able to join the rest of my Blumenthal relatives at Etta's funeral in May 1973, thirty-eight years, almost to the day, after the Accident. At that time, I was living in Hawaii with Jack and our two young sons while Jack performed his military service at Tripler Army Hospital in Honolulu. Knowing only too well how I would have done everything possible to find a flight back to Rhode Island in time for the funeral, my mother sent a letter to Jack at the hospital telling him the news and making sure he would be at my side when he brought the letter home to me. She also made sure no one in the family called me, so I did not learn the crushing news until hours after the funeral had ended. I understood my mother's reasoning, and she was right. I would have found a way, even if it involved flying many hours beyond the typical thirteen-hour direct flight, with multiple plane changes, to struggle to get there. But I didn't. When Jack's military assignment ended two months later, the first thing I did when we returned home was to visit Naomi and Bob in Providence. That day, Naomi tenderly showed me the nightgown Etta had been wearing when Naomi found her mother-in-law no longer breathing in her bed. She felt it still retained a faint aroma of my aunt. I knew Naomi would never discard it, and she never has.

Six years before Etta died, Ronnie was released from prison after serving thirteen years of his life sentence. Etta had worried about her adored nephew for those thirteen years, just as she had worried about her younger brother Hy during his years in the army during World War II, and gratefully welcomed Ronnie home and into her life. He attended her funeral even though he was in the process of ending his first marriage, drinking too much, working too little, and hanging around with Mafia types.

He was constantly seeking more money that he could borrow, but his Blumenthal cousins hadn't given up on him. Yet.

When I thought of the lady who never stopped loving our criminal cousin, the aunt who meant so much to me, and to everyone else in the Blumenthal family, I could not find enough words to praise her. She, of all people, had every right to rail at the skies, to become a bitter and resentful woman, to scream at the injustice of what happened to her one day in May 1935. I was convinced that had my aunt ever had the chance to meet Thomas H. Killourey after the Accident, she would miraculously have found the strength to forgive him for his crime. Hate never entered my aunt's heart, not even after the Accident. Instead, she turned out to be the Blumenthal clan's phoenix, for she was the one who rose up, whole and strong, out of the ashes of destruction.

While I will always believe that my aunt Etta was an angel sent from heaven, as perfect a person as any I have ever met, I must admit that many of us Blumenthals were far from innocent...there is no doubt of that.

CHAPTER NINE
Those Blumenthal Bootleggers

So how bad were the Blumenthals? Even Ruby?

I can easily answer that question by introducing yet one other recurring character in my family saga that I could not ignore, for it travels through the Blumenthal story like a wrecking ball, seemingly positive and vital, yet ultimately turning deadly and uncontrollable. I believed it all started with my great-uncle Ben Sass (my grandmother Rose "Teibe" Blumenthal's younger brother and my mother's uncle).

And I wouldn't be surprised if it even touched my uncle Ruby…in more than one way.

I'm talking about alcohol. Spirits. Booze.

Benjamin Sass was born in 1886, twelve years after my grandmother. He died in 1961, when I was seventeen, and although I met him at an occasional family get-together, my memory of him is slight. I knew he was married to Ida Torgan, but I remembered little about her as well. Ben and Ida had four daughters, Lillian, Edith, Dorothy, and Arlene, and one son, Sam. My mother was very close with her cousin Arlene when they were growing up in Providence. Many years later, when my parents began spending more time in Florida, where Arlene eventually moved, my mother and Arlene renewed their bond. I enjoyed watching how the two women acted years younger when they got together and reminisced about their lives as kids living one street away from each another. How I wish I had spoken to Arlene about the Accident and the Incident and the Sass family, but whenever I saw her in Florida when I was visiting my parents, it never occurred to me to discuss any of those matters.

Still, there were facts I knew. Ben and Ida Sass and their five children were in a higher class of society than their Blumenthal relatives. The Sasses had more money, fancier clothes, and a larger home than Phillip and Rose Blumenthal and their eight children. After all, Ben owned a catering company while Phillip owned and ran a tailor shop by himself. The Sasses were family, however, and lived near 7 Overhill Road, and Ben, in particular, had a strong connection to both his nephew Barney Blumenthal and his great-nephew Ronnie Blumenthal. To be specific, the connection was alcohol.

To keep it all straight, familywise: Sarah Sass, Ben and my grandmother Rose's older sister, married Tom Rosenfield. They had six children. One of their sons, Benny Rosenfield, owned a liquor store on Hope Street in Providence. However, Ben Sass (Benny Rosenfield's uncle) was the more successful "liquor man." During Prohibition, from the time the Eighteenth Amendment went into effect January 1920, which banned the manufacture, transport, importation, and sale of liquor in the United States, to its repeal in 1933, Uncle Ben did whatever he could do, mostly illegally, to make money from this forbidden item.

ALLEGED WHISKEY RAIDER HELD FOR GRAND JURY

Carl Northup Charged with Highway Robbery and Assault.

George Northup, 27, of Mineral Spring avenue, Pawtucket, charged with highway robbery and assault upon Benjamin Sass and George Press, was arraigned in the Sixth District Court yesterday morning and held without bail for the grand jury by Judge Rueckert. A truck owned by Abraham I. Specter and valued at $1500 is involved in the robbery charge.

Northup was identified by one of the Romano brothers of Wickford Tuesday as one of the men who held up the winery last winter, at which time Raymond McDevitt of Pawtucket was fatally wounded.

Ben Sass, my grandmother's younger brother, led the family into the liquor business. The 1923 *Providence Journal* article (top) details one of his bootlegging and rumrunning-related dust-ups. This ad from The *Jewish Times* (bottom) was for the kosher catering business that gave him a steady supply of wealthy Jewish customers for the booze he brought in.

Apparently, Ben Sass ran a pretty successful bootlegging business. He made great use of a still, which he kept behind his brother-in-law Tommy Rosenfield's barn on Sixth Street in Providence. The barn and the still, used to create alcohol by distilling liquid mixtures by heating to a boil and then cooling to condense the vapor, were right next to my uncle Lewie Blumenthal's house. Many in the Rosenfield family, including Sarah and Tom, my grandmother's sister and brother-in-law, lived in a cluster just a few streets away from Overhill Road.

Ben Sass made good money from his still during those Prohibition years and spent a lot of it on philanthropic activities. In 1924, four years after Prohibition began, he was one of the founders of Temple Emanuel in Providence. From its inception, the new synagogue was expected to be a vibrant Conservative congregation—more modern and not as strict as Orthodox Judaism, with some of the services in English. Over the next two decades the temple became one of the leading synagogues in New England. Ben and his wife, Ida, were involved in every aspect of the development and maintenance of that place of worship. I am curious as to whether members of the congregation knew that much of the money he was supplying to the synagogue came from the illegal still. Undoubtedly, however, he was not the only member of the temple who was in some way involved in this illicit but profitable bootlegging.

Ben Sass's money and energy were also devoted to the Touro Fraternal Association, which he helped establish in 1918, to integrate new immigrants into American society and provide them with necessary assistance. One of its important projects was to deliver coal during the Depression of the 1930s to needy members. The society pages of the Providence and Pawtucket newspapers, even during Prohibition, were filled with mentions of Mrs. Benjamin (Ida) Sass, and her involvement in multiple philanthropic organizations.

Before the repeal of Prohibition in 1933, while he was busy with his bootlegging activities, Ben ran a kosher catering business in Providence, providing the food for bar mitzvahs, banquets, weddings, and luncheons. Once Prohibition ended, Ben managed the LESDA Wine Company, Pawtucket's newest and most modern wine and liquor shop at the time. In 1935, the store distributed Carmel Rishon, LeZion Wines, and cognacs. Alcohol, indeed, was Ben's life support.

While Rhode Island and Connecticut were, to be clear, the only two states that did not ratify the Eighteenth Amendment, they were still obliged to observe the federal law. There is no ignoring the fact that my great-uncle Ben was one of the many who did run afoul of the law, since Rhode Island often turned a slightly blind eye to the large numbers of bootleggers in its state. Liquor figured strongly in Ben's life, a tradition carried on by his nephew, my uncle Barney Blumenthal, in his legal Boston liquor store. Bottles of alcohol, some legal, some not, filled the shelves in Ben's barn on Sixth Street in Providence and later, legally, in Barney's store in Boston.

I knew that Ben Sass and his Rosenfield nephew were bootleggers, but I was never aware that Barney and Ruby were too and that they ran Ruby's Providence drugstore together. (Druggists were allowed to sell alcohol for "medicinal" purposes.) Not surprisingly, the bootlegging wasn't mentioned in Ruby's obituary. Obviously, Barney had left his older brother and the drugstore before the Accident in 1935 and was living in Boston with his pregnant wife, Edythe, running his own liquor store. The bootlegging brothers, who were ten years apart in age, had to have been very close during their years at the drugstore. I can easily imagine Ruby being a part of his younger brother's new liquor venture in Boston. I could also visualize the twenty-nine-year-old Barney being distraught by his thirty-nine-year-old brother's death in the Accident.

My great-uncle Ben was one of many Jewish bootleggers during Prohibition. Bootlegging was a moneymaking business that allowed entrance to an appealing underground social scene. It is impossible to know the exact number of criminals involved in bootlegging during Prohibition. The leaders of the industry, the "gangster class," were, however, chiefly Jewish; in *Jews and Booze: Becoming American in the Age of Prohibition,* author Marni Davis says that 50 percent were Jewish, 25 percent Italian, and around 10 percent were Irish. Many American Jews were attracted to the illegal alcohol business because it helped them to assimilate, permitting the most prominent Jewish bootleggers to reach the upper echelons of society.

In America, the Jews who immigrated found that it was easier to enter the whiskey industry rather than the beer industry, which was controlled by German Americans. In the beer industry, the Germans hired only fellow Germans. The whiskey industry, however, didn't have a direct distribution system, which enticed Jewish entrepreneurs. Plus, unlike wine and beer, which had strong associations with the Old World, whiskey was characterized as an American drink. Not only did it serve as an avenue to economic success, it also provided a sense of patriotism. In this way, American Jews were contributing to the fabric of American culture. By 1900, Jews made up 25 percent of the whiskey distillers, rectifiers, and wholesalers in Louisville, Kentucky, a city where the Jewish population was only about 3 percent.

In truth, alcohol has always played an important role in Jewish life. Wine, particularly, is paramount to keeping Jewish tradition alive. On Passover, for instance, four cups of wine are consumed. Jews also followed the Torah commandment to offer a blessing over the wine they drink every Friday evening, during their Sabbath rituals.

Jews who kept a kosher diet often followed another commandment that forbid them to drink wine that was produced or even distributed by non-Jews, giving them another reason to be involved in the alcohol industry. This restriction created a profitable opportunity for the entire community. If Jews were to drink wine, a religious requirement, they had to be a part of every facet of its creation, from harvesting the grapes to handling the shipments. In a weird, most likely foolish thought process, perhaps my great-uncle Ben was just helping Jews follow a Torah commandment…while he got rich.

During Prohibition, rabbis were allowed to have sacramental wine for Jewish observances, from every Sabbath to numerous Jewish holidays, but Jewish bootlegging wasn't limited to providing sacramental wine. One well-known Jewish bootlegger, Samuel Bronfman, had Jewish bootleggers floating so much illegal booze into America over Lake Erie that it became known as the "Jewish Lake."

For every Meyer Lansky or Longie Zwillman, there were no doubt hundreds of other Jewish bootleggers who were important players during Prohibition, but their contributions are relatively unknown. Perhaps that is because these "contributions" were illegal and not the most honorable chapter in Jewish American history. Selling forbidden booze was how many Jews supported their families. As with my great-uncle Ben, many eventually became philanthropists as well, reaching the upper echelons of respectful society.

Despite the financial success of many Jews during Prohibition, Jews for the most part were staunch opponents of Prohibition. According to historians, Jews viewed Prohibition as part of a movement in America that wanted to keep immigrants and religions such as Judaism and Catholicism out of the mainstream. Many Jewish organizations opposed Prohibition, concerned that organizations pushing Prohibition, such as the Women's Christian Temperence Union and the Ku Klux Klan, would harm both their civil liberties and economic freedom.

As for the wine situation for Jews during Prohibition, thanks to Section 6 of the Volstead Act, the enforcement legislation of Prohibition, the ban on alcohol was removed for wine used for religious sacraments. This meant that rabbis and priests could legally possess wine. While this led a number of priests to turn to bootlegging, it led to even more bootlegger rabbis. Although the government worked to try to determine whether someone was actually a priest, the American rabbinate was more loosely organized and less supervised than the Catholic Church. Rabbis, or people pretending to be rabbis, and Jewish bootleggers worked the system to help keep wine in people's hands, whether it was used for religious rituals or not.

Many American Jews were outraged with this practice of bootlegging, thinking that its association with organized crime reflected badly on their community and would make it more difficult to assimilate into American culture. However, some thought bootlegging was the most American activity they could participate in. The gangster glitz and glamour were idolized. Indeed, there were many successful infamous Jewish bootleggers such as Meyer Lansky, Benjamin "Bugsy" Siegel, Moe Dalitz, and Abner "Longie" Zwillman.

The Bronfman family of Canada, founders of the Seagram's empire, was the most powerful Jewish family during Prohibition. Coincidentally, "Bronfman" means "liquor man" in Yiddish. In 1919, when the Volstead Act passed, brothers Sam and Harry Bronfman opened export houses along Canada's border with North Dakota. There, they bottled the legal minimum of distilled alcohol, mixing it with water, caramel, and sulfuric acid. The caramel helped achieve the whiskey color and the acid reacted with the oak barrel to create an aged taste. Sam made millions exporting alcohol to the United States. He cut distribution deals with Meyer Lansky and Arnold Rothstein. Al Capone ran Bronfman booze across the Midwest, and the Bugs and Meyer Mob (as in Siegel and Lansky) protected Bronfman liquor shipments coming across the border against hijackers.

Sam purchased a Kentucky distillery, dismantled it, sent the pieces north, reassembled it at home, and distilled his own whiskey. He also built an underground pipeline to pump alcohol into the United States. Sam's involvement in this illicit industry was far-reaching, but he is remembered primarily as a leader in the Canadian Zionist movement. Jewish bootleggers were icons of Prohibition, and their involvement continues a tradition of producing and selling alcohol that still continues, albeit legally, today.

While Ben Sass never achieved even a portion of the amount of fame or money that the Bronfmans did or gained the reputation of serious Prohibition criminals like Bugsy Siegel or Meyer Lansky, like his grand-nephew Ronnie, my great-uncle was arrested for his crimes. Ben was fined twenty dollars on a charge of possessing liquor unlawfully, on April 29, 1921, at age thirty-five. A couple of years later, still during Prohibition, Ben's name appeared again in the *Providence Journal*, this time for being the victim of a highway robbery and assault case. On August 9, 1923, George Northrup, a well-known bootlegger in Pawtucket, apparently held up the truck in which my great-uncle was riding and stole the truck, valued at the time at $1,500, and which was most likely filled with Sass liquor. Ben was lucky to have escaped with his life from this robbery and assault since Northrup had recently held up a winery, a robbery in which a victim had been fatally wounded. Bootleggers like Uncle Ben ran a risky business during Prohibition and had to concern themselves with not only evading the police but also evading other, more dangerous bootleggers.

I found it interesting that an earlier *Providence Journal* article, dated August 19, 1914, six years before Prohibition began, mentioned that the Board of Police Commission had refused the application of "Ben Sass, who runs a saloon at 307 Wickender Street and 16 Thompson Street to transfer his business to Blumenthal." The apparent reason for my grandfather wanting to accept the saloon from his brother-in-law six years before Prohibition became public knowledge a year later, on September 3, 1915, when Benjamin I. Sass filed for bankruptcy. On September 8, 1914, an auction was held at 16 Thomson Street and 307 Wickender Street. The articles at the public auction included "one 2nd class liquor license and one back bar with mirrors and one front bar with railing, one cash register and safe, one ice box, one pump, a set of copper measures, the stock of ales, wines liquors and cigars." Transferring the saloon to his brother-in-law was Ben's last hope to avoid bankruptcy. Why my grandfather, who had eight kids to feed at that time and a tailor shop, might have been interested in acquiring a saloon is yet another question.

Five years later, on October 16, 1920, an article in the *Providence Journal* explained what Ben Sass decided to do after he lost his liquor license and all the items in his saloon: He set up his own liquor business. That article described a raid on a house on Seventh Street occupied by Sass as well as the garage at his house. The Prohibition agents collected twenty-one gallons of alleged alcohol, whiskey, and other mixtures said to be "of intoxicating composition."

Three years later, it appeared as if Uncle Ben did a lot more than make gin and whiskey in his still on Seventh Street and was actively working in the bootlegging business. This time, on September 24, 1923, twenty-eight-year-old Ben hit the news in a pretty big way. On that day, Ben, along with six other bootleggers, including his twenty-two-year-old brother-in-law, Joe Rosenfield, was arrested, and a truck loaded with eighty cases of Scotch whiskey, valued at approximately $5,000, was seized in a surprise raid by five federal Prohibition agents. This time, Ben was arraigned before the US commissioner in Warwick, Rhode Island, on charges of violating the National Prohibition Act. According to the agents, that seizure was expected to put an end to the operations of bootlegging and rum-running crews who had built up an extensive trade among the most socially prominent families in the city.

The entire capture seemed like a scene out of the HBO series *Boardwalk Empire*. The Prohibition men, who had apparently been on the trail of Uncle Ben's gang for some time, had concealed themselves around houses and in bushes in the vicinity of Fred Smith's fish market in Longmeadow, a quiet, waterfront, residential neighborhood in Warwick, where it was thought the liquor might be landing. Shortly before midnight, those agents, after a long wait, saw a truck with seven passengers approach and stop in a dark spot near the shore.

Two of the men from the truck (it is unknown if Ben was one of them) rowed in a small skiff to a boat anchored about a half mile off the shore while the others stood guard over the truck, until the men returned with a cargo of liquor. After five such trips, the truck was then loaded to capacity. As the rumrunners prepared to leave with their highly prized stash of booze, on a prearranged signal, the federal agents leaped from their hiding places and, with revolvers drawn, arrested the seven men. The gang made no concerted attempt to resist arrest. One of the men, thirty-six-year-old William Haven of Longmeadow, was found to have been carrying a loaded revolver, which he explained he needed to ward off rum pirates.

The Prohibition agents brought their captives, together with the truck and its load, to Warwick. The seven men were locked up in the central police station for the night and the liquor was taken to a Providence warehouse.

Indeed, this sweep by the federal agents, three years into Prohibition, was a lot more serious than an arrest for possession of a still. There is no sign, however, that Uncle Ben stopped his bootlegging for the final ten years of Prohibition, nor is there any doubt that Ben and his family were far wealthier than the Phillip Blumenthal family. After all, how could you compare the proceeds of a one-man tailor shop to that of a catering business and the ill-gotten rewards of bootlegging? When Ben died in 1961, twenty-eight years after Prohibition ended, he was far more remembered for his extensive philanthropic activities than his illegal liquor activities.

The idea of this defunct, or at least temporarily put-out-of-business, gang of bootleggers servicing socially prominent families makes me wonder if Uncle Ben had many Jewish customers. Also, the fact that Ben supposedly sold mostly to wealthy Jews is, in itself, interesting, especially since he founded an organization to help newly immigrated Jews. His wife Ida's name was all over the society pages of the Providence newspapers, so he had access to lots of wealthy Providence and Pawtucket Jews.

Yet, for Ben to be a financially successful bootlegger he had to have many non-Jewish customers. The names of the other seven bootleggers arrested with him in Longmeadow, except for his brother-in-law Joseph Rosenfield, do not appear to be traditionally Jewish names. Thus, Ben Sass likely not only sold to non-Jews, he worked right alongside of them.

Many years later, Ben's great-nephew Ronnie Blumenthal may well have been thought of as the Jewish murderer, while the Accident victims must have stood out as being Jews as well. Yet, considering the fact that the driver of the car in the Accident was drunk, my uncle Barney owned a liquor store, and Ronnie became an alcoholic, then the image of a successful Jewish bootlegger in the Blumenthal family is important.

I cannot help wondering how the Accident of 1935 affected my great-uncle Ben Sass. After all, he lost his older sister, Rose, in the crash along with his nephew Ruby; his two great-nephews, Morty and Allen; and his great-niece Barbara, all of whom lived nearby. I could only imagine that Ben, far wealthier than his now-widowed and devastated brother-in-law, Phillip Blumenthal, might well have even paid for the expensive funerals of those relatives. Since Ben was a founding father of Temple Emanuel, I would have expected that Ben had been seriously involved in the funeral services conducted there.

I heard that, before the Accident, when my uncle Barney had been setting up his own liquor store, the Columbus Avenue

Wine Co. of Boston, he had been helped by his uncle Ben and Ben's connections. By the time of the Accident, Prohibition had been over for a year and a half, and there was nothing illegal about Ben and Barney's liquor business relationship. Yet, perhaps, the Accident, caused by a highly intoxicated driver shortly after Prohibition ended, resonated in a deeper way in my uncle Ben's mind.

Alcohol had now caused the death of his relatives, the same substance whose illegal sale had been an endeavor to which Ben had dedicated thirteen years of his life, from ages thirty-four to forty-seven, and from which he had earned some of his fortune. Many years later, there was no denying that his nephew Barney's son Ronnie was an alcoholic, an all-too-common disease that eventually paid a large part in Ronnie's myriad problems.

Uncle Ben's story is filled with excitement and financial and social success. Today, Prohibition is often looked as an unsuccessful and often ludicrous attempt to civilize unruly Americans by removing alcohol from their lives. This unsuccessful experiment had many unintended consequences, including the rise of organized crime and formation of the American Mafia. Unquestionably, the crimes my great-uncle committed during this failed experiment cannot be placed in the same category as vehicular homicide or murder in the second degree. Although he was pursued by federal agents, and might have spent a night or two in jail, Ben Sass was no Al Capone, let alone the drunken driver of the car that killed six of his relatives. But his reliance on the sale of alcohol puts him in an undeniable relationship with these two criminals, both of whom had blood on their hands. Alcohol held a negative and ugly place in the Blumenthal family saga, and the money it generated surely left scars on both Ben Sass's and Barney Blumenthal's hands.

CHAPTER TEN

Examination of a Life: Who Was Ronnie Blumenthal?

My family had wrongly believed that what had happened on May 14, 1935, was unquestionably the worst possible nightmare we would ever face. Had Thomas H. Killourey never found a pathway into the Blumenthal world, how different the lives of my family would have been. But other paths lay in front of us, and nothing good resulted from those junctures.

In search of answers to why bad things happened to our family we all insisted, "Look at our background! Look at who we are!" Cohesive, kind, hardworking people, always reminiscent of the 1935 tragedy that had decimated our family and taught us all that the world could be a dangerous place, that we could have been so much larger. For the cousins, losing our uncle and grandmother had removed such an essential part of our past. Shouldn't Uncle Ruby be upstairs at the pinochle table, laughing and smoking and yelling over a good or particularly bad hand? What specialties would our grandmother have brought to the Sunday table, or what stories could she have told us about her life in Russia? And no one could deny that losing three first cousins had forever diminished our group. Who knew what Morty, Barbara, and Allen might have brought to our gatherings? Those empty chairs would never fade from any Blumenthal mind.

So many of the thoughts about what was happening to the Blumenthal family revolved around our uncle Barney, Ronnie's father, born in 1906, the fifth child in the Blumenthal family. Uncle Barney was such a sweet man, a little on the plump side, but still tall, erect, and handsome, with a warm smile always lighting up his face. How could this man ever have had a hand in that evil deed as some rumormongers hinted? Barney was much loved by his four sisters and was especially close with his two older brothers, Ruby and Lewie, and his "baby" brother, Hy. Money was tight in the Blumenthal household in the early 1900s, but the family was close-knit, with the older children taking care of the younger ones. Violence never entered that home and few wandered far from 7 Overhill Road. Only Barney and my mother had married Boston people and followed them nearly a hundred miles from that house.

If we were searching for crime inside our family, then we had to be honest. We knew there were bootleggers in the Blumenthal family. It's possible—likely, in fact— that bootlegger Ben Sass's nephew, Barney Blumenthal, knew the liquor business well, which helped him own and operate a successful store, Hall's Liquors, on Tremont Street in Boston. As for more clues about what might have happened that July afternoon in 1954, maybe it all began with selling illegal alcohol during Prohibition. But how could a little bootlegging have influenced the Blumenthal genes? There was no denying that as he grew older our cousin Ronnie had a problem with alcohol, getting drunk way too often while hanging around with his teenage friends. But that was just typical teenage behavior, wasn't it? Were Ronnie's issues with alcohol some sort of karmic payback? Had the illegal bootleg booze during Prohibition harmed anyone? It wasn't unheard of....

Whatever we thought about Uncle Barney, my sister, Toby, had her own opinion about our aunt Edythe, which was a lot nicer than mine. After Toby suffered a miscarriage, she received a call from our aunt Edythe, who insisted on introducing Toby to her own highly respected Boston obstetrician, who then became Toby's doctor, eventually delivering her two babies. "Edythe was so attentive to me during that difficult time," Toby said. "She kept telling me that I was beautiful. She could not have been nicer." That particular story made me wonder briefly if my aunt might have been more complicated, and kinder, than I might have assumed. That thought was indeed brief. Future events convinced me that Edythe's act of benevolence had been a rare moment.

My cousin Fred Brown, one year younger than Ronnie, was one of Ronnie's closest friends from childhood. You could not imagine two more unlikely friends. Fred was the oldest of three in a family where money was rarely available, a serious, hard-working man from his earliest age, aware of his family responsibilities and deeply committed to all members of the Blumenthal family. Years later, it would be Fred and his wife, Sandra, whom Ronnie chose as the godparents of his one and only child.

There was never a streak of wildness in Fred, but somehow the two cousins, despite the personality differences and the distance between Brookline, Massachusetts, and Providence, Rhode Island, saw plenty of each another, especially as they grew older. As soon as Ronnie got his license and a fancy car to go with it, he frequently drove down to Providence to spend time with Fred. Fred never had a problem finding nice girls who might want to go out with his well-dressed, handsome, and fun-loving cousin, who arrived in a sporty new Chevy Bel Air convertible with plenty of money in his wallet.

Fred often came into Boston to visit Ronnie, who never failed to make their evenings memorable and nerve-wracking, driving his brand-new convertible faster than his usual over-the-speed-limit pace, ignoring Fred's shouts at him to slow down. "He'd smile and slow down, but just a very little," Fred told me. "He was a wild kid used to getting everything he wanted. He always had beautiful clothes and owned a camel-hair topcoat that I loved. He was a big, husky guy, so it might not have fit me even if he had ever decided to give it to me, but I would have loved it." Yes, Ronnie ignored the speed limit, but as we searched for glimpses of what might have been a violent cousin Ronnie, none of us has any memories of him losing his temper or being aggressive or cruel.

Mel Lipson, whose mother, Esta, was one of Barney's younger sisters, was one year younger than Ronnie. According to Mel, "Ronnie might have been handsome, but I thought he was a spoiled brat, and his mother was snotty. Still, he could be fun to be around, and I enjoyed my visits to his house at 80 Beals Street in Brookline. I remember Uncle Barney's liquor store being rather small, but he generously supplied the liquor for family celebrations."

Mel remembered one time he went out for lunch with Ronnie and two other cousins in Providence. "The three of us didn't have much money so we ordered maybe a hot dog, while Ronnie got a full meal with Salisbury steak and dessert. It didn't bother us. It was just the way it was. He was an only child and privileged. And also arrogant."

Considering how much my aunt and uncle doted on their only child, it always confused me that in 1945, when Ronnie turned ten, my aunt and uncle sent him off to the Riverside Military Academy in Gainesville, Georgia, which recently changed its name to Riverside Preparatory Academy. According to President Stanley Preczewski (*Gainesville Times*, October 5, 2022), "We will continue using the military model of education including required uniforms, earned leadership responsibilities, and codes of conduct, as we have for more than one hundred years."

In many respects that sounded like it would have been the perfect thing for my cousin during his later teenage years. By then he had grown more undisciplined—neither school nor rules mattered, and cash, fast cars, and pretty girls were the focus in his life. I cannot, however, comprehend why, years before he became a teen, a ten-year-old boy who was the light of his mother's eyes, her adored "Ronnalah," was suddenly uprooted from his parents and sent more than a thousand miles away to a Southern town. A Jewish boy in the 1940s yet, a time when anti-Semitism was far worse in the South than back in Boston. Although "Hebrew" is printed clearly on his school record under the heading "Church," the name "Blumenthal" could not have been a common or especially welcomed one in Gainesville, Georgia.

In truth, Bobby Gordon, Ronnie's wealthy cousin on his mother's side, had gone to Riverside a few years before Ronnie, which was obviously how the family heard of the school in the first place. Perhaps this was yet another example of the Blumenthals trying to keep up with the far-richer Gordons. After all, Riverside was not free, as were the Brookline public schools, so the idea of having a child in a private school, especially a boarding school, had to offer some extra clout to my aunt's social standing. Still, it would have been a bit of an extreme attempt to climb up the social ladder.

I recently read some of the following comments about the school published in *Niche Reviews* of all-boys preparatory schools close to the years that Ronnie was there. The comments comparing the school to a prison have a special significance for Ronnie's future "education": "This school is the most pathetic excuse for an academy that is supposed to help kids! The bullying and the punishments are so bad they make your kids terrified. This school is worse than a prison."

There were also positive comments such as the following: "I spent six years at RMA ('58–'63). It was, without doubt, one of the great experiences of my life. No, it's not an easy place; it's a challenge, and it produces men who can deal with challenges."

Another, more understandable, reason for Ronnie's two years at Riverside could have been related to our family's assumptions that my aunt and uncle had been having marital problems. If that was the case, that might have been the reason to send their son away from a house where nasty arguments were frequent and escalating. If it had been the reason, however, there were many boarding schools closer to Brookline than one in Gainesville, such as the prestigious Phillips Andover Academy. And why a military school? Unlike his brothers, Ruby and Hy, Barney had not fought or had any type of involvement in either World War I or World War II, nor did he appear enamored with the military. Was there a specific reason that Barney and Edith suddenly believed ten-year-old Ronnie needed strict discipline at a faraway military school? Had something so egregious happened that they had felt compelled to resort to such a drastic change in their young son's life? Or did they honestly believe that two years at a military school would benefit him in innumerable ways?

Whatever the reasoning might have been for Ronnie's exile, no answer to those questions ever came from the Providence Blumenthals. The only sign of those two years I can personally recall was the photo of Ronnie in a military uniform, his cute, round, smiling face topped with a military cap that my aunt Etta kept on a mantle at 7 Overhill Road. I'd heard how she fretted for the three years her "baby" brother Hy was in the service in Europe. Maybe she was worried that her adored nephew Ronnie might eventually face danger in a future upheaval. What could a ten-year-old have done to merit such a change in the entire family's life? Like so many questions concerning my cousin's life, that one remains unanswerable, but it does qualify as a red flag. Something happened at 80 Beals Street (a few doors away from 83 Beals Street, where Joe and Rose Kennedy lived many years earlier in the 1910s) that caused Barney and Edythe Blumenthal to pack their son's suitcase and drive more than fifteen hours to deliver their adored fifth grader to a military school in Georgia.

In Ronnie's record at the school there appeared no reason why he would not return after 1947. After all, as they clearly noted, his grades were average and his discipline satisfactory. Indeed, those grades were pretty run-of-the-mill: eighty-eight and seventy-four in English; seventy-one and seventy in arithmetic; eighties in science and reading; seventies and eighties in penmanship; and high nineties for spelling. These scores were much higher than the ones he would later earn at Brookline High School. In the photo of Ronnie in his Riverside military uniform, his round, cherub-like face displaying a bright smile, Ronnie was simply adorable. My mother also kept a small photo of Ronnie in his unform in a frame on her bureau, but my aunt Etta's photo was far larger and in a more prominent place on her living room mantel. So many times I saw her smile as she pointed out the special photo to me. "Such a precious *punim* [face]," she told me, and I would nod my head in agreement.

A year after Ronnie's return from Riverside Military Academy, he celebrated his bar mitzvah in 1948 at Congregation Kehillath Israel in Brookline, a truly joyous family occasion. At age five I was apparently too young to have been invited, but my older cousins remember it as a fun affair, with a smiling Ronnie at the center of it all. Thanks to home movie film of the three-day celebration, I finally witnessed that lavish and joyous occasion. Lots of food, music, dancing, hugging, and kissing fill the video, with Ronnie beaming and basking in the spotlight. I watched that video multiple times, seeing how, dressed in a stylish blue suit and designer tie, my thirteen-year-old cousin solemnly and nearly perfectly recited his Torah portion before heading off to the fancy and lively celebration in his honor.

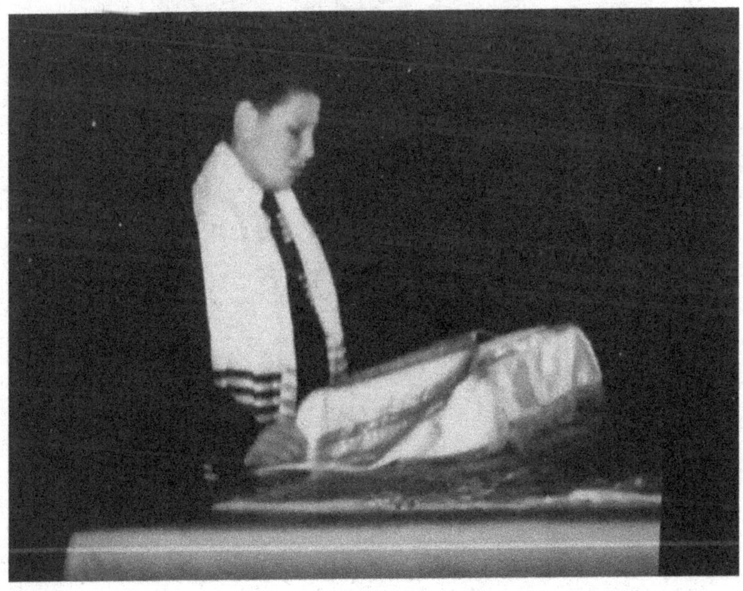

Scenes from Ronnie's 1948 Bar Mitzvah.

I have been riveted to the beginning of the video, where I saw Ronnie, looking quite pleased, walking up the stairs to the esteemed synagogue, settled comfortably between his proud parents. He initially appeared a bit serious, but after the services, his face was filled with that huge, inimitable Ronnie smile.

He was nearly exactly the same age as our cousin Morty Blumenthal—killed in the Accident—whom we never met. The photos of Morty that filled the front pages of dozens of newspapers after May 14, 1935 (thirteen years before Ronnie's bar mitzvah) show a dark-haired Providence boy, twelve years old, dressed in a white shirt, print tie, vest, and tweed suit jacket, looking serious and incredibly handsome. I was always entranced by that formal photo of my cousin. Where and when was it taken? Born in 1923, Morty was only twelve when he died in the Accident, too young to have had a bar mitzvah at Temple Emanuel on Taft Street in Providence, just a few doors away from his own home at 84 Taft Avenue. Morty had two older Blumenthal cousins, Irma and Elaine Blumenthal, daughters of Uncle Lewie, four years younger than his father and ten years older than my mother. At that time, unlike boys, girls were not permitted to have a bat mitzvah. One can only imagine the joy his Blumenthal grandparents would have felt for this heir to their name to be called to the Torah as a man. The fact that Morty died with his grandmother Rose and his father before he reached the age of thirteen seems even more poignant and heartbreaking.

When Ronnie Blumenthal was called to the Torah as a man in the eyes of Jewish law, however, great joy permeated the synagogue and the celebratory parties. After all, he was the only male heir to the Blumenthal name since both his uncles, Hy and Lewie, had produced daughters. In so many scenes of the party following the services, Ronnie is hugged by multiple relatives, including every one of his Blumenthal aunts and uncles, and he dances sweetly with all who reached out to him. The dances with his mother, however, are the most fascinating. The bar mitzvah boy whirls his mother joyously around the dance floor as his father watches, pride filling his face. The film shows nothing except a happy, wealthy Jewish family celebrating the future of their one son, a future filled with hope and endless possibility.

We could only guess what might have happened to Morty if he had lived, especially after Pearl Harbor was attacked six years later. Would he have been drafted or enlisted and served in World War II? Probably. Would he have survived the war? Maybe. We do know that by the time Ronnie was seventeen, he was already getting into serious trouble. Some of his classmates at Brookline High School were describing Ronnie as explosive and temperamental, with one describing a scene in a burger joint in which Ronnie slapped the face of his date.

That skirmish wasn't the only one to tarnish my cousin's reputation. A far more serious and dangerous one happened in June 1954, one for which Ronnie was legally cited. This time he threw a lit firecracker into an open convertible, nearly causing the teen girl driver to lose control of her car. Thinking about the crash that destroyed the lives of six of Ronnie's relatives, the rest of the family cringed. How could he be so reckless? It was a miracle that the terrified driver safely brought her car to a stop. What was my cousin *thinking?* That this was funny?

In school, Ronnie was not the danger he was on the open road. There, he ran at a far slower speed. The news that his academic record was so bad that he would not be graduating with the Brookline High School Class of 1953 must have disappointed his parents. They quickly enrolled him in Huntington Prep, a private school in Boston, in the hopes that he would change his ways and earn his general education diploma, and then, like his Blumenthal cousins, head off to college. Several months into Ronnie's first semester at Huntington Prep, however, the headmaster made it more than clear that graduation would not be in the cards there. The only subject that was earning Ronnie's interest there was the extracurricular sport of boxing, for which he was physically well-suited. However, his poor academic standing dashed his hopes to form a boxing club with another classmate.

All that remained in Ronnie's corner that discouraging year when his former Brookline High classmates headed off to college were a fast car, a handsome face, expensive clothes, plenty of spending money, and an array of pretty girls who were more than happy to enjoy those benefits. Since all the girls in his class at Brookline were off to college, that year Ronnie drove his Chevy Bel Air convertible into Newton, where he began dating a pretty girl named Barbara, managing to get to her high school every day just in time to drive her home in his hot car.

As an eighteen-year-old who was left behind by his Brookline class of 1953, Ronnie never appeared particularly disappointed to be spending a year at prep school. He still had strong access to his former classmates, as well as to the girls who were a year behind them. Yet, events happened that year that may well have impacted the carefree life of a teenager who worried little about his academic or professional future. After all, what did it matter if he never got his high school degree or went to college? There was always the liquor store. The store would be his whenever he was ready to join his father there and, down the road, take over the business.

The world outside Ronnie's comfortable Beals Street home was changing. The Korean War (1950–1953) had claimed the lives of more than thirty-six thousand American soldiers and injured ninety-two thousand of them. Wisconsin Senator Joseph McCarthy's fears of Communist infiltration in the United States made daily headlines, as did the rumblings of a conflict in French Indochina, which France was busy losing to the locals in 1954, the country now known as Vietnam. Edythe and Barney understood, even if Ronnie did not, that the Selective Service Act of 1948 was still in effect and that an unmarried eighteen-year-old who was not enrolled in college could end up getting drafted. His parents most likely called in a favor from a close Rhode Island family friend, Lenny Holland, an Army Reserve officer, to get Ronnie into the 101st Engineer Battalion of the local Massachusetts Army National Guard troop in Medford. For six months, beginning in March 1954, Ronnie could continue at Huntington Prep in his quest for his GED and a possible path to college while attending weekly sessions at the Medford Armory. It was hoped that if he followed that plan, he would remain relatively exempt from any future military action. While his time at the armory was not my cousin's first stint in a military unform, the smiling ten-year-old Ronnie at Riverside Military School bore little resemblance to the teenage reluctant guardsman.

CHAPTER ELEVEN

The Murder: July 27, 1954

"Will you tell me why I done it?"

While the details about the Accident are clearly explained in Thomas H. Killourey's court documents, questions remain about the second hideous family event, which many of the family call the Incident, seventy years later. Only two facts of the Incident have any degree of certainty to them: (1) Ora Schonarth, fifty-two, was viciously murdered in her home at 68 Cypress Street in Brookline, Massachusetts, on July 27, 1954; and (2) my eighteen-year-old cousin, Ronald S. Blumenthal, of 80 Beals Street in Brookline, was taken into custody and transported to the Brookline Police Department at 4:30 a.m. on July 29, 1954. At 6:10 a.m., while Aunt Edythe and Uncle Barney remained at 80 Beals Street in states of shock and hysteria, Ronnie admitted in a statement, which remained unsigned, that he murdered Ora Schonarth in her home sometime around 4:00 p.m. on Tuesday, July 27, 1954.

More than seventy years after that murder, many other details remain fuzzy. For instance, on Wednesday, July 28, at 11:15

a.m., Ora's younger sister, Mary D. Smart, discovered Ora's body in the Cypress Street apartment and called the police. When they arrived, she told them, "My sister is on the floor inside, she's dead, she has been stabbed." When the police entered, they found the apartment orderly except for a few soiled dishes in the sink. The magazine section of the *Boston Sunday Record* from July 25, 1954, was on top of the bed in the bedroom. In the living room, where the body was found, a bloodstained cushion from one of the living room chairs lay on the floor, and several bloodstains marked the wall. Ora's handbag sat on the couch among some newspapers, the most recent of which was the *Boston Daily Record* dated July 27, 1954.

Ora was on her back, on the living room carpet. Her legs were together, the ankles bound with a piece of blue cloth. A pair of men's khaki pants were tied around her neck and a knife was stuck in her chest. A rolling pin, wrapped in waxed paper and stained with what seemed to be blood, was on the floor, near her left arm. One of its handles was missing. Also, some more pieces of the blue cloth that was tied around her ankles lay next to her left arm. The police found no evidence of forced entry to the apartment, although the back door was open. The crime scene was every bit as ugly as the scene of the 1935 Connecticut car crash, though in the Brookline apartment only one hideously shattered body was found rather than six and there were no signs of an accident.

The Boston medical examiner, Dr. Thomas Kendrick, would soon report that Ora had died from repeated blows of the rolling pin, which had fractured her skull in eight places. How cruelly coincidental is the fact that the cause of death for five of the six in the Connecticut crash was also a fractured skull? A rolling pin covered in waxed paper and controlled by human hands broke

Ora's skull. Skulls fractured as bodies were thrust forward during a violent car crash ended five lives. One can only pray that those five deaths were quick; Ora's death, regrettably, might not have been so quick.

Indeed, Dr. Kendrick's preliminary autopsy report stated that a bread knife with a six-inch blade had been plunged into the victim's chest after she was dead. In a later and ultimately final report, judging by the appearance of rigor mortis, however, the pathologist changed that conclusion and said Ora was still alive when the knife was plunged into her heart. His pathology report also indicated that particles of cultivated blueberries and milk were found in Ora's stomach. Initially, he concluded that her death may have occurred within a period of four hours after she ate that food and drank the milk, but he later amended that report to say that the crime could have occurred within a twenty-four-hour period of the discovery of the body. Those time details have always muddied the story, making it difficult to fit every piece of the puzzle into a solid, unquestionable image. When I read the coroner's report of the Accident, as hideous as it appeared, it was simple and to the point—there were no questions as to how each of the six victims died and who caused their deaths. Ora's death report, however, as hideous as it was, appeared far more indecisive.

What is also undisputable, however, is the fact that within hours of the discovery of Ora's body, the headlines of the Boston newspapers announced SLAYING IN BROOKLINE: DIVORCÉE BEATEN, STABBED AND STRANGLED IN HER OWN HOME; ROLLING PIN, KNIFE, NEAR BODY OF DRESSMAKER; FOUR TIMES MARRIED NURSES AID AND DRESSMAKER FOUND BLUDGEONED, STRANGLED AND STABBED TO DEATH IN HER BROOKLINE APARTMENT.

As the police began zealously investigating the crime, the first report claimed—falsely, as it turned out—that a man closely associated with Ora was under intense questioning by police, who hinted that an arrest was imminent. A chemical test had apparently shown that the suspect's hands and arms had been in recent contact with blood, and he was unable to account for how that contact had been made. Now the police had established that the woman had been killed between 2:00 and 3:00 a.m. on Wednesday morning. They also revealed that a good set of fingerprints had been obtained from the crime scene and that there had been no sign of a struggle and the house had not been ransacked. The next report by Dr. Kendrick stated that the victim had been killed by at least eight blows from the rolling pin to her skull, which had been "crushed like an eggshell." The stab wound had gone through the left side of her chest and into her heart. He concluded that the murder had apparently taken place sometime after midnight on Tuesday. Brookline detectives had been rushed to the scene followed by state police attachés of the district attorney of Norfolk County, along with a team of medical experts from the Harvard Bureau of Legal Medicine.

As for the whereabouts of the man who would be accused of the murder, thirty-six hours before his arrest, my cousin Ronne was paying a visit to two female friends, Lois Kane and Vicky Prince. Around eight o'clock on Tuesday evening, July 27, 1954, nine hours before the body was discovered and the police began their investigation, and four hours before one incorrect official guess about the time of death, "sometime after midnight on Tuesday," Ronnie Blumenthal calmly recounted every detail of the murder that the police would soon investigate, boasting to his startled listeners about "the perfect crime." Lois, seventeen at the time, had graduated Brookline High a few months earlier and knew Ronnie only slightly. She had little to do with him until she went to visit her girlfriend Vicky and found him there. After a few minutes, Ronnie suddenly asked the two girls, "If a woman was stabbed in the heart, would you believe she was dead?"

Lois and Vicky had replied that the question was silly, but Ronnie continued with his gruesome tale of a "perfect murder," using "someone" instead of "I" in his recitation. When the girls started to make fun of his ghastly and unbelievable tale, he once again repeated the grisly story, this time in the first person. Telling them the murder victim lived on Cypress Street, he left out her name but included every detail of the murder itself, explaining calmly how *he* had strangled her, hit her with the rolling pin, and then stabbed her. He even told them about tying her up. The girls were rightfully horrified, barely able to believe him. At first, Lois thought Ronnie was the type of guy who tried to make an impression by saying something so thoroughly horrible that it would make his listeners' skin crawl. Annoyed that the girls didn't believe his story, Ronnie told them, "You'll believe me when you read it in the newspapers," and at 9:00 p.m. he left.

There is no way anyone who knew Ronnie could read the police report and not assume that the Ronnie they knew had lost his mind. How could he ever murder a woman in such a vicious and hideous manner and then calmy relate the story of what he had just done to two girls who were just friends and not intimates? It made no sense. My cousin Ronnie was now as big a mystery as was the murder.

As the newspaper account of this hard-to-believe scene reported, Vicky left Brookline for a family vacation the next morning, but Lois repeated the story to her mother as soon as she woke up on Wednesday. When they didn't see anything about a Brookline murder in the morning newspaper, Lois and her mother assumed Ronnie had made up the whole story. But when the Wednesday *evening* newspaper was filled with details about the divorcée who had been viciously murdered in her Cypress Street apartment, the details of the crime exactly what Ronnie had described to her less than twenty-four hours earlier, Lois told her father everything she had heard at Vicky's house.

Mr. Kane then called a friend, a *Boston American* newspaper executive, who came to the Kane house so that Lois could repeat the story to him. Satisfied that Lois was not a flighty teenager who had made up a crazy story and convinced that Lois held the key to the murder investigation, the friend arranged a meeting with Norfolk County District Attorney Myron Lane at the Brookline police station. Here, Lois spent the next two and a half hours repeating her testimony of the previous evening's events. Then she went home. At 4:30 a.m., the police headed to 80 Beals Street to pick up Ronnie, whose boasting about "the perfect crime" had provided them with the necessary suspicion to arrest him at his home on Thursday, July 29.

Whenever I've contemplated that evening over the years, I wondered if my cousin was living in another world, even aware of what he was doing. If he had indeed committed that murder, had he done it to impress two girls he barely knew? No, that doesn't seem right. Was he a psychopath with a personality disorder characterized, according to the *Merriam-Webster Dictionary*, "by persistent antisocial behavior, impaired empathy and remorse, and bold, disinhibited and egotistical traits"? Hmmm, possibly. Or was he trying to cover for someone else? Also a possibility, but then why say anything to anybody? All I knew for sure was that a woman was dead, and my cousin Ronnie did everything he could to look guilty as hell short of walking into the police station himself and spilling the beans.

Several days after Ronnie was arrested, another *Boston Herald* story surfaced about a call that he had made later on the same night he visited Lois. In that story, Ronnie also confessed his crime to yet another Brookline girl, a former girlfriend named Esther Brown. Apparently, Esther had called her present boyfriend after Ronnie had been arrested and told him about the call she had received from Ronnie on Tuesday night, July 27. Ronnie told Esther that he was in trouble, that he had killed the dressmaker Mrs. Schonarth, and that he wanted her to know why. "It's worth going to the electric chair to save my family," he apparently told Esther. "I asked her [Ora] to give him up—I mean my father—but she only told me to mind my own business." Those haunting lines, "It's worth going to the electric chair to save my family," were repeated and dissected countless times in newspaper stories, lawyers' discussions, and family conversations.

As for her call from Ronnie, Esther also told her boyfriend that Ronnie had complained some time ago that his father was having an affair with the redheaded dressmaker. He had told Esther that his mother had discovered his father's infidelity, that their home was breaking up as a result of the affair, and that his mother had gone to Mrs. Schonarth's apartment several weeks before to discuss the matter with her. Esther also related that on Thursday, July 29, two days after Ronnie had called her, my aunt and uncle had been in touch with her and warned her not to discuss the incident with anyone until she had talked with them. That same day, Ronnie's lawyer, Herbert Callahan, called Esther and told her not to discuss the case with anyone, that what Ronnie had told her on Tuesday was "just his version and a rumor and a mistake." I repeated those words, "just his version and a rumor and a mistake," many times to myself and to my relatives. How wonderful if Callahan had been right. If only

Ronnie's version of what he had told Esther, as well as Lois and Vicky, was a mistake. Looking back, I realize we were all just deluding ourselves because we wanted our cousin to be innocent.

Callahan told Esther he would be in touch with her later. Because Esther's family refused to allow her to testify in court about this highly revealing phone call, filled with important details about Ronnie and his parents and "the dressmaker," Esther never reached the heroine status that Lois Kane achieved after her brave report to the police.

The newspapers had more than enough details to keep the press hot on Ronnie's trail. As they avidly recounted, before Ronnie had visited Lois, and even before he had gone to see Ora, he had enjoyed a busy Tuesday. He spent much of the morning of the murder at the home of Mr. and Mrs. Leon Leshefsky in the Waveland section of Hull, near the Nantasket home his parents sometimes rented in the summer. It was from there that he apparently went directly to Ora's Cypress Street apartment. According to Mrs. Leshefsky, known as "Bobby," she and her two daughters, Harriet and Myrna, "thought the world of Ronnie. He was such a nice kid. Ronnie was a member of our circle. We will never understand this. It's heartbreaking. Ronnie was at our house all Tuesday morning and he and the girls didn't even go to the beach then. He acted as normal as apple pie that morning and did everything he usually did. We have nothing but high praise for Ronnie, and my family will do everything we can to help him."

Myrna, four years younger than Ronnie and living in Cambridge, Massachusetts, remembered that day well. Although Ronnie was closer to Myrna's older sister, Harriet, who died in 2005, Myrna double-dated with Ronnie several times. "He was a big guy, kind of like a big teddy bear," she said. "He didn't stay at our house very long that day. He said he had to get back to

Brookline." As for what happened when Ronnie indeed returned to Brookline, Myrna always believed what everyone around her said: "His father was having an affair with the woman. That was why he did what he did." As for her mother's description of Ronnie that July day, "normal as apple pie," it would be a very long time, perhaps never again, that anyone would describe Ronnie as "normal as pie," apple or any other kind.

When Ronnie left Nantasket Beach that fateful Tuesday, he gave a boyhood chum a ride in his convertible. According to that friend, Ronnie drove him about a mile from Paragon Park to D Street. "He seemed in a good mood, joking and having fun," Myrna said. But just an hour or so after he gave that boy a lift, Ronnie allegedly clubbed and stabbed a woman to death. Nothing stopped the newspapers from insisting that my cousin had committed the murder just for the "thrill of it," like teenagers Nathan Leopold and Richard Loeb back in 1924.

On the trail from the very beginning, newspaper reports of that warm July night showed that Ronnie, after coming back from Nantasket, after viciously killing Ora Schonarth, and after visiting Lois and Vicky, drove with a few friends to the Howard Johnson's restaurant at Cleveland Circle in Brighton. They noted that Ronnie, speeding in his black Bel Air convertible, skidded, with his tires screeching, into the parking lot of that frequent rendezvous spot for Brookline and Newton high schoolers. When he went inside to get something to eat, he reportedly exchanged harsh words with twenty-one-year-old Edward Fontenarosa, an employee of the restaurant and a psychology major at Suffolk University, who was working behind the counter. According to Fontenarosa, Ronnie had been "quarrelsome and belligerent" that evening. "He came in here with a chip on his shoulder like he had something on his mind and wanted to take his peeve out on somebody. He was with a student at Boston College and got very loud."

The trouble began when Ronnie started complaining about the price of the food, yelling it wasn't worth the price. "I told him I didn't make the prices, that I just worked here," Fontenarosa said. "He had a stern look on his face, as if something was bothering him. Then I heard him make insulting remarks about the other counterman, Leo Hajab, of Dorchester. I told him if he had something to say, say it to Leo's face, that I didn't like people talking behind other people's backs. Then I told Ronnie if he didn't like the prices, say so, and he told me, 'I don't like you either.' I told him that was too bad and he said, 'What do you want to do about it?'"

During the argument, the Boston College student who was standing behind Ronnie gestured with his hands that Ronnie had been drinking and not to pay any attention to him. "I didn't smell any liquor on his breath," Fontenarosa insisted. "He didn't stagger. He didn't look drunk. He seemed alert and wide awake. But you could tell he had something on his mind. He was looking for an outlet. Ronnie finally left but not before arguing with the manager on the way out."

Yet another acquaintance of Ronnie's described his friend's behavior that night at Howard Johnson's differently. He said that Ronnie seemed quiet, as if he had something on his mind. He didn't join in the conversation like he usually did, especially if the talk was about cars and how fast they could go.

These two differing descriptions of Ronnie made the bewildering scene even more perplexing. Perhaps that made perfect sense: Ronnie was two different people, not just that night, but, most likely, for a far longer time.

As for Wednesday, July 28, the day Lois Kane spoke to her parents and to the police, Ronnie had another busy day. A police report about Ronnie's activities on that day indicated that he had been in Dennis, Massachusetts, about an hour-and-a-half drive from Brookline, selling a watch and a wallet to a gas station attendant there. I cannot help but wonder why Ronnie needed the money that day. Was he planning to take off and evade the consequences of what he had supposedly done the night before? Or did he just often sell his belongings, knowing his parents would always replace them?

According to one Beals Street neighbor, Ronnie "seemed just as unconcerned as ever when he drove up to his house that day about quarter to six in his black Bel Air convertible, a good-looking blonde with him. She had her arm around him. They got out of the car and went into his house together." For some reason there appeared to be no mention of this blonde in any police reports. Maybe the neighbor was hallucinating. Maybe everything that happened on July 27 and July 28 were hallucinations. But this was no mirage; it was a nightmare. Around ten hours after that supposed sighting of a "good-looking blonde" in his car, Ronnie Blumenthal was woken in his bed by the police.

At 4:30 on that Thursday morning, seven Brookline policemen arrived at 80 Beals Street. My uncle Barney answered the door and, understandably more asleep than awake, nervously asked Captain Joseph Mahoney and State Police Lieutenant William Delay, "What's the matter?"

"We want to talk to your son," Captain Mahoney told him. Aunt Edythe, who had gotten out of bed by this time, became hysterical at the sight of the policemen in her house. The officers found Ronnie sound asleep in his bed on the first floor. Within minutes, while my uncle watched helplessly and utterly confused and my aunt grew more distraught, the police officers moved throughout the house. In the basement, they removed a pair of bloodied khaki pants and a sweatshirt from the washing machine, as well as the water in which they were soaking. From under Ronnie's bed, they retrieved a pair of light-gray buckskin shoes. In minutes, the officers were gone, having taken Ronnie into custody. The police also brought Ronnie's 1954 black Chevy Bel Air convertible to the police station to be examined by a chemist and photographed. The scene at my aunt and uncle's house had to be painful. The shock of the police at their door, the removal of their barely awake son to police custody, the bloodied clothes in the washing machine, the screaming of my aunt—how could this possibly be happening to this supposedly loving family of three?

Thanks to Lois Kane's statement hours earlier and Ronnie's complete cooperation, events moved at a stunningly fast pace. One of the first things that Ronnie reportedly said to the arresting officer when they arrived at the police station was, "Will you tell me why I done it?" That is the question that remains in my mind today, the answer for which I, and most of my relatives, am still searching.

Brookline Girl, 17, Solved Slaying

Her Calm Story Led to Arrest

A pretty 17-year-old Brookline girl with a sense of public responsibility bred into her at her home and nourished at her school solved the slaying of Mrs. Ora Schonerth.

Lois Kane, the daughter of Kane Furniture Company president Louis Kane of 573 Washington St., could have kept the secret confession of Ronald S. Blumenthal, 18, also of Brookline, sealed behind her lips.

But because her parents and her teachers had taught her the responsibility that goes along with the benefits of life in a democracy, she spoke out.

Her speaking enabled police to arrest the youth who now is charged with the "extremely vicious murder" of the attractive Brookline dressmaker last Tuesday.

It was to Lois and a girl friend

LOIS KANE

At 5:10 on Thursday morning, July 28, the police began interviewing Ronnie about the Schonarth murder. At 6:10 a.m. he admitted in a statement that he had murdered Ora Schonarth in her Brookline home sometime around 4:00 p.m. on Tuesday July 27, 1954. At 6:40 a.m., the police officers drove Ronnie to 78 Cypress Street, where he cooperatively reenacted the crime.

There, according to detectives, Ronnie described exactly what had happened, giving them more details than he had offered Lois and Vicky some thirty hours earlier. In an unemotional tone, he told them that at 4:00 on Tuesday afternoon, he went alone to the Cypress Street apartment to ask Mrs. Schonarth to stitch his raincoat, and when she finished, he gave her a dollar. Then she left the room to make change, and when she came back, "I grabbed her by the throat and choked her. She fell to the floor. I went into the kitchen and got a rolling pin and beat her on the head. She was bleeding pretty badly. I went into the bedroom and found a pair of men's brown shorts in a drawer. I tied them around her good and tight. [According to the police report, he tied the shorts around her legs.] Then I picked up some cloth from the sewing machine and tied that piece of cloth around her neck. I went into the kitchen then and I got a knife. I stabbed her in the heart. I then went out and got into the car which I'd parked on Durham Avenue and I drove back to Coolidge Corner."

When he was asked what motivated him, he said that the impulse just came over him. "I just had a sort of obsession. I can't explain it. I don't know. I just done it. I must have gone berserk." The word "berserk" has floated around in my head for years. What did he mean by that? Had he just lost his mind? How could my cousin have transformed from a self-centered and overindulged eighteen-year-old into a brutal killer in an instant?

Shouldn't someone in the family have noticed some aspect of "berserk" behavior before that afternoon?

Whether my cousin went berserk or not, at 9:00 a.m. on July 29, with Judge Frank A. Crehan presiding and every Blumenthal relative waiting for the decision, the case of Ronald Blumenthal was continued to August 5, 1954. Ronnie was remanded to the Norfolk County Dedham jail without bail.

On the way to the jail, Ronnie reportedly asked Probation Officer Robert C. True, "What happens now?" Officer True said Ronnie asked the question with casual unconcern. "He was so calm it seemed as if he didn't know what was going on. I told him that he'd be back in court next Thursday, then probably held for the Grand Jury, and it might be quite a while before he actually went to trial. He just nodded."

This detail was added to the pile of hard-to-believe details that Ronnie's relatives dissected ad nauseum. Who was this person the newspaper reporters claimed was our Ronnie? Had he no idea the seriousness of the crime to which he had just confessed and the havoc it had caused to all who loved him, as well as to those who loved Ora Schonarth? It was obvious he was not "berserk," but rather catatonic and stupefied, or, more awful to contemplate, a dumb murderer.

From the moment that the first newspaper article appeared linking Ronnie to Ora's ghastly murder, the interest in the story intensified. People far from Ronnie's family wanted to know every single detail of what he had or had not done. Maybe the local news in Boston that summer was slow and uninteresting. The Red Sox ended up finishing forty-two games behind the first place Cleveland Indians, so we didn't even have their games to distract us. Whatever the reason, that murder captured the spotlight, and reporters could not seem to supply enough stories to satisfy their readers' cravings. The trial itself was expected to be one of the most dramatic, bizarre, and brutal in Norfolk County history. After all, here was a young, wealthy, handsome, Jewish teenager who was accused of brutally murdering a woman three times his age for reasons readers could only imagine.

Sure, things were happening in the world beyond Brookline in 1954. The French lost Dien Bien Phu to the Viet Minh, West Germany was admitted into NATO, the Supreme Court banned segregation in public schools in the *Brown v. Board of Education* decision, and the USS *Nautilus* was commissioned as the first nuclear-powered submarine. *On the Waterfront* with Marlon Brando and Eva Marie Saint, winner of eight Academy Awards, opened on July 28. Bill Haley and the Comets' version of "Rock Around the Clock" had been recorded by the American Decca label on April 12 and was playing on radios all over the country. Elvis Presley had just released his first two commercial recordings, "That's All Right" and "Blue Moon of Kentucky" on July 19. The first doses of the polio vaccine had been injected five months earlier in February. The Joseph McCarthy hearings had been televised from April to June and were now over. None of these events, however, could compare to the murder that had happened on one of Brookline's quiet streets on a lovely summer afternoon.

The papers continually filled their pages with copious details about my cousin's activities before and after the murder, along with statements from his high school friends, acquaintances, teachers, and neighbors in an attempt to satisfy their readers' appetites for Ronnie minutiae. The Boston reporters dug and dug, and the photographers snapped and snapped, and the readers read and read about the Blumenthal murder. Yet, surprisingly, not one reporter reached out to Ronnie's relatives in

Providence or Boston to ask a question about Ronnie. For all I know, Ronnie's uncle, a Boston philanthropist and property owner, made it clear that all of Ronnie's relatives were off limits to reporters. At one time, Maurice Gordon, married to Edythe's sister Dorothy, owned fourteen thousand rental apartments in Boston and another $15 million worth of real estate in Miami. His many philanthropic gifts included a men's dormitory and a $100,000 music scholarship to Brandeis University. In 1968, because of student charges that he was a "slum lord," he canceled a $500,000 donation to Boston University toward the construction of a new facility for their School of Nursing. While the Gordon name may have been sullied by some bad publicity at that time, it was nothing compared to his Blumenthal nephew's crime stories. Still, it was obvious that Maurice and Dorothy considered Ronnie's freedom an important philanthropic cause.

Most of the headlines of the stories about their nephew were anything but subtle, such as the front page of the July 30, 1954, *Boston Daily Record*, with its THRILL KILLING RIVALS LEOPOLD-LOEB CASE headline, accompanied by several photos of my cousin, some looking like a typical eighteen-year-old kid, others ferocious and scary. This was the story of the summer, and the Boston papers concentrated on it from July 27 straight through until its inevitable conclusion on October 1, relentlessly continuing their sensational coverage. It makes sense that local radio and television news coverage followed suit. And why not? The story had all the necessary elements to keep the readers glued to its details: handsome, husky, wealthy, Jewish, spoiled, eighteen-year-old prep school son of a liquor store owner; a fifty-two-year-old, petite, redheaded, four-time divorcée with a penchant for younger men, a remarkable talent with a needle and thread, and a bit of a checkered lifestyle. Add in a possible sex scandal, a vicious murder, a confusing motive, and a couple of pretty teenage girls with attachments to the suspect, and the story, with each new detail that could be unearthed, grew even more mesmerizing. It became more surreal each day to the family that was struggling to accept the fact that one of its members had most probably killed a woman in her own home in cold blood. Six members of that family had been murdered by a drunk driver eighteen years earlier. Now we had become a murdering family? How did *that* happen?

While we struggled with this agonizing conundrum, the papers made hay. The center of all their attention remained inside the Dedham jail. Ronnie, while not catatonic, seemed eerily disinterested and unruffled. Although he was housed in the east wing cell block near other prisoners, it was reported that Ronnie made no effort to converse with them or the guards. The questions he had asked on the way to the jail for the first time were rephrased and reprinted dozens of times: "What happens to me now? What's my sentence going to be?" Readers were understandably shocked when told that when Ronnie had been asked if he wanted to contact anyone or send any messages, he said he did not.

Jail officials reported that the suspect remained calm and devoid of emotional display during visits with his father and his lawyer. Ronnie's seeming obliviousness of the effect of his crime on the public became more apparent each day as evidenced by his genuine surprise at the crowds that appeared when he was finally in public view for a court appearance. "Why are they all looking at me?" he asked a court officer more than once, appearing astonished that anyone was interested in him.

All Boston newspaper readers were now aware that Ronnie no longer wore his expensive preppy shirts and pants but instead he wore the white cotton trousers and blue jacket of the Dedham jail, and, although most of the prisoners ate in a mess hall, my cousin preferred to have his meals in his cell. Although he exchanged only one-word greetings with "trusties" (nonviolent inmates who have been sentenced to time in the county jail) and guards who entered the cell block, Ronnie's attitude, as described in the newspapers, was "neither sullen nor taciturn but rather introspective." Those words seemed a bit out of place. Ronnie had never been described as possessing the powers of introspection.

One *Boston Evening American* story, along with many other similar newspaper stories, reported that Ronnie's parents had been understandably traumatized when District Attorney Myron Lane, Brookline Police Captain Joseph Mahoney, and a score of patrolmen had descended on their home to arrest their son. It had been their first inkling that the boy on whom they had lavished everything they could afford stood charged with Brookline's most appalling crime in its history. Every day after that morning, veteran detectives continued to express amazement and bewilderment at Ronnie's blasé attitude. "He hasn't shown a single sign of consciousness of guilt," one of the investigators declared. "He just doesn't show any emotion at all in so far as the murder is concerned."

Boast of Perfect Crime to Girl Friend Traps Youth in Brookline Slaying

Parents Stunned as Police Arrest Son at 4:30 A. M.

SLAYING

Blumenthal a 'Friendly Boy'

Murder Story Shocks Neighbors

Narse Genevieve Receives Medal at Ike's Hands

Pals Say Suspect No Student but 'Nice Guy'

Blumenthal Got 'Dear John' Note

F. D. Jr. Attacks Watch Tariff Hike

Bar Honeymoons, Funerals as "Business Expenses"

What Happens Now? Asks Boy on Way to Jail

Comic Dictionary

PATIENCE

Formal Complaint Against Student

SPEEDING

THE BOSTON DAILY GLOBE—THURSDAY, JULY 29, 1954

SLAYING

Continued from the First Page

The murderer then plunged a bread knife with a six and one-half inch blade into her heart after death, bound her feet with a pair of men's shorts and knotted around her neck a piece of cloth apparently taken from the sewing machine with which she made her living.

The body of the victim, a part-time nurses' aid at Boston State Hospital in Mattapan, was found by a sister, Mrs. Mary Smart of Walter av., Brookline, who was called to investigate when suspicions were aroused because Mrs. Schonarth was not seen about her apartment.

Medical Examiner Thomas P. Kendrick said last night the body had lain in the front room of the apartment for about 10 hours.

Lane and Brookline police questioned a neighbor who reportedly heard screams about 1 a. m. Police declined to divulge the neighbor's name and disclosed only that the person "heard something this morning."

Assisting police in the investigation were the victim's fourth husband, Joseph Schonarth, a Kenmore sq. restaurant manager; a brother Charles Dwelley of Hanover; a nephew, Roger Moore, 30, of Chestnut st., Brookline, and the sister who discovered her body.

Police said all had volunteered to give what information they could in an effort to solve the brutal slaying.

Schonarth, police said, told investigators he had not seen his former wife for about a year. The couple, married in Dedham Feb. 12, 1948, were divorced on April 15, 1953. She charged cruel and abusive treatment in the Norfolk Probate Court contest.

RELATIVES OF MURDER VICTIM—Roger Moore, 30, of Brookline, a nephew, and Charles Dwelley of Hanover, a brother, aided police investigating murder of Mrs. Ora Schonarth.

VICTIM'S SISTER—Mrs. Mary Smart of Brookline.

McCarthy Tells Cohn Adherents He Will Use Ex-Aid in Probes

School Supt. Thomas of Dover, Sherborn Shifts to Franklin

HARVARD FELLOW—Geraldine Murphy of Watertown has been named the first James Bryant Conant fellow in the Harvard Graduate School of Education. An English teacher, Miss Murphy will continue her graduate studies in education under the fellowship established in honor of the former Harvard president.

Aly Khan Coming to Unsnarl Tangle Over Child With Rita

Canada and Israel Plan to Exchange Ambassadors Soon

Rep. Martin Finally Gives Rhee a Country

8 U.S. Airmen Die in Korean Crashes

Audrey Hepburn's Mother Unhurt as Car Crashes

Boy Tells Thrill Killing

'Was Berserk, I Guess'

BOSTON DAILY RECORD, FRIDAY, JULY 30, 1954

Boast to 2 Brookline Girls Brings Murder Confession

Ronald S. Blumenthal, 18, confessed "thrill killer" of Mrs. Ora Schonarth, 52, in one of Massachusetts' most vicious murders, was in a cell in Dedham jail last night because he sought an even greater thrill by boasting of committing a "perfect crime."

In his frenzied quest after sensation, the

Mrs. Ora Dwelley Schonarth, 52, Brookline divorcee for whose murder Tuesday afternoon Ronald Blumenthal, 18, husky athlete is being held. Blumenthal was arrested early yesterday. He confessed to the crime shortly after being taken into custody.

husky, 6-foot, 210-pound prep school student from a wealthy Brookline family recounted every detail of the murder to two high school girls four hours after he had bludgeoned the tiny red headed divorcee to death in her Cypress st. home.

APPEALS FOR SECRECY

"Where do you get that stuff?" the girls asked him.

He said he had read about the murder in a detective story magazine and the girls asked him to get them a copy.

"I'll let you read it one of these days," he told them and then started for the door. He turned back to beg them not to tell anyone he had told them about the lurid crime.

After he had sworn them to secrecy, he said suddenly, "If you stabbed a woman in the back, would it kill her?"

He then left hastily.

GIRLS TELL PARENTS

When the girls read of Mrs Schonarth's murder hours later, they told their parents and that brought about Blumenthal's arrest.

The slaying of the four times wed divorcee—one of the few thrill murders ever to take place in Massachusetts—had a close parallel to the country's most sensational thrill murder of all, the slaying of 14-year-old Bobby Franks in Chicago in 1924 by Nathan Leopold and Richard Loeb.

Leopold and Loeb were both 18—just Blumenthal's age. They came of wealthy families and attended good schools—just as Blumenthal did. And they killed because of an obsession—just as he says he did.

A few hours after his arrest as a result of a tip to the Record-American, Blumenthal was arraigned in Brookline Municipal Court. He entered a mandatory plea of innocent and Judge John

RONALD BLUMENTHAL
Poses for Rogues Gallery

J. Crehan ordered him held without bail for a hearing Aug. 5.

He apepared cool and calm in the courtroom and spoke only to give assent when Dist. Atty. Myron Lane asked for a week's continuance. The murder charge was then read by Mrs. Dollie B. Murphy, court clerk, and the not guilty plea was entered.

UNCLE VISITS BOY

His parents, Mr. and Mrs. Barney Blumenthal, of 80 Beals st., Brookline, have not seen him since he was taken from his home and confronted with the murder evidence.

Early last night, however, an uncle, Louis Franke, accompanied by Atty. Harry J. Williams, visited the boy at the jail and talked with him briefly.

Shortly after they left, young Blumenthal, housed in the same cell block which has known such notorious killers as Sacco and Vanzetti and the Millen-Faber gang, retired for the night.

Deputy Master Edwin H. Downs said the young man fell almost immediately into sound sleep and appeared exhausted after the day's events. He ate a substantial meal before retiring.

GETS SOLITARY

Young Blumenthal will be kept in solitary confinement over the week-end. Starting Monday, he will be allowed a half-hour of exercise in the prison yard daily.

On the way to the jail the blond good-looking Huntington prep school student asked a court officer:

"What happens to me now. What's my sentence going to be?"

Asked if he wanted to contact anyone or send any messages, he said he did not.

The only explanatio nhe gave for killing the petite red-headed woman who had been his mother's dressmaker for 20 years was:

"I went berserk I guess."

In his confession, he was alleged to have told authorities that he killed for the thrill.

"He has told us everything," said Norfolk County Dist. Atty. Myron Lane.

In his circumstantial account of the killing, he related that on Monday afternoon he drove to

Continued on Page 6

Speed Prank Also Charged

When Ronald Blumenthal is brought into Brookline court next Thursday to face a charge of murder he will find another charge: that of speeding, awaiting him.

Police charge that on June 19, young Blumenthal tossed a lighted fire cracker into an open convertible in which two girls were riding along Beacon st. and then fled in his own car.

LYNN MAN DROPS DEAD

J. Ernest Stone, 63, a retired salesman, dropped dead of a heart attack on the sidewalk in front of his home at 16 Sutcliffe rd., Lynn, yesterday.

RONALD BLUMENTHAL, 18, LEAVES FOR MURDER SCENE
Powerfully Built Youth Showed Authorities How He Slew Divorcee

'Nice Kid, Wild,' Classmate Says

A Huntington School classmate of Ronnie Blumenthal, the accused young Brookline slayer, said yesterday that Ronnie impressed him as "a nice kid, although maybe a little on the wild side."

"He wasn't any wilder than most kids, but he liked to speed cars and stuff like that," explained Robert Dorn, 24 Colwell ave., Brighton.

"He never talked to me about

RONALD BLUMENTHAL
"What Happens to Me Now?"

looking for 'thrills' or anything like what I read about him in the papers," Dorn continued. "I could hardly believe it when I heard about his being accused of murder.

"I never knew him to do anything vicious or talk about anything involving violence. He always seemed like a nice kid to me."

Dorn said he and Blumenthal were quite friendly at school, but that he saw little of Ronnie socially.

DIDN'T DISCUSS GIRLS

"One time we were going out on a double-date, but it flopped. Ronnie just told me 'forget about it.' He never told me the reason.

"I never went on any parties with Ronnie. Mostly, we talked about cars. He had a '50 Ford at school. We'd read articles and argue which cars were better and why.

"Ronnie told me he was going with a girl. They broke up for a while, he told me, but later they went back together again.

"He didn't discuss girls any more than the average fellow does."

Dorn, who plans to enter University of Massachusetts next fall, unless the Army gets him first, said he met Blumenthal for

Continued on Page 23

Tip to Record Solves Murder

Here's how the Record-American solved the slaying of Mrs. Ora Dwelley Schonarth within 16 hours of the time her body was discovered.

Only a short while after he had strangled, bludgeoned and stabbed the red-headed divorcee to death, Ronald S. Blumenthal called at the apartment of a girl who was his former classmate at Brookline high school.

He told the girl in detail about a boy who "had just committed the perfect crime." He revealed how the victim was a woman, and that she had been beaten over the head with a rolling pin and then stabbed through the heart with a knife.

While he was telling this lurid tale, a second girl dropped in and he repeated the story to her.

The girls asked him where he ever dreamed up such a fantastic

Continued on Page 23

BOY, 18, ADMITS THRILL KILLING

Tells Police He Slew Brookline Divorcee

MURDER VICTIM AND YOUTH HELD FOR CRIME—Police say Ronald S. Blumenthal, 18, of Brookline (above), prep school student, confessed to slaying of Mrs. Ora Schonarth, 52, at her home. Officials say confession details indicate it was a "thrill" murder.

Boasted of Murder to Girl—Her Father Gave Tip to Police

Went to Dressmaker's to Have Coat Mended

By ROBERT E. HEALY

A stocky 18-year-old preparatory school student early this morning confessed, police announced, to the brutal murder of a four-times wed Brookline dressmaker.

Police charged Ronald S. Blumenthal, 18, of 80 Beals st., Brookline, with the Tuesday afternoon slaying of Mrs. Ora Schonarth, 52, whose body was found in her apartment at 78 Cypress st. at 10:30 a. m. yesterday.

Investigators indicated that in his confession the boy had said he killed for the thrill.

He had openly boasted to a girl acquaintance that he had staged the perfect crime. After

Suspect Also

Ronnie's oblivious attitude, his guards said in newspaper interviews, could have been attributed to his exhaustion from being awoken and arrested in the early morning at his home, grilled at the Brookline police headquarters, driven to the victim's apartment for a reenactment of the crime, and then delivered to the jail. The guards added, "Even exhaustion would not have permitted a nervous man to go back to sleep in a short time." Obviously, despite many attempts to figure out my cousin, he was as puzzled as all who had the chance to see him at close range. That didn't include the dozens of news reporters, who never got close enough to get their information from Ronnie himself.

After Ronnie's first full night at the jail, the accused youth, jail guards reported, arose shortly after daybreak and eagerly awaited his breakfast. Deputy Superintendent Edwin H. Downey said that aside from a lawyer and Ronnie's uncle Abraham Frank (my aunt Edythe's brother), Ronnie received no visitors that day.

CHAPTER TWELVE

The Victim: Ora Schonarth, the Enigmatic Dressmaker

While all this media attention was focused on the apparent murderer, too little was focused on the clear victim. Yet this unfortunate victim deserves every bit of the effort to clarify who she was. That is the very least I could do for her.

So who was Ora Schonarth? "That woman" was far more than "the fifty-two-year-old Brookline murder victim." Because my mother once referred to her as "a woman of ill repute," I assumed this was not only true but also the sum total of who she was. My mother was not alone in her opinion, which was shared by so many of Ronnie's relatives, who tried mightily not to see her in any ray of a sympathetic light. After all, if she was just a "loose woman," then maybe she had done something to Ronnie to justify his killing her. It wasn't like she left behind a grieving husband or heartbroken children. Those details made it easier for our family to push her aside and concentrate on "our poor Ronnie."

As absurd and cruel as this rationality was, I understand it now. I also came to understand that it wasn't true. While it was difficult to obtain a totally clear view of a woman who has been dead for over seventy years, there is still enough information available through police reports and newspaper stories to at least piece together a view of who she was when my cousin confessed to ending her life.

In many ways, Ora Schonarth led a rather odd life. She was not a typical woman of the 1950s, nor was she typical of the people who lived in the affluent town of Brookline, Massachusetts. She had no children, even after four marriages, three of which ended in divorce and one that made her a widow.

Described as a petite redhead, Ora grew up in a family filled with children. She was born on March 31, 1898 (making her fifty-four as opposed to the age of fifty-two described at her death by the media), in Lee, Maine, a small town of forty square miles in Penobscot County with the 1900 US census showing a population of 801 residents. Ora was the oldest of seven children, three boys and four girls, of Bertha and Albert Dwelley. At the time of Ora's death, her widowed mother, age seventy-four, lived near Ora, on 28 Walter Avenue in Brookline, at what turned out to be the same address as Ora's three younger sisters, Calista, Clymena, and Mary. Charles, one of her brothers, lived in Hanover, Massachusetts, while another, George, lived nearby, as did her devoted nephew Roger Moore, Calista's son.

It must have been quite a culture shock for Ora to have left that small town of Lee and have headed to the big city of Boston, where she eventually married four times. Three of Ora's husbands had been younger than she. Ora's first marriage was to a man with the last name of Johnson, about whom nothing else is known. Her second marriage, at age thirty-seven, on

November 23, 1935, was to a Boston police detective named Gordon H. Douglas of the Bureau of Records, who died of a heart attack two short years later, on August 16, 1937. Her third marriage, at thirty-nine, was to Dr. William F. McMahon, formerly of Tremont Street, Roxbury, who was a police surgeon at the Roxbury Crossing Station.

Eleven years later, on February 12, 1948, at age fifty, she married her fourth and final husband, Joseph Peter Schonarth, whom she divorced six years later in 1954.

Unquestionably, Ora did well financially in her new city, even becoming a property owner. That was quite a feat for an independent woman in the 1950s. In 1952, before her fourth marriage ended, Ora, who had just received a $17,000 settlement for an auto accident, had purchased a two-story, four-family apartment building at 78 Cypress Street in Brookline. It was in this building, which had formerly been a Simmons College dormitory, where she was murdered. In their five-year marriage, Ora and Joseph Schonarth had lived at three different Brookline addresses—Washburn Place, Vernon Street, and Tappan Street—before moving into the Cypress Street building.

After her body was discovered, one of the first people the police interviewed was Ora's latest ex-husband, Joseph Schonarth, who, at that time, worked as a counterman at a Kenmore Square restaurant. The police brought Schonarth from the restaurant to the police station, where they interviewed him about his ex-wife. He explained that he had not seen Ora since their divorce three months earlier. Joe Schonarth, who had been with Bambina (Lena) DiPalma, the mother of his young son, Vincent, on the evening of July 27, was not considered a suspect. At the time, he lived with his father and stepmother on Wilder Street in Dorchester, although he married DiPalma a few months later, and the two remained together, raising Vinny, for the next sixteen years until Joseph's death at age forty-nine in 1970.

Yet, despite some of these difficult marital times, Ora remained deeply connected to her family throughout the four marriages, right up until the time of her death. She was close to her thirty-year-old nephew, Roger, who lived nearby with his wife, Alice, in the Cypress Street Veterans Housing Project. He had come to Ora's house on the evening of July 27, as was his usual custom every Tuesday night, to take her trash barrels from her backyard to the curb. When he saw that the lights in the apartment were not on, he mistakenly assumed that she was out for a few hours before going to her job, as she worked the 11:00 p.m. to 7:00 a.m. shift at the Boston State Hospital in Mattapan. Roger never imagined that his aunt was, at that moment, lying dead on her living room floor, a matter of feet from where he was standing.

It was not surprising that it was another member of Ora's close-knit family who discovered the murder in the first place. Ora's youngest sister, Mary Smart, who lived nearby on Walter Street, had been concerned when Ora did not answer the phone on Wednesday morning. She knew her sister had not been feeling well and was worried when she was unable to reach her. Mary went to the apartment around 11:00 a.m. When she saw both back doors were open, she peered into the first-floor window of the apartment and saw her sister's crumpled body lying on the rug of her sewing room. Racing into the house, she dropped to her knees beside her sister. Failing to get a pulse, she called the police. When they arrived, Mary was standing outside the apartment building. "My sister is on the floor inside, she's dead, she has been stabbed!" she told the officers. It wasn't until she returned to the body the second time that she noticed the knife was still sticking out of her sister's chest.

Ora's funeral, on Friday, July 30, 1954, was held privately at the Lacey Funeral Chapel on Harvard Street in Brookline and was officiated by Reverend William Leslie of St. Mark's Methodist Church on Park Street in Brookline. After the service, Ora was buried in the same plot in Fairview Cemetery in Hyde Park as her second husband, Gordon Douglas, the Boston police detective who had died during their brief marriage, seventeen years earlier, in 1937.

It was en route to the funeral service that Mary Smart offered a shockingly kindhearted interview regarding her sister's alleged murderer, Ronnie Blumenthal. "I can feel no hatred for the boy," Ora's grief-stricken sister told the reporters covering the funeral. "I feel sorrow. He must just be sick. But I don't wish any harm to his family. Sure, his mother must feel as bad, knowing that her son did this thing, as my mother does knowing that her daughter was murdered. As for me, I am relieved that the suspense of wondering who killed my sister is done."

It seemed inconceivable that a woman, who, less than forty-eight hours earlier had discovered her older sister's badly beaten and stabbed dead body, could manage to offer such a gentle act of forgiveness. I must admit, sadly, that I was never even remotely as kindhearted or generous regarding Thomas Killourey, my relatives' murderer. I was not proud of that fact, but I would not attempt to deny it. It would be impossible to know if Ora had been as benevolent or magnanimous as her sister, but it is obvious that somewhere in Ora's family such compassion had been present. After all, Ora seemed in many ways the center of her large family, nearly all of whom lived within a few miles of their oldest sibling. This was a supportive family that obviously cared for their daughter, sister, and aunt. They may all have started out in Lee, Maine, but at that time the center of their family life was near Ora, in Brookline. That family had been irrevocably shattered by that brutal murder.

Ora's will and final testament, which had been filed four months earlier, in February 1954, stipulated that her property on Cypress Street would go in a trust to her mother, Bertha Dwelley. On her mother's death, however, this property and the rest of her estate would go to her devoted nephew, Roger Moore. While Ora had no children of her own, there were many indications of her deep connection to Roger.

In trying to unravel the mystery of this financially independent woman, it should be noted that Ora had two separate incomes as she worked tirelessly at two dissimilar jobs. Unlike the typical homemaker of her generation, Ora had always been employed. An expert seamstress, who for thirty-five years was considered one of the most fashionable "modistes" in Brookline, Ora had been the proprietor of a stylish dress shop. At the time of her death, however, she no longer operated that dress shop and instead saw customers inside her Cypress Street home. She also maintained a concession in a store at C. G. Howes Company, 258 Harvard Street, Brookline, where, since February 1953, she had kept another electric sewing machine and an ironing board. She had not been seen in the store for about six months prior to her death.

Indeed, at the same that Ora was still doing seamstress work, she had begun a second job under the name of Ora Dwelley in November 1953, eight months before her death, as a nurse's aide, in the Medical Building at the Boston State Hospital, which was a state mental hospital. She worked the 11:00 p.m. to 7:00 a.m. shift three times a week, with Wednesday and Thursday nights off. Her salary was $45.97 a week, and her weekly take-home pay was about $37, which would be worth around $435 in 2024. She assisted the nurses assigned to the medical wards, and her patients were all women.

Murder July 28, 1954 Case of: Ora Schonarth

Interview: 

[redacted] stated that he was in Maine for the weekend and returned at 10:30 P.M. Sunday; parked his car on Davis Avenue while waiting for Mrs. Schonarth to move her car, which she did about 11 P.M. when she went to work, dressed in white.

He then parked his car in the yard and on Wednesday, July 28, 1954 about 7:30 A.M. when he went to use it the driveway was blocked by a Buick Convertible owned by Mrs. Schonarth. He then went to the back yard to see if she was there. Not finding her he went to the front door and rang her bell once and while waiting, the telephone in her apartment started to ring. After 5 or 6 rings it stopped. He thought Ora was answering it and waited awhile (2 or 3 minutes), then rang the bell a total of three times and left for work (7:40 A.M.).

One day last week a 1954 light tan sedan, containing three men, came to Ora's apartment and the men entered. In about 10 minutes they came out smiling and drove away.

#1 - 35-45, 5-4, 160, stocky build, dark hair, olive complexion

Unable to give further description, except that all had olive complexions and one was taller than the other two.

A lot of entertaining...all men.

Ptl. J. Lawlor Capt. Robert J. Maloney

BROOKLINE POLICE DEPARTMENT
BROOKLINE, MASS.

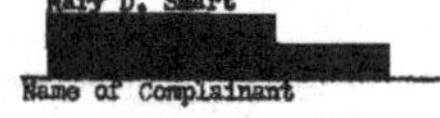
Mary D. Smart

Homicide Investigation — Offense | July 28, 1954 — Date | Name of Complainant

-2-

Case Re: Ora H. Schonarth (deceased)
78 Cypress Street
Brookline, Massachusetts

kitchen - were open. She entered the apartment and shortly thereafter discovered her sister's body on the living room floor. Failing to get a pulse beat, she notified the police by telephone. She said that it wasn't until she returned to the body, the second time, that she noticed the knife in her sister's chest.

Mrs. Smart identified her sister as follows:

Ora H. Schonarth
About 53 yrs. - divorced
Maiden name: Dwelley
Born: Lee, Maine
Father: Albert
Mother: Bertha
Previously married four times -

1. Dr. Wm. E. McMahan
2. Gordon Douglas
3. Herbert Johnson
4. Joseph Schonarth

She divorced her fourth husband, Schonarth, some time in 1953, according to Mrs. Smart

Mrs. Smart said that her sister lived alone, since her divorce, and that in addition to being employed as a nurse's attendant at the Boston State Hospital, conducted a dressmaking business from her Cypress Street apartment. Mrs. Smart said that she last saw her sister alive on Monday, July 26, when she visited with her and her mother at [redacted].

After interviewing Mrs. Smart, I conducted an examination of both the interior and exterior of the Schonarth apartment. This building located at 78 Cypress Street, Brookline is a 2½ story frame dwelling. The building is divided into four separate apartments. Mrs. Schonarth, who owned the building, occupied a first floor apartment on the southerly side of the house. Her apartment consisted of five rooms, namely, a living room, sewing room, bedroom, kitchen and bath.

In examining the apartment there was no evidence that a forcible entrance had been gained to the same. As stated previously, Mrs. Smart said she found the back doors open and she was certain that the front door, leading to the outer vestibule, was closed when she found her sister's body. There were three windows open in the apartment and these three windows were screened.

Investigating Officer

Brookline Police reports, July 28–August 2, 1954.

BROOKLINE POLICE DEPARTMENT
BROOKLINE, MASS.

Homicide Investigation	August 2, 1954	Mary D. Smart [redacted]
Offense	Date	Name of Complainant

Case Re: Ora H. Schonarth (deceased)

Interview: Miss Robinson
Supervisor of Nurses
Boston State Hospital

At 12 Noon, Monday, August 2, 1954 these officers interviewed a Miss Robinson, who is supervisor of nurses at the Boston State Hospital in Mattapan. This interview was conducted in Miss Robinson's office at the Hospital.

Hospital records indicated that Ora H. Schonarth was employed as a nurses aid in the Medical Building at the Boston State Hospital between the dates of November 29, 1953 and July 26, 1954. She was employed under the name of Ora Dwelley, with an address at 78 Cypress Street in Brookline. She worked the 11-7 shift five nights a week and her regular days-off were Wednesday and Thursday nights. Her salary was $45.97 a week and her take-home pay was about $37.00 weekly. Her duties were to assist the nurses assigned to the medical wards and her patients were all females.

Miss Robinson described Mrs. Schonarth's record at the Hospital as very satisfactory. She was clean and neat and very conscientious about her work. Her attendance record was good.

Miss Robinson said that on Friday, July 23, Mrs. Schonarth asked that her days off be changed the following week. She requested that she be given Tuesday, July 27, off as she had a date to go to the track. This was the first time she ever asked for a change of day-off.

Miss Robinson said that Mrs. Schonarth was very close-mouthed and the only employee she confided in was a Mrs. Garland who at this time (Aug. 2) is on vacation.

Det. J. K. Leary

James C. Rourke -Sergeant of Police
Investigating Officer

As indicated above, the supervisor described Ora's record at the state mental hospital as very satisfactory, indicating that her work was clean and neat and that she was conscientious about her duties. Her attendance record was considered good. She had requested to be off on Tuesday, July 27 (the day of the murder), because she had a date to go to the racetrack. That was the first time she had ever asked to change her shift for a day off. To be able to do that type of nursing, which could often be depressing and difficult, in such a satisfactory manner for the prior eight months painted Ora as a compassionate as well as reliable worker.

Between her two jobs and the $17,000 auto settlement, as well as the rents she received for the apartments in her building, Ora did not lack for money. Nor was she the type of person who appeared content to sit around idly, waiting for someone else to support and take care of her.

Even with the second job as a nurse's aide, Ora's reputation as a talented seamstress was stellar at the time of her death. My aunt Edythe, as well as her wealthier sister, Dorothy Gordon, and Dorothy's daughter, Lola Jacobson, had all availed themselves of Ora's expertise for many years, refusing to bring their designer clothes to any other seamstress in the Boston area. As a matter of fact, it was Lola who introduced Ora to Aunt Edythe. "I always regretted that I did that," she said. "And, truthfully, I didn't think she was all that attractive. She wore too much make up and sometimes her face looked like a clown's." This comment, it must be remembered, came from one of Ronnie's first cousins on "the other side," albeit a guilt-ridden one.

With Ora in her fifties at that time, her beauty might indeed have been fading, but apparently there were still men who thought otherwise. Perhaps, as later did come to light, Uncle Barney was one of them. I find the thought of my stout uncle having an affair of any sort with this tiny lady a bit jarring. Ora was obviously slighter than my aunt, as well as a far more independent woman. Also, my uncle's access to Ora would not have been hard to manage. After all, she lived alone, and he could have found a multitude of excuses to drop in on his family's dressmaker. There had to have been opportunities for him to bring some of his own clothes that might need to be hemmed, taken in, or let out, as well as to pick up his wife's or son's freshly altered clothing. While I'd rather not try to visualize Ora and Barney's encounters, I have to accept the fact, according to the police records, that these encounters occurred. Ronnie, as well as Maurice Gordon, who had asked the police to keep those details quiet, knew about them.

It is also probable that Uncle Barney was not the only man removing some of his clothing in Ora's presence. In the time since 1952, when Ora had bought the big, gray, two-and-a-half-story building at 78 Cypress Street where she lived and worked as a seamstress, some of her neighbors had already formed their own unique pictures of their landlady, especially about Ora's time not spent at her sewing machine or at the hospital. It was evident from the beginning of the police investigation into the murder victim's life that her neighbors were all too willing to discuss their opinions and observations of the now-famous resident of their neighborhood.

Some of those neighbors saw Ora as more than an independent woman who worked two dissimilar jobs. Several reported that she loved life and fun, lively traits manifested in her unique mannerisms. They considered her a stylish dresser and were impressed that she drove a flashy, late-model Buick convertible. Since her neighbors all seemed to know Ora had received a large settlement from her auto damage case, few could understand why she worked so many hours, at the hospital or at her sewing machine.

One of the occupants of an apartment at 78 Cypress Street said that she only saw her landlady on the days that she brought Ora her rent and that even though she tried to chat with Ora the two rarely exchanged many words. When asked about her landlady's activities around the time of the murder, another neighbor reported that on Friday afternoon, July 23, a swarthy man had an argument with Ora and came out of the house with Ora running after him. The two exchanged words in a foreign tongue before he walked toward Boylston Street. The same neighbor also stated said that there was a lot of "entertaining" with men in Ora's apartment and that some men stayed for days.

When Ora was not at the hospital or working at her sewing machine, she often visited night spots in the Brookline Village where she was well-known to the regular customers. She was also a frequent visitor to both the horse and dog tracks. It turned out that the last person to see Ora alive may well have been a coworker at the hospital whom she had driven home on the morning of the murder. Ora had told the coworker that she had been looking forward to taking that evening off and visiting the track with a date.

Eighteen-year-old Ronnie Blumenthal seems to have known Ora Schonarth since he was a little boy. During the many years Ora had been a seamstress for his parents, Ronnie had frequently accompanied his mother to the Cypress Street apartment. Some of the neighbors believed that Ora showed a preference for younger men and that one frequent visitor had been described by more than one neighbor as "a tall, good-looking blond boy" whom Ora once passed off as "my son." Those same neighbors expressed surprise when the murder victim's obituary made no mention of a son. That youth, they said, used to drive what they assumed was her car, a black convertible, on many occasions. It is, of course, highly possible that the "tall, good-looking blond boy" was Ronnie Blumenthal, who was driving his own late-model black convertible, his Chevy and Ora's Buick being similar enough to confuse the casual observer.

Another neighbor, who lived one floor above Ora, said that she was certain Ronnie arrived for reasons other than alterations. One evening, a week before the murder, the neighbor reported that Ronnie had knocked on her door a little after 9:30. He'd seemed as surprised to see her as she was to see him. Blushing, he then explained that he'd meant to go to Ora's place but had gotten confused. Without another word, he had hurried to Ora's apartment.

A Brookline acquaintance of Ronnie's told authorities that not long before Ronnie had confided to him that he frequently visited Ora's home by himself. Also, a girl who often doubled-dated with Ronnie commented that Ronnie possessed an unusual attitude about older women for a boy in his teens. She recalled one occasion when she was riding in his car along with some of his friends and he expressed admiration for a fashionably dressed older woman who was walking down the street. The other guys in the car thought that was hilarious and teased Ronnie. Ronnie put up a strong defense of middle-aged women. The girl also remembered Ronnie mentioning his family's dressmaker, Ora Schonarth, in a conversation. "He told me that he hoped I would look as good as that divorcée when I was fifty-two."

Investigations, once attorney Herbert Callahan took over Ronnie's case, continued to illuminate a picture of the victim different from that of a hardworking seamstress and nurse's aide at a state mental hospital. After all, it was in his client's best interest as, unfortunately, it had also been to some of Ronnie's relatives, that Ora Schonarth not be seen as too sympathetic a victim. For example, the headlines of the August 6 edition of the *Boston American* blazed USER OF DOPE above stories detailing Ora Schonarth's drug-filled episodes. One newspaper piece revealed that one of her closest friends, a woman who was a frequent visitor to her apartment, apparently had a history of narcotics use as well as multiple alcohol-related convictions. Investigators also found that within the last year of Ora's life, police were often called to her Cypress Street apartment on the complaints of her neighbors. On one occasion, the police found both Ora and her visitor under the influence of drugs. The police records, however, show no arrest for either of the women that evening, which makes one wonder about the veracity of that report.

In the year prior to the murder there were reports of police responses to her neighbors' complaints about groups of Brookline High School students sitting in cars behind her apartment, smoking marijuana. One of the neighbors insisted this was a recent event and had not happened before Ora had moved in. One cannot help but wonder why the reporters never searched for more positive stories about this woman who worked so many hours aiding mentally struggling women at the Boston State Hospital. While those types of stories could also have been found an attentive audience, clearly lurid scandal made for more eye-catching headlines and sold more papers.

The onslaught of unfavorable articles continued to fill the newspapers, whose readers seemed to prefer more sensational stories. One such story relied on the Suffolk Court Probate records, which detailed Ora's divorce proceedings from Dr. William E. McMahon. Dr. McMahon, the third of her four husbands, was granted an uncontested divorce from her on his charges that he lived with her "in constant fear of my life."

In his divorce testimony, the physician, who had been a police surgeon for the Roxbury Crossing police station, said that one night when he attempted to kiss Ora, she ran wild with a baseball bat, broke three windows and several door panels, damaged the dining room table, and succeeded in hitting him once.

"I lost thirty-eight pounds in six months, and I was in such constant fear of my life that I called in a friend to stay for two weeks," Dr. McMahon told the court in his case to win his freedom from his wife. One of the terms of the doctor's divorce was a $4,000 cash settlement to Ora in lieu of alimony.

According to that divorce suit testimony, Ora lavished all her attention on a dog and was so absorbed with the animal that she had no time to think of children. This perhaps explains the fact that Ora's love for animals, as well as her hardworking ethos as seamstress and proprietor of an exclusive dress shop, might have contributed in some part to the fact that children were not part of any of her four marriages. No one will ever know exactly why Ora Schonarth had four husbands but no children.

Another negative story that received wide readership had to do with Ora's fourth marriage. Her final husband, Peter Joseph Schonarth, more than twenty years younger than Ora, was a decorated World War II veteran, having served in the infantry in the 100th Division in Europe, where he was wounded and awarded the Bronze Star and the Croix de Guerre with palm. Ora and Joseph married on February 12, 1948, and divorced on April 15, 1953, three months before her murder. In Dedham Probate Court, Ora claimed cruel and abusive treatment by Joseph. The last act of cruelty listed allegedly took place in the

78 Cypress Street apartment, which Ora purchased around the time of the divorce.

Coincidentally, I happened upon a genealogy blog that mentioned a woman by the name of Angie Schonarth, whose father-in-law, I discovered when I contacted her, was Peter Joseph Schonarth. Although Peter had already died twenty-five years prior, when she married his son, Vincent, Angie had heard a great deal about Ora from her husband.

Vinny Schonarth, who died on February 28, 2019, never met his father's first wife. As a matter of fact, Vinny, whose mother was Lena DePalma ("Bambina"), was born in 1947, before Joseph Peter Schonarth married Ora in 1948. After his divorce from Ora, Joseph officially adopted Vinny, and he and Lena raised him together until Joseph's death in 1970. According to Angie, Vinny never heard a kind word about Ora in all the stories told by his parents. "Vincent said that Ora took his father for all he was worth, including the house he was living in and the car, and even harmed his business, a Howard Johnson franchise," Angie said. "Quite simply, she was just not a nice woman." Vinny was especially fond of one black-and-white photo of his father in his highly decorated military uniform. "Joe was a hero in Germany, when he was in charge of his unit there," Angie added. "No one ever spoke a bad word about him. But that woman was horrible. I'm so sorry she had such a terrible death, but the truth is she was a terrible woman."

Vinny clearly remembered the trip to the Brookline police station he took as a five-year-old right after Ora's murder. "He sat with his mother outside the room where they were questioning his father," Angie said. "He was frightened by the loud noises and was so happy when his father finally walked out of the room and the three of them went home." Vinny always said Bambina, who died in 1976, and Joseph, who died at age fifty in 1970 at the Jamaica Plain Veterans Administration hospital from an infection he contracted at the hospital, had a loving marriage.

What was most evident in all these stories about Ora Dwelley Schonarth was the fact that few people who knew her well managed to offer stories about their friend or relative. While the motive for her death also remained as much a mystery as her real character, what was known for sure was that she was brutally murdered in her own apartment sometime on July 27. She was found there, on her back, on the living room carpet, clothed in a blue dress with a white top, red high-heel shoes, and no stockings. Her fashionable clothing did not appear to be disarranged in any way. The only solid evidence the police discovered when they entered her home was that the apartment was orderly except for a few soiled dishes in the sink, bearing the remains of blueberries and milk. While Ora and her murder soon became the subject of dozens of sensational newspaper articles that reached beyond the confines of her Brookline life, what was most likely the last newspaper she had ever read, the magazine section of the *Boston Sunday Globe* of July 25, 1954, was lying neatly on top of the bed in the bedroom.

I no longer believe my mother's story that Ora was nothing more than a woman of ill repute. Yes, she liked men and married four of them. As a single woman, she certainly had the right to have entertained some others in the privacy of her apartment. What I knew for sure was that after an intense investigation by police and attorneys, no one was ever been able to understand exactly why Ronnie Blumenthal was in her apartment the day she died. Yes, he had a coat that needed to be repaired, but was that the only reason he had walked into her home? How true was the story that his father, Barney, was having an affair with her, as related by one reporter, an idea floated in the rumor mill for years to come? Was Ronnie having his own affair with her? Had something inexplicably awful happened between the two of them the afternoon he appeared with his torn raincoat? All I can believe is that there is an excellent chance that Ronnie was at 78 Cypress Street for a reason more important than merely to have a torn coat sewn up, a visit with catastrophic results.

CHAPTER THIRTEEN
The Murder Case: What Will Happen to Ronnie?

Newspapers reported on Ora Schonarth's funeral and her sister's kindhearted message of forgiveness to Ora's murderer, but equal space was allotted to the report that this alleged killer was having a noontime meal of baked fish and a potato, served on a tray to him a few miles away from the Lacey Funeral Chapel at the Dedham jail. The newspapers also reported that Ronnie appeared calm and silent, was eating and sleeping well, and had not yet been allowed out of his cell for exercise.

Ronnie was returned to the Dedham jail after his hearing on August 6, 1954.

While Ronnie was in jail and unavailable for interviews, even more new details of how he had spent the days leading up to the murder were grabbed up by reporters and dished out to their eager readers. One rather odd story about Ronnie's whereabouts on the day of the murder related that he had gone to Coolidge Cleaners on Beacon Street in Brookline at 5:00 p.m. on July 27. He was dressed in khaki pants, a sweatshirt, and buckskin shoes, and he had come to pick up some dry cleaning. The garments he picked up included gray trousers, blue trousers, a blue dress shirt, a gray jersey, and a gray shirt, all of which had been left on July 19, for the price of $2.66. Considering he had admitted to killing Ora around 4:00 p.m. that same afternoon, apparently dressed in the same clothes he wore to the cleaners, clothes that were later found bloodstained and in the washing machine of his home, that report was a bit puzzling. Perhaps the records of the dry cleaner were incorrect or the time of the murder was wrong. These were more questions that needed answers. Of course, there was one particular question whose answer Ronnie's family wanted as desperately as the police, who conducted more than one hundred interviews with his friends and acquaintances: *Why?* Where was the motive to explain my cousin's "berserk" state of mind?

An interview conducted by the police with Captain Joseph Rizzo of the 101st Engineer Battalion of the National Guard organization had offered what might be considered a ray of light on this subject. As Rizzo had explained, Ronnie had accompanied his unit to Camp Drum near Watertown, New York for a two-week training period, from July 10 to July 24, 1954. On July 20, 1954, Ronnie received a "Dear John" letter from Barbara from Newton, the beautiful girl he had picked up after school while he was at Huntington Prep. There had been so many girlfriends in Ronnie's teenage years, however; this Barbara, whose last name was never printed in any newspaper story about the murder, must have been the one for whom he had fallen hard and possibly with a hideous consequence.

Because Ronnie immediately became very upset after receiving the letter and made a scene, Rizzo called him to his command post. The two talked for over an hour while Rizzo recounted his experiences in World War II with soldiers who had received similar letters. After this talk, Rizzo was certain Ronnie felt much better and was thinking, *The hell with her*.

However, after their long chat, Rizzo heard that Ronnie had cried a great deal at night, and the next morning he had dramatically torn up the letter before a group of men. He'd even taken his girlfriend's pictures from his wallet and passed them around, insisting they keep all the photos. According to Rizzo, however, after that emotional scene, the final four days of the two-week training period passed without incident, and, other than receiving the letter, Ronnie appeared no different from any other man in the company. Captain Rizzo could not have been more incorrect in that assessment. The unit returned to Medford from Camp Drum on Saturday, July 24, and that was the last time Captain Rizzo saw Ronnie Blumenthal.

But the question always lingered over how connected were this mysterious Barbara and the tiny dressmaker whose life ended on July 27, 1954?

It had appeared that Barbara crushed Ronnie's heart with one letter. The newspapers knew little about Barbara, except that she was beautiful and from Newton and that she wanted to break up with Ronnie. We have no idea if there was another boy involved in her life or the exact reason for the letter she sent to Ronnie. It's interesting that she sent the letter just a few days before Ronnie was due to come home from New York. Was she afraid to tell him in person? If so, why? Did she just not want to see the despair and confusion on his face when she told him their relationship was over?

While I had obsessed for years over exactly how Barbara from Newton had affected my cousin's life, recently I was finally able to find some answers surrounding this mysterious woman. With a bit of sleuthing, I was able to locate Barbara, who, in her eighties, well remembers Ronnie and the "Dear John" letter. Because she has never discussed the Ronnie event with her family, she wants to remain as anonymous as possible. However, she will never forget her relationship with Ronnie. Nor the murder.

"I only went with him for around seven or eight months. I was sixteen at the time," she said. "He was always sweet and never lost his temper or was out of control. He never frightened me or was tough acting. The reason I broke up with him was because that summer, I had decided that he was going to be trouble with the whole school thing. I mean, he had no direction and hadn't graduated high school and wasn't going to college, so I didn't see him going anywhere. It was time to end our relationship."

It was how Barbara ended the relationship that will always create a conundrum. She had gone on a six-week cross-country trip for teens that summer and was having a terrific time. "But I was thinking about Ronnie a lot and was certain the relationship would have to end," she said. "One day, we were at Mt. Hood, and it was snowing in July, and I was sitting with a friend when I told her I wanted to break up with Ronnie. I told her I hated to do it to his face, and she suggested I write him a letter. That seemed like a good idea so that was what I did.

"A week later, I got a phone call from my mother, which was pretty unusual as she rarely called or wrote me. She told me I had to come home right away. I told her I wanted to stay on the trip and had no intention of leaving it. Then she told me that Ronnie had committed a murder, and it was all over the news that I had written him a letter."

Indeed, Barbara was put on a plane back to Boston early the next morning. And when she arrived there, her parents informed her they had packed a suitcase for her, and they were all heading straight to New Hampshire. "We need to lie low for a few weeks," her mother had said. "Until this all passes over." So, they did their best to stay out of the news, remaining in New Hampshire and refusing to allow Barbara to be interviewed by the police or any papers when they returned.

But Barbara did admit that she had found things very strange inside the Blumenthal home on Beals Street. "Really weird stuff, like the way Edythe acted around her grown son. I spent a lot of time at Ronnie's house and every time I was there, Edythe was wearing a negligee. She never got dressed. And her physical behavior around Ronnie was downright strange. Flirty and nothing like a real mother would act. It wasn't fun to be there. I think he was trying to be a mama's boy in lots of ways. It was pretty awful in that house."

As for Barney, Barbara hardly ever saw him as he was working most of the time. But she did see enough of him to decide "he was pussy whipped."

Barbara said it was obvious Edythe did not like her, but Barbara couldn't have cared less. "Edythe had a bulldog face and similar body," Barbara said. "There was nothing attractive about her. She was built like meat box, yet she was parading around in her almost see-through negligee like she was gorgeous."

Barbara is convinced, however, that there was no relationship between the letter she wrote Ronnie and the Schonarth murder.

"I can't ever believe that my letter was an excuse and had anything to do with the murder. It had absolutely nothing to do with me that he killed her. If he did it, it was because his father was having an affair with the woman, not because of a craziness or being so upset over the letter. He never even answered the letter. Or if he did, my parents never showed it to me."

Still, Barbara will never forget the afternoon in 1997 when she answered her phone and heard, "Hi, Barbara. It's Ronnie." She was so shocked she nearly dropped the phone. While she has little memory of what Ronnie said to her, she does vividly remember what she said to him before she hung up the phone. It was simple and direct: "Never call me again." It has been more than twenty-five years since that call and, until our recent conversation, Barbara has never discussed Ronnie, the murder, or the letter.

The concept of Ronnie suffering a "Dear John" rejection while at Camp Drum became the subject of more than one newspaper report. Unlike Barbara's insistence that the letter had nothing to do with the murder, there were those who did believe it was, indeed, the catalyst for Ronnie's state of mind one week after he received it. According to Ronnie's close Brookline friend, eighteen-year-old Barbara Wasserman, it might have been. As Barbara Wasserman explained to more than one newspaper, on Monday afternoon, July 26, two days after Ronnie returned from Fort Drum, Ronnie had told her about the Dear John letter. "I knew Ronnie well," Miss Wasserman told the reporters. "He was like a brother. He told me everything. He was just the most wonderful boy. I can't believe it. He must have been out of his mind. He had been going with another girl named Barbara. When school closed, she went to California on a teen tour, but she did write to him, and Ronnie was very happy with that.

"When he came over Monday, he told me about Barbara's final letter when he was at Camp Drum, and he was crying. He was very depressed. He wasn't the same boy. He was very unhappy. He was such a wonderful fellow, very popular. He had everything he wanted, a beautiful home, a new car, money, great clothes, and yet he just didn't seem to know what to do with himself."

Barbara Wasserman wondered when she could visit Ronnie in jail. She added that Ronnie had many friends who would stand by him. Barbara's father, who operated a store on Harvard Street in Brookline that sold newspapers and magazines, emphasized this too. "He was a good boy," Mr. Wasserman said. "A fine boy. Don't worry. When the right time comes, his friends will be there to help him."

As the evidence piled up against Ronnie, perhaps it was inevitable that there were few who cared about him and more who either didn't care or who found plenty of reasons to distance themselves from their "friend" who had always had lots of money to spend. As a Jewish kid in trouble in the 1950s, Ronnie provided more than one Jewish parent with a reason to disassociate their child from that "bad apple." Jews were concerned enough about anti-Semitism in Boston; they knew that a Jewish boy mentioned in newspaper headlines as an accused murderer wasn't good for any of them, any more than Leopold and Loeb were to Chicago's Jews thirty years earlier.

Until his name was splashed across the front pages of the Boston papers, Ronnie appeared to have more than one caring girlfriend. He apparently found time to visit one of them on the same day he met Barbara Wasserman and once again expressed his pain over his rejection. This time, around 7:30 p.m. on Monday the 26, he called his good friend Toby Mendelson. Immediately, he told her about the rejection letter and then arrived at her apartment about twenty minutes later. The two then took a short ride in his car. Toby suggested they drive by Esther Brown's home on Rawson Road, but they did not stop there, instead driving on to Vicky Prince's house on Dean Road. Toby told Ronnie that Vicky was sick and Toby wanted to see her. They stayed at Vicky's house until sometime around 8:30 p.m., when they left because Toby had a date. Ronnie drove her home, and that was the last time Toby, like most of his friends, saw or heard from him.

Toby never heard Ronnie mention Mrs. Schonarth and never knew the woman existed before her murder. She knew he was very upset upon receiving the rejection letter, but still, he hadn't showed any bitterness toward anyone. Toby, like so many of those who knew Ronnie, was at a loss to explain his actions the next day.

Once the story of Ronnie and the Dear John letter was released, numerous newspaper stories included that new detail in their versions of what happened in Ora Schonarth's apartment. Now headlines such as JILT GIRL ENTERS BLUMENTHAL CASE appeared in Boston newspapers, explaining that Brookline police were anxious to question a girl named Barbara who had sent a Dear John letter to Ronnie while he was at Camp Drum. As always, the air of mystery surrounding our cousin Ronnie was firmly in place.

However, there were other interesting and accurate stories depicting Ronnie's actions on the day before the murder. On Monday night, July 26, after he had spent some time in the afternoon with Barbara Wasserman and, at 8:30 p.m., had dropped off Toby Mendelson, Ronnie spent some time with an old friend from Brookline High School, eighteen-year-old Chesley Gray. Chesley didn't move in the same social circle as Ronnie but said they had been friends anyway and offered this story to the eager newspapers. Sometime Monday night, Chesley had been walking near Coolidge Corner when Ronnie stopped to pick him up. Three other youths from Brighton were already in Ronnie's car at the time. Ronnie told Chesley about the relationship with Barbara that ended while he was at Fort Drum. He said the full impact of that letter didn't hit him until he got home. "While I was away at camp, I guess I didn't realize she meant we were really finished," Ronnie told Chesley. "I guess it was a case of out of sight, out of mind. But it hit me in the face when I got home. I just wish she had waited until I got home."

Sometimes it seemed as if Ronnie's friends and acquaintances were simply standing in front of the newspaper offices, desperately waiting to tell their Ronnie story. One teen, who did not reveal his name, who said he "was in Ronnie's group" told more than one reporter that it would have been typical of Ronnie's vanity and lack of sensitivity to boast about his crime to two girls less than six hours after he committed it. "Ronnie would figure that there was no point of it if he couldn't talk about it afterwards," that same teen remarked. "Especially to a couple of girls."

When a teen wasn't available to talk about Ronnie, there was no shortage of stories about the murder itself. For days after Ronnie's arrest, stories like this one in the *Boston Herald*'s July 30 edition appeared: "Petite Mrs. Schonarth struggled against the youth, twice her size, then collapsed unconscious. He let her drop and went into the kitchen where he seized the rolling pin and reportedly smashed it over her head, fracturing her skull eight times. He returned to the kitchen and picked up the bread knife and plunged the six-and-a-half-inch blade into her heart."

I compared the newspaper coverage to that of the Accident in 1935. Each was sensational in its own right, with gruesome details splashed on the pages. I understood that Ora Schonarth's death was a murder and Allen Halpert and my uncle Ruby, along with the other four relatives in their car, died as a result of what was then classified as an accident but today would be called vehicular homicide or vehicular manslaughter. I guess the more things change, the more they stay the same.

As for Ora Schonarth's murder, a new detail presented by the coroner soon became available to make her murder even more shocking. Dr. Thomas P. Kendrick reported unequivocally that the cause of death was indeed stabbing in the heart, not strangulation by the khaki pants tied around the victim's neck. Not eight skull fractures from a wax paper–covered rolling pin. His report stated that Ora did not die when strangled but was still alive when Ronnie allegedly stabbed her multiple times in the heart. While other doctors offered the opinion that she would have died from the strangulation, which might have been relatively quick, now it seemed that her death would have been slower. It was horrific to think of how that poor woman suffered. When Dr. Kendrick's report also added there were no signs of sexual attack, the ceaseless interest in the story only increased.

The *Boston American* reported that investigators were also probing every possible aspect of Ronnie's relationship to the murder victim, promising "a tangled skein of human emotions so explosive in nature that the testimony will uncover a facet of Ronnie Blumenthal's life which he tried to keep secret." One such story appeared in the *American* on Tuesday, August 3, 1954, insisting that "these detectives, who have painstakingly probed every shadow of the teenager's relationship with the petite divorcée, have uncovered so sensational a 'why' for the crime that they have refused to discuss it." The newspaper assured its readers that the Blumenthal trial would reveal a motive more definite than just a teenager going berserk and being momentarily obsessed. In other words, my cousin must have been doing more with Ora Schonarth than just making use of her superior sewing skills.

Captain Joseph Mahoney, acting chief of the Brookline Police Department, spurred on those stories by hinting that his men might be on the track of that obsession, declaring, "There is more to the murder than has come out. I never swallowed that 'obsession' story of his. The reason for the murder goes much further than that."

On August 2, 1954, the *Boston Daily Record* featured a headline that screamed, RONNIE'S SECRET TOLD: KILLED IN LOVE ROW, typical of dozens of others discussing the sensational aspect of the murder. Captain Mahoney's further comment that "sex comes into the picture in this case," provided even more possibilities for those stories.

Still searching for answers about Ronnie, Brookline police detectives continued to question Ronnie's friends and acquaintances about the day and evening of the murder, attempting to unravel the mysteries of the murder. According to newspaper stories, promising one of the most dramatic trials in Norfolk County history, the investigators didn't believe that Ronnie drove all the way from Nantasket to Brookline on the afternoon of July 27 merely to have a rip mended in his raincoat. They believed there was more evidence that he knew the woman better than he claimed on the day of the alleged murder. Could this seamstress have been the older woman about whom he was bragging to one of his friends? How often did he come to her apartment with nothing to be mended? Had something happened between the two of them on the day of the murder that had nothing to do with a torn raincoat? There were far more questions, each newspaper reported, about that bizarre relationship than there were answers.

So many members of our family had pondered each of those questions, thinking that we might know more than these investigators. Since I was only ten at the time, I was not part of those discussions, but I learned later that my older cousins, including my sister, Toby, who was fourteen at the time, were. All I knew about the murder at that time was from a newspaper I discovered tucked away in a kitchen drawer. I had been at camp for the month of July and returned home on August 1 to a strangely tense atmosphere in the house. When I brought the newspaper, with its large photo of my older cousin Ronnie under the headline THIS IS THE FACE OF A MURDERER to my mother, she burst into tears. She then told me it was all a horrible mistake and I should never talk about it to any of my friends. I followed her instructions but knew that my mother was always distraught and our phone never stopped ringing. When my parents suggested I join a couple of my friends at an overnight Girl Scout camp for the last two weeks of August, I was more than happy to get out of that house.

It was so many years later that I learned my uncle Lewie, Barney's older brother and more or less the head of the Blumenthal family since Ruby and my grandfather had died, had raced from Providence to Brookline as soon as he heard of his nephew's arrest and tried to be of any possible assistance. Aunt Edythe was in seclusion at her sister Dorothy Gordon's house, receiving no one, and was under a doctor's care for her physical and mental collapse. Uncle Barney was valiantly struggling to hold himself together, trying to comfort his distraught wife and to remain strong for his son. The word "shocked" would not even begin to describe his psychological state. Lewie remained a few days but returned to Providence, disappointed that he was unable to see Ronnie or to be of any help to his brother and sister-in-law, as confused about the "why," "how," and "if" as any Brookline detective assigned to the case. Ronnie's relatives read as many of the newspaper articles as they could tolerate and shook their heads in despair over the stories about their nephew and cousin. There had been so many tragic newspaper stories about the Accident eighteen years earlier, but these new stories were ugly and confusing and just as painful to bear.

CHAPTER FOURTEEN

"The Big Story": Fact or Fiction?

While the newspapers continued to offer a never-ending assortment of stories about Ronnie and the murder of Ora Schonarth, not all of which were true, television entered the Ronnie Blumenthal scene. After World War II was over and "big business" ended its war production and went back to making consumer goods, the new invention of television had indeed begun to make inroads into the American household. It started slowly but rapidly picked up speed. In 1948, when Milton Berle ruled TV, only 1 percent of American households had a television. By 1955, when Jackie Gleason and *The Honeymooners* had taken over from Berle, 75 percent of homes had a set. So it's not a surprise that a television series called *The Big Story*, in which newspaper reporters wrote scripts about the events they covered, produced a show about Ronnie and the Schonarth murder. Based on a popular radio series also called *The Big Story*, the series ran from 1949 to 1959, with each episode lasting thirty minutes and telling a different reporter's story chosen from newspapers across the country, albeit with the names changed.

Law & Order continues that technique today, using ripped-from-the-headlines stories. On *The Big Story,* comments from the actual reporter opened and closed each show, the permanent narrator drove the plotline, and a featured actor dramatized the reporter's role. The reporter received $500, was interviewed on air, and was acknowledged in the interview. The radio series was adapted for television, where it debuted on NBC on September 16, 1949. The series continued to air on NBC until June 28, 1957, after which it appeared in syndication until 1958. The series was hosted by Robert Sloane, Norman Rose, Ben Grauer, and, finally, Burgess Meredith.

The episode about Ronnie and the Schonarth murder aired in Providence on September 23, 1955, on Channel 10. It may also have aired on Boston TV. As part of season seven of *The Big Story*, the episode was produced by Robert Louis Stevenson, narrated by Ben Grauer, and was the story of reporters Tom Sullivan and Jim Donahue of the *Boston American.*

For some reason, my cousin Fred heard about the show and was the only family member actually to watch it on September 23, 1955. "I don't remember much about it," he said. "But someone called to tell me to watch it, and I did. It was about a year after the murder and was not shown in Massachusetts, but I was asked to watch it and report if there was any damaging, untrue remarks. As I recall, it was all on the up-and-up. Again, it was so long ago that my memory is fuzzy."

I tried unsuccessfully through multiple sources to get a copy of the episode. While nearly all the other episodes of *The Big Story* appeared to be available in various media and university libraries, that particular episode was always missing from the list. However, thanks to an incredibly resourceful researcher named Jared Walske at the Brookline Public Library, I was able to retrieve the script of the episode from Box 30, Folder 17 (1949–1955), University of Wisconsin—Madison Digital Collections. After reading the fifty-nine-page script, I sent it to Fred. When Fred finished reading the actual script, more than sixty years after he first watched the show on a Providence television station, he said, "I felt sick in my stomach." I couldn't agree more with my cousin's reaction.

The Schonarth murder episode begins with the following descriptions of Brookline and an introduction to the reporters and the crime they include in their "Big Story":

Bobby continues sulking about the fact that his mother has gone to New York to visit her sister and he is home alone with his father, who is always working. The dressmaker, Sophie, ridicules him, telling him how he has everything he could want and is never satisfied. When she angrily tells him to leave and never to return, he begs her to let him stay, before he finally stops talking and brutally kills her.

After the two reporters head to the scene of the crime and see Sophie's dead body, the story shifts to the police station where one of the dressmaker's ex-husbands is being interrogated for the murder. The suspect's loving father waits anxiously at the station, proclaiming his son's innocence and refusing to leave while his son remains there.

The next scene is the Martin's "Living Room, Wealthy People," where Bobby is badgering his father to take a family vacation.

Bobby continues to beg his father to go away on a vacation, which only makes his hardworking father angrier. Before his father finally leaves for work, Bobby offers an ominous warning to him.

Next, the story shifts to the Brookline colonial home of a teen named Betty, where Bobby is telling her about the murder. She is aghast and can hardly believe him.

Meanwhile, the two *Boston American* reporters continue to work the case and hear from the neighbors about a blond boy named Bobby who used to visit the dressmaker often and who was seen leaving her apartment the night of the murder. Meanwhile, Bobby returns to Betty's house and tells her he was making up the story about killing the dressmaker. He lightly kisses her before he leaves, and she believes him.

Hours after Bobby leaves, however, the newspaper describing the murder is delivered to Betty's house and she realizes he was telling the truth when he told her he had killed the dressmaker. She and her family relate her conversation with Ronnie to the reporters.

While the police, with the help of the two intrepid newspaper reporters, are putting together the story about Bobby and the dressmaker, Mr. Martin returns home to find his devastated son on the couch. Bobby begins to sob like a little boy in his father's arms, as the two reporters arrive to interrogate him.

Mr. Martin, defending his son, manages to get the reporters to leave and promises Bobby they will go on a trip. He even packs their bags. Soon, however, the police arrive to arrest Bobby, who is taken to the police station. The final scene shows the police releasing another suspect, the dressmaker's ex-husband to his own father, who, never having given up believing in his son's innocence, hugs his son tightly. Bobby's distraught father now takes that joyous father's now-empty seat at the police station.

I suppose some of the story is accurate, but the key takeaway is that Bobby felt unloved by his parents and was desperate to make his hardworking, rich father notice him. Bobby killed the dressmaker because she ridiculed him about being spoiled and then tried to throw him out. In other words, Bobby became a killer because his father didn't show him enough love and the dressmaker rejected him, too. Considering the stories about my uncle's affair with the dressmaker, I suppose we were all lucky that the two reporters did not focus on that aspect of the story.

Obviously, that episode of *The Big Story* was just one example of how widespread and notorious the story had been to have it made into a television episode less than a year after the trial itself. At the time, you couldn't ask for more enthralling theater. I wouldn't watch this missing TV episode if I could find it, nor even if it had been made into a two-hour Hollywood film starring teenage Robert Blake or Ricky Nelson as Ronnie, Piper Laurie or Rhonda Fleming as the redheaded seamstress, and teenage Shirley Jones as the girl who solves the murder. Aunt Edythe, should she have been so lucky, could have been played by Agnes Moorehead, and Uncle Barney by William Bendix. To the family who lost Ora and the one who loved Ronnie, however, nothing about this tragic story was farcical or even plausible.

While I was not a party to family discussions during that July and August, I knew that over the next thirteen years, my mother was in frequent touch with her sister-in-law Edythe and her brother Barney and that every sensational newspaper article that followed the murder was personally agonizing to her. So was the idea that all her brothers and sisters and nieces and nephews were as much in the dark about the murder as were the authors of the newspaper stories. That one line Ronnie had supposedly spoken to Esther Brown reverberated in everyone's minds: "It's worth going to the electric chair to save my family." What did that mean? Was he so attached to his parents that the thought of their marriage being shattered by his father's affair had made him berserk? Who could possibly know what had gone through his mind that July afternoon?

Every day since the murder Ronnie's family's confusion and pain grew as investigators continued searching for a lengthier relationship between Ronnie and Ora, a concept that police felt existed from the beginning of their own investigations. It was not news to the Brookline police, as Esther Brown had revealed in the discussion of her phone call with Ronnie, that Uncle Barney was having an affair with Ora Schonarth. On August 6, Larry Goldberg from the *Boston Post* called the Brookline police to say that the information he had on the murder was that "Barney Blumenthal had been playing around with Ora." Goldberg added that "Morris [Maurice] Gordon, married to Mrs. Blumenthal's sister, would talk." Needless to say, the dissemination of this information stung the Blumenthal family deeply. It would be bad enough to suspect that a much-loved member of our family might be having an affair, but to have it blasted all over the news was crushing. First, the murder. Then, the affair. What could possibly be next?

Next, indeed, came the scandalous story of Barney Blumenthal's teenaged son having his own relationship with the woman with whom his father "had been playing around." In such a scenario, repeated in multiple newspaper stories, the son would have gone to see the dressmaker on the afternoon of July 27 with the torn raincoat as a cover story. Perhaps the two had quarreled that afternoon over something more serious, and Ora had threatened to reveal their own relationship. Or his father's. Whatever the reason, Ronnie had, the reporters theorized, panicked and killed her. The idea that both the father and the son were involved with the same woman created limitless fodder for "new and revealing" stories about the already shocking crime. An innocent woman was dead, a teenager had confessed to her brutal murder, and a father's extramarital affair was all over the news. It seemed to be a story of biblical proportions, perhaps Greek tragedy or a Eugene O'Neill play. Questions still abounded and answers were few, but none of that stopped the explicit stories, filled with theories and suppositions, from appearing day after day.

During the chaos, Ronnie remained almost completely silent in cell number eight at the Norfolk County Jail in Dedham. This was where he would remain, except for his brief appearance in court on September 12, until the law decided what course it would take with his life. In his present location, as it was reported daily, the confessed murderer said little to the other prisoners or to the guards who brought him food. He ate the prison fare with little comment and displayed minimal interest in what went on around him. He spent his time, except for the daily hour of exercise he was permitted outside his cell, either walking back and forth in his cell, lying on his bed, or rifling through the magazines and newspapers provided for the inmates of the Dedham jail, paying little attention to the chaos his alleged murder was causing back home. He was allowed two visitors per week, with his father being the most frequent visitor.

Of course, the newspapers quickly picked up the fact that Aunt Edythe was absent from the initial jailhouse visits. Attorney Callahan reported that Edythe was a very sick woman and that was the reason she had not been to see her son since his arrest. He said she was under a doctor's care and had been in seclusion at the home of friends on the South Shore since her collapse on the night of her son's arrest. Most of that was correct and understandable.

Ten days after my cousin had been remanded to the Dedham jail, however, on August 6, my aunt, accompanied by my uncle, visited Ronnie for a half hour for the first time. Ronnie was reported to have thrown his arms around his mother when he first saw her. Whenever I thought of that particular scene playing out in the Dedham jail, I could not help but think about the bar mitzvah service and celebration, held in Brookline years earlier, when an adorable thirteen-year-old Ronnie danced quite gracefully with his beaming, blonde mother, both of their smiles dazzling the camera, their arms lovingly wrapped around each other. How could anyone have guessed what would happen five years later? As everyone in the family knew only too well, life was precarious and you never knew what disaster could come out of nowhere.

So, while my cousin sat in that small jail cell, apparently showing little concern about his situation and the heartache he had already caused one family and was still causing to another, and the newspaper reporters knocked themselves out finding people to talk about him, Ronnie's legal team got to work. There was much work to be done to save Ronnie Blumenthal from the electric chair, which he had obviously deemed a small price to pay for saving his family. Fortunately for him, the same family was willing to pay the price to keep him out of that chair.

CHAPTER FIFTEEN
Days in Court

Aunt Edythe and Uncle Barney originally engaged attorney Harry Williams of Brighton with offices in Pemberton Square in the Government Center area of Boston to represent my cousin in his first court appearance. However, it didn't take long for Williams to be replaced by a more prestigious trial lawyer, Herbert F. Callahan. Naturally, the reporters were on top of this development. Within hours of that decision on July 29, photos appeared in multiple newspapers of Callahan accompanying Uncle Barney, who was bringing toothpaste and a toothbrush to the Dedham jail.

Since I was only ten the summer of Ronnie's trial, I am quite certain my parents did all they could to shield me from the dreadfulness of the situation. We never discussed the one newspaper article I had seen when I returned home from camp the beginning of August. Although they were diligent about removing future newspapers about the murder from my view, there were television reports that I occasionally caught. My parents had owned a television for a year or so and had watched a lot of the McCarthy hearings that past April. When I caught a rare glimpse of a television report about the murder, my mother either ordered me from the room or turned off the TV. I knew that she and her sisters and brothers in Rhode Island discussed every item they read or saw on TV or heard from Barney and Edythe about the case. To say that they were all obsessed with the murder is an understatement. After all, it wasn't only their nephew who was on trial, it was their already wounded family.

My mother had made it quite clear that this was a private family matter and not one that I should share with my friends. She instructed me that if any of my friends or their parents asked me about my cousin, I should just say that I had no idea what was going on. Yet, I found it nearly impossible not to at least tell my best friend, Janie Driscoll, a little about what was going on. When I told her that my cousin might have killed a lady, she reacted, as expected, with shock. When she couldn't remember which cousin he was, I did manage to sneak a copy of one of the newspapers my mother tried unsuccessfully to hide from me and show her. This one was of my uncle Barney bringing some personal items like toothpaste and a toothbrush to the jail. I wasn't exactly proud of what I told her, but, still, it was news about my family, and, as my best friend, Janie deserved to know everything important about it, and this was pretty important. Janie, unlike me, could hold a secret and never told any other friends or her parents about my "family secret." Still, it was good to have someone to talk to about all the tension in my house and the constant phone calls to and from my aunts and uncles about the "situation." My sister, Toby, at fourteen, knew more than I did. I knew she felt really sad about it all, but she did not want to talk about it with her younger sister.

I didn't think the front-page newspaper photo of Uncle Barney was such a big deal, and the only thing Janie said when I somehow managed to show it to her was that my uncle looked a little fat and nothing like my mother, who was very slim. Still, how that photo distressed my poor mother. I found her staring at it more than once. I knew from the conversations I overheard between her and my father that she was filled with anger over the fact that the photographers didn't leave her brother alone for a minute. Besides, she was certain he looked heartbroken and distraught. Looking more carefully at that same photo today, I can understand what she meant. Simply the thought of a father having to deliver those items to a jail cell where his only child was imprisoned had to be heart-wrenching for my uncle, especially when photographers were constantly outside his house as well as the jail, never allowing him or his wife one second of privacy.

Naturally, Ronnie's ever-growing legal case had my mother and her sisters and brothers frantic. While her nephew's case would be the first one Norfolk County Attorney General Myron Lane was prosecuting since he had taken office only a few weeks earlier, the reputation of Ronnie's new lawyer was almost legendary. Reading the reports many years later, I also learned that seven years before the trial, Callahan had won an acquittal in the highly publicized case of Charles Russell Goodale, accused of slaying Ruth McGurk, a pretty Cambridge girl who was lured to her death from a dance hall at the start of her summer vacation. In a second case, just four months before Ronnie's, Callahan had secured freedom for sixteen-year-old Paul T. Hines, a Boston housing project resident, charged with the stabbing death of seventeen-year-old Richard Cushman.

Callahan no doubt came with a price tag worthy of such a high-profile lawyer. I heard my parents discussing another newspaper report that said Aunt Edythe's brother, Boston real estate guru Maurice Gordon, had used his reputation and financial position to help secure the involvement of such a prestigious lawyer in his nephew's shockingly difficult case.

As was also expected, when District Attorney Lane and attorney Callahan began to prepare for their cases, the Boston papers ran even wilder scoops and photos, none of which escaped my mother's pained scrutiny. Lane indicated that he would be ready to present evidence to the grand jury on September 7. Despite prospects of a temporary insanity plea (which famous lawyer Clarence Darrow chose not to use in the defense of Leopold and Loeb), the DA would apparently press for a first-degree murder indictment, asserting he had enough evidence to show premeditation. There was no doubt my cousin's lawyer was going to have to fight an uphill battle.

Newspaper stories reported that the formal complaint the DA ultimately submitted stated that "Ronald Sheldon Blumenthal on the 27th of July did assault and beat Ora Schonarth of said Brookline with intent to kill and murder her by manually strangulating and stabbing her and by such assault and beating did kill and murder such Schonarth."

Every word of that complaint was a stab to every Blumenthal's heart. There was no immediate indication of exactly when Ronnie would go on trial, although it was expected that an indictment would be returned against him. The DA repeatedly stated that the evidence showed premeditation and that he would press for a first-degree indictment, which could result in a death sentence by electric chair. The mere mention of the electric chair put my mother and all the Blumenthals into a state of hysteria. Capital punishment was in effect in many states in the country, including Massachusetts.

All of my relatives, like most Jews in the 1950s, vividly remembered the electrocution, just a year earlier, of thirty-seven-year-old Ethel Rosenberg and thirty-five-year-old Julius Rosenberg, amid the McCarthy-era anti-Communist sentiment. The Rosenbergs were accused of passing on atomic secrets to the Soviet Union in a case that remained controversial until decoded secret Soviet communications that proved their guilt were released over forty years later. They were electrocuted in New York at Sing Sing Prison on Friday, June 19, 1953, after being sentenced to death in April 1951. The couple were the first civilians in US history to be executed for espionage, and they were Jewish.

A story appeared in the August 1, 1954, *Boston American* with (Attorney General Myron) "Lane, asserting he had enough evidence to warrant the first-degree murder charge which could lead Ronnie Blumenthal to the electric chair." In the same story he emphasized that Ronnie, if convicted of first-degree premeditated murder, would face life imprisonment or the electric chair. Obviously terrified by such a possibility, my aunt and uncle had little choice but to put their son's life, as well as their money, in the hands of Herbert Callahan, considered a specialist in so-called "lost causes." Everyone was relieved that the celebrated attorney moved quickly, serving notice that as Ronnie's counsel he would insist the state produce evidence to show probable cause as to why Ronnie should be held for the grand jury. The case had been rescheduled from August 5 to August 12 so the newly appointed attorney could familiarize himself with the case he had just taken over from Harry Williams.

From the moment Callahan took over Ronnie's defense, however, a crucial element of the case was given great deliberation: the mystery concerning the exact time of death for Ora

Schonarth. When Ronnie had detailed his account for the police (as well as for Lois Kane and Vicky Prince) of strangling, clubbing, and stabbing Ora in her apartment, he had explicitly stated he was in the apartment at 4:00 p.m. on Tuesday, July 27. Yet, the conflicting reports from the pathologist, Dr. Thomas Kendrick, cast confusion on that crucial detail. After first examining the contents of Ora's stomach, Kendrick indicated that the time of death, as Ronnie had stated, was around 4:00 p.m. However, in a later pathology report, Kendrick declared the time of death was 1:00 a.m. on the twenty-eighth, pinpointing the death nine hours later than his original assumption of 4:00 p.m. on the twenty-seventh. This made no sense to any of my relatives. After all, at 8:00 p.m. on the evening of the twenty-seventh, Ronnie had described exactly how he had murdered Ora to Lois and Vicky. But, according to Kendrick's latest report, she may not have even been dead then.

My cousin's new lawyer used that discrepancy as a reason to examine every aspect of Ora's private life, which was revealed to be more than a little questionable. Reports came to light that men, "lots of men," according to her neighbors, came and went at a high frequency. Ronnie's private life and that of my uncle had been exposed to the distress of all their relatives. Now even poor dead Ora would not escape such unpleasant exposure.

I imagined how Thomas H. Killourey would have made out if the State of Connecticut had held a real trial for him. Stories of his drinking escapades, especially on the day of the Accident, would have been splashed across the newspapers instead of being hidden in a file no one outside the courtroom got to read for over eighty years. At that imaginary trial, no one would have heard a negative word uttered about any of the six victims. Could Killourey's lawyer have unveiled a traffic report showing that

Reuben Blumenthal had once been cited for speeding? Or that one of the grandmothers or the three children had committed any crime whatsoever? I truly doubt that. I also have no idea if the fact that the six victims were all Jewish and the drunk driver of the car that killed them was Irish could have possibly made any difference. There is no denying during this time in the mid-1930s that anti-Semitism was rampant in the US. The virulently anti-Semitic Father Coughlin, who supported Nazi Germany and Fascist Italy, was reaching an estimated 30 million radio listeners, approximately one-fourth of all American citizens, during his weekly broadcasts.

As for Ronnie's case, Captain Joseph Mahoney, the acting head of the Brookline police detective division, had also made it clear that the investigation was not complete. His mention of another visitor to the Cypress Street apartment in the early hours of July 28 strongly altered the scenario of the murder and gave our family a tiny ray of hope. Yes, Ronnie had confessed to the murder, but who knew what had made him say he had done those awful things to Ora? My mother was far from the only member of her family who adamantly believed that Ronnie had not killed her. They were certain the truth was finally coming out. "We have witnesses who saw someone enter the victim's Cypress Street home early Wednesday morning nine hours after the boy said he murdered Mrs. Schonarth," Mahoney disclosed in his report. "One woman neighbor [later identified as a Mrs. Tucker] said a man, wearing a white T-shirt and khaki pants, went through the front door at 1:30 a.m. and she heard an unearthly scream from the house at 2:45 a.m." That unidentified scream, which might have been from a man or a woman, was apparently so loud and chilling that it woke up other residents of 68 Cypress Street.

Mrs. Tucker also reported that when she returned home about 10:45 p.m. on Tuesday she saw a light on in the Schonarth living room. She was awakened by a car about 1:30 a.m. Wednesday and heard someone coming into Ora's apartment. About 2:45 a.m., she heard a horrible scream but saw nothing. Then between 3:20 and 3:30 a.m., she heard heavy steps on the piazza and heard the bushes rattle. Looking out a window, she saw a man's legs and saw a figure run down Cypress Street toward Washington Street. She heard a motor start but did not see the car.

After both Dr. Kendrick and Mrs. Tucker's reports, Ronnie's confession that he had killed Ora at 4:00 p.m. on Tuesday the twenty-seventh was in doubt. Callahan seriously investigated the identity of the male visitor to Ora's apartment. Was this mystery man perhaps one of the frequent flow of male visitors that Ora's neighbors cited appearing at her door? Had he arrived at the apartment for an "appointment" with Ora? There was much discussion about what kind of an appointment it might have been, but I am sure no one in my family thought it could have been to have his pants altered at 1:30 in the morning. Instead of whatever he intended, had he instead found her body before the police were called to the apartment? If that were the case, he would not have wanted to be caught going into her apartment at such an hour.

While that insinuation did not clear Ronnie, it did smear his victim and leave room for conjecture about the murder itself. The idea of men going to the apartment at all hours would be consistent with a police report that Ora and an unidentified man had once been arrested for "lewd and lascivious behavior" as well as in agreement with my mother's insistence that her nephew's victim was a "woman of ill repute." The concept of "blame the victim" resonated loud and clear, but to the lawyers working to save Ronnie from the electric chair, all restraints were off. The Brookline Police Department had steadfastly avoided such direct mentions of the murder victim's "unwholesome" past, yet Ronnie's lawyer showed no hesitation in revealing those details, which the reporters eagerly developed for their publications and which brought my relatives a few sad rays of hope. Maybe, *just maybe,* there were so many other men in Ora's life, that one of *them* could have been her murderer. It was a long shot, but my relatives were grasping at whatever straws they could.

According to Mahoney, who secured Ronnie's alleged confession, Brookline police also actively probed the theory that Ora was still alive when Ronnie concocted his perfect murder formula and that he angrily went back to erase Lois's and Vicky's sneers of disbelief by putting his plan into operation. That theory would explain his appearing at the cleaners at 5:00 p.m. that afternoon in his unstained clothes, but it certainly didn't clear him of the crime.

Perhaps instead Ronnie returned to the scene of the murder to collect an item he had mistakenly left there. In such a scenario, the "unearthly scream" could have been Ronnie's when he realized exactly what he had done hours earlier. Any way you looked at that explanation, it wasn't good for Ronnie's case.

Yet another idea being floated suggested that Ronnie had talked about the murder to someone other than the two girls, most probably a man, perhaps even his father, and that person had gone to the apartment in the middle of the night to see if Ronnie had been telling the truth. The possible involvement of Barney Blumenthal in the murder was a recurring theme that brought additional misery to my family. Not only did the whole world know, thanks to some newspaper articles, that my uncle had been having an affair with Ora, but they were told he might well have also murdered her. As if that wasn't shocking enough, the new theory surfaced that Barney, unlike his son, had a staunch reason for murdering Ora and would have been convicted of premeditated murder in the first degree and been sent to the electric chair. How on earth would a father, especially a Blumenthal who had lived through a car crash resulting from a drunk driver that had killed so many members of his family, do such a thing to his own son, the son he had named in memory of his older brother Reuben, one of the six victims of the crash? That absurd and ugly theory lived on for many years, even to the present. I well remember, years after the murder, talking to people who asked me questions about my cousin, who was out of prison by then. Most of them would state that they had believed my uncle had committed the murder. My own in-laws insisted that was the real story.

No matter what Ronnie's relatives thought of all these equally hopeful and hideous details, the case was in the capable hands of Ronnie's defense lawyer. Herbert Callahan had a dramatic sense of presence and a thatch of white hair often hidden beneath a wide-brimmed hat. He was to be aided by his son, Herbert F. Callahan Jr., amid frequent reports that the defense to save the youth from the electric chair would be based on disclosures of a sensational nature bearing on the legal aspects of the alleged confession. That assertion was interpreted in police circles to mean that the defense would try to keep his client's confession out of the trial or at least attempt to discredit it as a statement attained by force or duress. All my relatives knew for sure was that Barney had paid a small fortune to the lawyer, and they prayed the two Callahans would be worth every cent.

As details of the upcoming case continued to be dissected and discussed by every member of my mother's family, my mother often had more news to report to them. After all, her three sisters and two of her brothers lived in Providence and she lived in Boston, where the newspapers and TV stations covered the case in minute detail. According to the reports, in preparation for the August 12 hearing in Brookline District Court, Callahan had made it clear he would have his own stenographer but did not anticipate producing any witnesses. The relatives were concerned, however, when the district attorney announced that he would call three witnesses at the hearing. One would be the Brookline policeman who found Ora's body. The second would be the stenographer who captured Ronnie's admission of the crime. The third would be the medical examiner who conducted Ora's autopsy. Even though my relatives had to agree that those witnesses made sense, the announcement made everyone in the family even more worried.

CHAPTER SIXTEEN
Punishment

Finally, amid intense public interest and the family's mood of high tension, at 9:00 a.m. on August 12, 1954, in the Brookline courtroom, with Judge Martin Colten presiding, the examination to determine if the prosecution had enough evidence to justify holding Ronnie for the grand jury began. When lawyer Herbert Callahan first appeared in the courtroom on Ronnie's behalf, the family was pleased to see that he was a forceful presence, serving notice to the new DA, who had yet to try a murder case, that the defense would battle all the way to prove to a jury that the teenager should not be found guilty of murder despite his confession. As a result of Callahan's questioning, the Brookline detectives admitted that Ronnie had not actually signed the statements he had given them, which were later described by Lane as a "full confession." The police officer who found Ora's body testified that developments had moved so quickly in the four hours following Ronnie's arrest early Thursday morning, July 29, that the defendant had been photographed, fingerprinted, arraigned, and sent to the Dedham jail before the statements he had made could be typed by the police stenographer. Because Ronnie had not been represented by counsel at his arraignment on July 29, an automatic plea of innocent was entered for him during that brief process. As a result, his lawyers questioned whether their client had actually confessed or if the unsigned confession that he'd given to the Brookline police Thursday morning had been delivered by threats and intimidation.

As the two-hour hearing continued, over persistent objections by District Attorney Lane, very few of which were sustained by Judge Colten, Callahan produced more testimony from Mahoney, asserting that police had been told a man came out of the Schonarth apartment around 2:00 a.m. on Wednesday, July 28, ten hours after the state had said she was killed by Ronnie. During Kendrick's questioning about the time of death, the medical examiner stated it was about twenty-four hours before he first saw the body on July 29. When Callahan prodded him for his changes about the time, Kendrick replied that he had made his final decision on the time when rigor mortis was complete.

According to the reports my relatives zealously read about the two-hour hearing, Ronnie, wearing a tweed sports jacket, an open-collared shirt, and dark slacks, kept ducking his short-cropped head out of sight below the side panels of the prisoner's dock. Neither of his parents was in attendance, although scores of women and girls crowded the entrance of the Brookline Municipal Court that morning, hoping for a glimpse of the handsome and infamous alleged killer.

Although Herbert Callahan had raised crucial elements of misconduct regarding the handling of Ronnie's arrest and confession, as well as of the time of death, Judge Colton found probable cause to hold my cousin without bail for the Norfolk grand jury, which would be convened in September. In addition, the judge also filed a complaint for a pending ticket against Ronnie for June 19, 1954, the night he had thrown a firecracker into a car driven by two girls. That news hadn't surprised the family as we had all heard that awful story before, but its revelation made an understandably big splash in the newspapers. At the completion of the hearing, Ronnie—flanked by Deputy Sheriff Robert True and court officer Guy Hopgood, as well as by Callahan, with the admiring crowd of girls still in place for another glance and having submitted his innocent plea—was returned to the Dedham jail.

My mother continued to follow every second of the court events, both in the newspapers and on TV, speaking to her brother Barney or her sister Etta at least once a day, trying to understand what was happening with her nephew, as well as how Barney and Edythe were holding up. When she wasn't talking to her brother or sister, she talked to my father, often in tears, discussing every detail with him, unable to leave the house or speak with her friends. I've often thought about how, eighteen years earlier, well before she had met my father or had her own family, she had been the Blumenthal family member who had received the phone call from the Connecticut State Police, informing her about the Accident. Before the murder it seemed as if she never stopped worrying that something awful would again befall her family. Finally, it had.

On September 10, a month after his two-hour hearing, Ronnie returned for his next court appearance, an event once again closely followed by a throng of gawking young women who were desperate for even a glance of the "celebrity," as well as by his relatives, who made phone calls to one another sharing any possible tidbit they might have picked up. While newspapers reported that the prisoner looked uninterested or unaware of what was happening to him, his aunts and uncles all thought he looked haggard and stunned, and even wondered if he had been drugged in some way.

Mostly, they studied his face in the newspaper photos, which were always accompanied by the words "motiveless murderer," "boy killer of divorcée," "thrill killer," and "son of wealthy Brookline parents." They tried, unsuccessfully, to compare the nephew they knew with the stranger on the front pages of the *Boston American* or *Boston Traveler*. All the relatives had decided that attorney Herbert Callahan was a smart guy. They knew Barney would somehow find the money to pay him, most probably from his wealthier relatives on his wife's side of the family such as his brother-in-law Maurice Gordon; that he'd do whatever it took to save his son's life. If he called any of them for help, even the Blumenthals who had little money of their own would help out in any way they could. How I wish my parents were still alive and I could ask them if they contributed toward Ronnie's defense. I would not have been surprised to hear that they did.

On September 10, Ronnie appeared under a heavy guard of deputy sheriffs and was handcuffed to another prisoner, James Lunnin of Roxbury, who was to be indicted for the slaying of Mary Isles. Together, the two prisoners walked the five hundred yards from the Dedham jail to Dedham Superior Court, where Ronnie was expected to be indicted by a Norfolk County grand jury for the murder of Ora Schonarth. There were two counts under the Blumenthal indictment. One said the victim died of assault and beating, while the other charged Ronnie "with the intent to murder Ora Schonarth by strangling her and by stabbing her with a knife and by such assault did kill and murder her." Obviously advised by his lawyers, Ronnie refrained from making a plea in answer to the charge.

After the murder indictment was read, Callahan requested no plea (neither guilty nor not guilty to first-degree or second-degree murder) be entered at that time and asked for twenty days in which to submit special pleadings against the bill. Instead, Judge Frank J. Donahue granted fourteen days for Callahan to submit his pleadings. District Attorney Myron Lane said he hoped to schedule the murder trial for a special session in late October or early November. Naturally, the words "murder trial" terrified my mother, and I could not ignore the aura of fear surrounding our house.

Out of respect for the Jewish High Holidays, which occurred in late September that year, it wasn't until Friday, October 1, 1954, more than the fourteen days originally granted to Callahan to request his plea, that Ronnie, dressed in his customary outfit of dark slacks, open-necked white shirt, and tweed sport jacket, appeared for his final court appearance at Norfolk County Superior Court in Dedham. I am certain that all my relatives had spent Rosh Hashanah and Yom Kippur at their synagogues praying for a miracle and Ronnie's release.

On the same five-hundred-yard path leading to the courthouse, which he had walked on September 10, Ronnie was again handcuffed, this time to Deputy Sheriff Del Turner. During the walk, in which he paid no attention to the usual crowd of gawking females, my cousin was reported to have asked the guards who won the World Series the day before. Told that the New York Giants had beaten the Cleveland Indians, Ronnie had supposedly said, "Good," and grinned. My mother and her sisters and brothers could not believe that was all he had said and told one another that this was yet another example of newspapers simply making up stories to sell copies of the paper. Perhaps no one wanted to admit that the gravity of what was about to happen to Ronnie inside the courtroom had not fully registered with him. Perhaps, since the day or evening of the murder, it never had.

As the newspapers also insisted, there had been numerous discussions between the DA and Herbert Callahan about whether Ronnie would plead not guilty and opt for a jury trial. After all, what about the fact that Ronnie had not signed the confession? Or the fact that he had not been advised of his legal rights as soon as he was taken to the police station? What about the unearthly scream heard hours after the time Ronnie had confessed to killing Ora? And what about the confusion over the time of death?

However, the decision had been made that Ronnie would plead guilty to murder in the second degree, the unpremeditated intentional killing of another, a lesser charge than first-degree murder but more serious than manslaughter. Ronnie would save himself and my aunt and uncle a long, expensive, and, most probably, sensational trial. He would be saving Lois Kane and Vicky Prince, and even possibly Esther Brown, from the strain of having to testify in front of a jury. And Ronnie would save himself from the electric chair.

As expected, multiple newspaper articles on October 1, 1954, concluded their coverage of this sensational story, reporting that "the playboy son of wealthy Brookline parents pleaded guilty to second degree murder in Dedham Superior Court today." The *Boston American* described Ronnie, who was standing in a cage with three other defendants, as appearing "bewildered" when Judge Frank J. Donahue ordered him to stand up and plead to the murder charge.

"Ronnie glanced inquiringly at his attorney who then walked to the bench and conferred with the judge, before whispering words to Ronnie. Then Ronnie repeated in a clear but faltering tone, 'I am guilty of so much as charged of murder of the second degree.' Ronnie flushed and hung his head as the clerk imposed the sentence, while his father, who was sitting in the first row of the spectators' section, buried his head in the crook of his elbow and broke into tears."

My mother said it was almost unbearable to read those words in the newspaper or to discuss them with her sisters and brothers. My older cousins who were the same age as Ronnie remember their parents talking in whispered tones about the case, refusing to talk about it to them.

Aunt Edythe, who was still in a precarious state of mind, was not present in the courtroom when Ronnie heard the court clerk say these words: "You are sentenced to prison for the rest of your natural life. You are to be removed to the state prison at Charlestown to spend one day in solitary confinement and the balance of your sentence at hard labor." Unlike the reporters, my aunt did not see Ronnie's eyes fill with tears, which, according to the *Boston American*, "he wiped away hastily."

Ronnie was immediately removed to an anteroom where he spent twenty minutes talking to his attorney and his father, who lit a cigarette for him and held on to his hand. I could not help but wonder if the reporter for the *Boston American* was in this room or whether Callahan related these private details to him afterwards, but their papers reported that my uncle kept wiping Ronnie's brow and stroking his head and neck in some sort of gesture of consolation. The story also included the detail that Callahan offered Ronnie advice on how to handle himself in prison, urging his client to "pick the right associates" and realize the full seriousness of what he would be up against inside the prison walls. The story concluded with Ronnie offering a weak smile to both men and then regaining the same calm demeanor he had supposedly been maintaining since his arrest on July 29.

Trying to imagine what was going through my eighteen-year-old cousin's mind as he sat in that room with his attorney and father, and maybe a reporter, is almost impossible. Maybe, just maybe, in some absurd way, Ronne was relieved. Perhaps being sentenced to prison could release him from day-to-day responsibilities that he found difficult to deal with and expectations that he found impossible to live up to.

From a social anthropology perspective, less than a decade removed from World War II and, given the enormous changes in the world between 1945 and 1954, plus the ongoing military draft, I would not be surprised to learn there were a lot of Ronnies in Brookline and Newton. They might not have had the opportunity or the inclination to murder anyone, but perhaps they could have. Instead, they abused alcohol and drugs...and, usually, that never made the news. In 1955, a year after Ora's murder, the movie *Rebel Without a Cause* starring James Dean was released, showing a generation of disaffected teenagers, dissatisfied with living lives like their parents, instead seeking thrills and trying to feel alive and adult. If Hollywood was making movies about this, it was already happening in real life. Perhaps it was not so crazy to think that Ronnie was rebelling against a society that expected conformity and good behavior, a wife and kids, and a lifelong job, as well as having the pressure of success from a successful family heaped upon him. And for him there was the added pressure of being the golden child, the last hope of the Blumenthals, from the moment he was born six months after the Accident.

In a way, it was easier for Ronnie to go with the flow of his peers. For a kid with money, he could afford to be resentful of his parents. He was given everything and never had to work for it, so he didn't have the natural appreciation that comes with hard work and earning your own money. He didn't care about grades because he had a guaranteed job waiting for him at the liquor store. He was marking time with girls, fast cars, and booze until he could be out on his own and away from his smothering parents. Maybe Barney wasn't smothering, but Edythe was. Maybe Barney was a hands-off parent fooling around with other women, working long hours at the liquor store, while Edythe ran the household. Ronnie was her "Ronnalah," her prize, the big, handsome boy who had her coloring and looked as good as her rich sister's two children, Lola and Bobby Gordon. Barney must have set a poor example to Ronnie in the way he let Edythe run their home and social life—it's Jim Backus in an apron straight out of *Rebel*.

Like many teenage boys, whose hormones kick in before their brains are fully developed to handle new emotions, Ronnie was prone to anger and depression. This can end with poor decision-making and thrill-seeking, like throwing a lighted firecracker into an open convertible. To him, that was funny, a prank, not anything dangerous or with consequences. Nothing in Ronnie's life had consequences...until he murdered a woman.

Ronnie was lucky to have received the sentence he had just been given. For many years later, my mother would mention the unsigned confession and the confusion over the time of Ora's death and shake her head, wondering if the lawyers had really earned their money, although from a legal standpoint they knew what they were doing. With the limited information the Blumenthal relatives had received, none of us would ever completely understand what had happened, either in Ora's living room or in the courtroom.

Thanks to the presentencing negotiations, it could not have come as a surprise to Ronnie or his parents that he would be heading to the archaic Charlestown State Prison. Charlestown just so happened to house an electric chair. Seven years earlier, Philip Bellino and Edward Gertson, convicted of murdering nineteen-year-old Robert "Tex" Williams, had been electrocuted there. It turned out to be the state's final executions even though the death penalty in Massachusetts was not ruled unconstitutional until 1984. The famous prisoners, anarchists Nicola Sacco and Bartolomeo Vanzetti had been executed there in 1927 for murders committed during a 1920 armed robbery of a shoe company in Braintree. Their case unfolded against a background of discrimination against Italians, against immigrants, and against anarchists. There was a firm belief in some circles that Sacco and Vanzetti were innocent when another of the alleged participants in the robbery confessed to the murders. But all appeals had been denied.

As so many newspapers reported and as his relatives agreed, my cousin held inside his closely guarded secret of why he strangled, bludgeoned, and stabbed Ora Schonarth. The questions we all asked about the murder remained unanswered. At the Dedham jail, on October 1, 1954, Ronnie's nineteenth birthday, the papers reported that he ate a meal of baked fish, vegetables, and milk. At 1:00 p.m. he was taken to the Charlestown State Prison, where my aunt and uncle were allowed to visit him three days later, on Monday, and twice a week from then on. Memories of his glorious bar mitzvah day six years earlier seemed impossible to evoke. Instead, as we all read in the papers, tears filling up our eyes, Ronnie spent the rest of his birthday showering, dressing, and having his hair shaved before going to sleep in isolation. As he fell asleep in the jail cell he had to know, as did all his relatives, that many more birthdays would pass before he would ever again celebrate the gift of freedom.

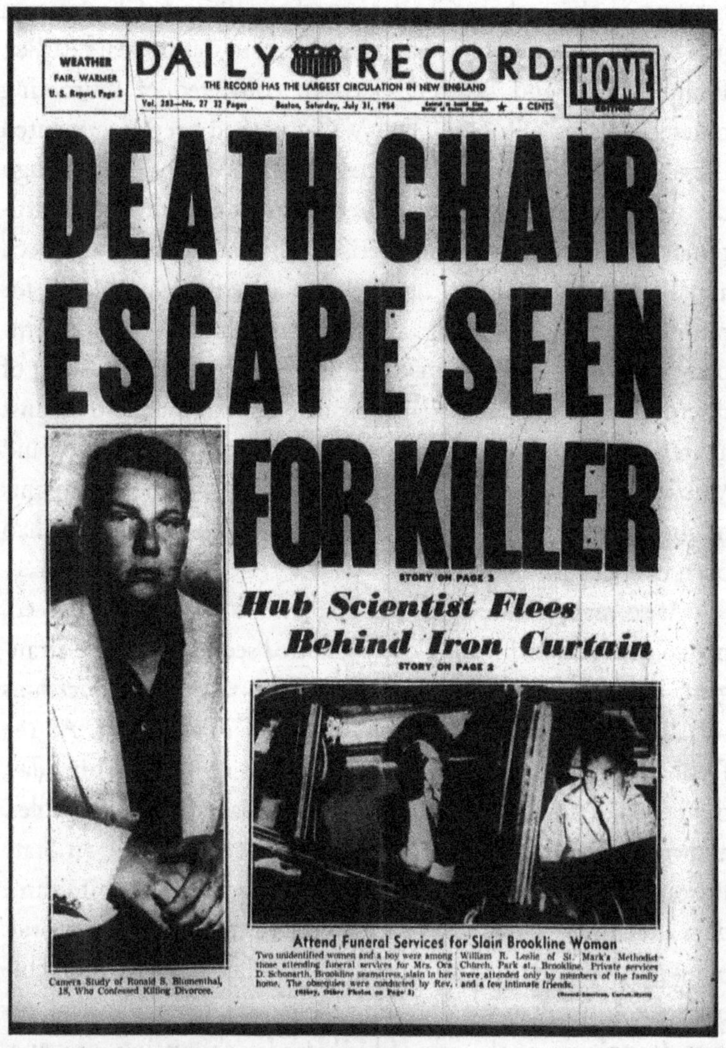

WEATHER
FAIR, WARMER
U. S. Report, Page 2

DAILY RECORD

THE RECORD HAS THE LARGEST CIRCULATION IN NEW ENGLAND

Vol. 283—No. 27 32 Pages — Boston, Saturday, July 31, 1954 — ★ 5 CENTS

HOME EDITION

DEATH CHAIR ESCAPE SEEN FOR KILLER

STORY ON PAGE 3

Hub Scientist Flees Behind Iron Curtain

STORY ON PAGE 2

Camera Study of Ronald S. Blumenthal, 18, Who Confessed Killing Divorcee.

Attend Funeral Services for Slain Brookline Woman

Two unidentified women and a boy were among those attending funeral services for Mrs. Ora D. Schonarth, Brookline seamstress, slain in her home. The obsequies were conducted by Rev. William R. Leslie of St. Mark's Methodist Church, Park st., Brookline. Private services were attended only by members of the family and a few intimate friends.

(Story, Other Photos on Page 3)

Quiz Ronnie's Pals; Insanity Plea Seen

Questioning of scores of girl and boy friends of Ronald Blumenthal, 18, was begun yesterday by Brookline police in an effort to find a motive for his apparently senseless "thrill slaying" of Mrs. Ora Schonarth, tiny, 52-year-old copper-haired divorcee.

Dissatisfied with the husky blond ten-ager's explanation that he killed the little dressmaker because of "a sudden obsession," authorities believe some deeper motive lies behind one of Massachusetts' most colorful murders in which the victim was strangled, bludgeoned, and stabbed through the heart.

But as the case stood yesterday, with the motive undetermined, it appeared that a plea of insanity would be used to save Ronnie from death in the electric chair. Such a plea could be founded on Ronnie's only explanation for the "thrill murder" so far, that he suddenly went berserk and strangled, bludgeoned and stabbed the dressmaker.

BURIED WITH 2D HUBBY

Police believe some Brookline school chum may unwittingly possess the key to the entire case.

Since Ronnie's loose-tongued talking led to his arrest, they believe he may have talked as freely to girls or boys of his acquaintance, any one of whom might come up with the clue to why the crime was committed.

Police began questioning Brookline teen-agers as private funeral services for the murder victim where held at the Lacey Funeral Home in Brookline and she was buried in the same plot in Fairview Cemetery Hyde Park, as her second of four husbands, Gordon Douglas, former Boston police officer.

A few miles away in Dedham Jail, her confessed murder remained calm and silent in his cell. He eats and sleeps well and will not be allowed out of his cell for the next few days. His meals are served to him on a tray. He had baked fish and potatoes for noonday dinner.

PARENTS STAY AWAY

He had no visitors yesterday and his parents, Mr. and Mrs. Barney Blumenthal have not yet been to see him. They are in strict seclusion in their Brookline home and Mrs. Blumenthal is in a highly nervous condition.

Also in strict seclusion and reported under a doctor's care are the parents of a girl named "Barbara," who wrote Ronnie Blumenthal a "Dear John" letter while he was at Camp Drum, N. Y., with the National Guard.

Ronnie, who had been going steadily with this girl for two years, is reported to have broken into tears after he received the letter which declared their close friendship was all over.

Atty. Harry Williams, counsel for Ronnie, declared yesterday that he had no comment on the strange case at present, but that he would visit his client at Dedham Jail during the next few days.

As Williams practice is largely confined to civil cases, it is not improbable that Ronnie's parents may hire a noted criminal lawyer to defend their son.

Dist. Atty. Myron Lane of Norfolk County yesterday praised Lois Kane, 18-year-old Brookline girl who gave authorities the information which led to the arrest and confession of Blumenthal in the thrill murder of Mrs. Schonarth.

"This girl, in coming forward with her information, performed a tremendous public service," Lane declared. "The example of good citizenship which she gave might well serve as a shining standard for the rest of us.

VISIT WAS MERE CHANCE

"By her action, she enabled us to make a speedy arrest in what was a thoroughly brutal crime."

Although Lois graduated from Brookline high school two months ago, she knew Ronald Blumenthal only slightly.

It was mere chance when she visited a girl friend at 8 p. m. Tuesday and found him there. She had no idea that only four hours previously he had choked and beaten the tiny red-headed dressmaker to death.

Here, in her own words, is exactly what happened when she met Blumenthal that night.

"For a while we, Ronald, my girl friend and myself, talked about various subjects of no importance. There was nothing to indicate what had happened to Mrs. Schonarth until suddenly he asked us, 'If a woman was stabbed in the heart, would you believe she was dead?'"

THOUGHT QUERY SILLY

We said that of course she would be and that the question was silly. Then he started telling us this weird tale of murder but he told it in the third person. That is, instead of saying "I", he would say "someone."

"It was so gruesome that we didn't believe him. We joshed him and asked if he had gotten it out of some detective story.

Awaits Fate

CHARACTER STUDY OF RONNIE BLUMENTHAL, 18
Police Probe Into Past Life of Brookline Teen-Ager

Ronald S. Blumenthal, 18, Brookline youth who confessed to slaying of Mrs. Ora Schonarth, arrives at Brookline Court with Det. John Dwyer. Funeral for the victim was held yesterday. Boasting of committing a "perfect crime" to two Brookline girls led to his arrest.

MRS. ORA SCHONARTH
Victim of Slaying

Lois Kane, 18, Brookline, who gave police the information which led to the arrest and confession of Ronald S. Blumenthal, was highly praised by Dist. Atty. Myron Lane for giving police solution to

Victim's Kin Feels 'No Hate for Boy'

As private funeral services were held for Mrs. Ora Schonarth, tiny red-haired murder victim, in Brookline yesterday, her sister, Mrs. Mary Smart declared she felt no hatred for the confessed killer, Ronald Blumenthal.

"I can feel no hatred," Mrs. Smart said. "For the boy I feel sorrow. He is sick. He must be."

GLAD SUSPENSE IS OVER

"I don't want any harm to his family. I'm sure his mother must feel as badly to know that her son did this thing as my mother does to know that her daughter was murdered."

"As for me, I'm relieved that the suspense of wondering who killed my sister is gone."

A few minutes after making this statement, Mrs. Smart attended the funeral at the Lacey Funeral Chapel on Harvard st., Brookline. Burial was at Fairview Cemetery, Hyde Park.

Accompanying her to the services were her two married sisters and their husbands, and her mother.

BURIED IN HYDE PARK

Two nieces and a nephew, Roger Moore, attended as did Mrs. Schonarth's friends, Mr. and Mrs. George Storm and Mr. and Mrs. Joseph Powers.

The services were conducted by Rev. William R. Leslie of St. Mark's Methodist Church, Park st., Brookline.

It was Mrs. Smart who found her sister murdered in her Cypress st. home last Tuesday morning.

RONNIE BLUMENTHAL, RIGHT
With Officer Ernest True

2 BATTER, ROB STORE OWNER

After slugging a Hancock st., Quincy, variety store owner with gun butts, two bandits yesterday dragged the victim into a rear room, emptied his pockets and fled after scooping up only bills of large denomination from the cash box, leaving the coins and $1 bills. The amount taken was not immediately established.

Harry Koelis, 65, of Gilson rd.,

The press coverage was devastating for the family.

The original caption for this photo that ran in the *Boston Globe* on October 1, 1954, (Globe staff photo by Charles McCormick), read: "Brookline schoolboy, Ronald Blumenthal, 18, shown at Dedham this morning where he got life term for murder of Mrs. Ora Schonarth. The 220-pound youth is flanked by Deputy Sheriffs Del Turner and John Winters."

CHAPTER SEVENTEEN
Doing Time

The day after his nineteenth birthday, Ronnie officially began his life sentence at Charlestown Prison. There had been so much press about Ronnie's lack of emotion, how he just seemed oblivious to what he had done or what was happening to him as he'd spent those past nine weeks in his cell at the Dedham jail. It was impossible to imagine my cousin devoid of emotion as he was driven in a police van to that daunting prison. Paul Dever, governor of Massachusetts from 1949 to 1954, at the groundbreaking for the Walpole prison in 1956, described Charlestown Prison as "a bastille that eclipses in infamy any current prison in the United States…a disgrace to our Commonwealth." One hundred fifty years old and believed to be the oldest penitentiary in the country, Charlestown Prison was further described as the "cramped compound of blackened granite and dilapidated brick buildings, the most disreputable prison in the country, damned as a verminous pesthole, unfit for human habitation." My aunt and uncle had to have driven by the prison before Ronnie arrived and must have been barely able to breathe when they imagined their son spending the rest of his life in such a hideous place. If there had been any truth at all to the rumor that Uncle Barney had committed the murder, one glimpse of that place would have caused my uncle to rush to the police station to admit his guilt and free his son from such a primeval prison.

My cousin Fred did not consider any of these descriptions of Charlestown Prison an exaggeration. As expected, as soon as Ronnie's sentence was given, Uncle Lew brought both Fred and Mel, contemporaries of Ronnie, from Providence to Charlestown to visit their cousin. "I drove in from Providence with Uncle Lewie to visit Ronnie almost immediately after he was sent there," Fred told me. "I remember how nervous I was, but I did what I had to do. Charlestown was a prison like you would see in a horror movie. Numerous floors, guards everywhere, etcetera. Just awful."

Despite the haste with which Fred left Providence, Aunt Etta had handed him a box of strudel with raspberry jam, nuts, and yellow raisins for Ronnie. Fred felt ridiculous carrying that box into the prison, which, of course, was taken from him the minute he walked in. That was also the last time anyone ever brought only one helping of anything to Ronnie. From then on, there were always two identical, perfectly wrapped packages: one for Ronnie and one for the guards. No one except Ronnie's parents and lawyers had been allowed to visit him during the ten weeks he had been in the Dedham jail, so prison visits were all new to the Blumenthal relatives. We quickly learned the rules of keeping Ronnie as protected as possible. We had no idea what was going to happen to our Ronnie, but we were all going to do our darnedest to make sure he wasn't going to starve and would know that we loved him.

When Ronnie was sent to Charlestown Prison, the population was around six hundred, and the conditions in most of the prison were indeed deplorable, with many cells having a bucket for a toilet. Meals were often handed to prisoners through bars. None of us had any idea if food we brought for Ronnie would make it into such a cell, but at least we could try.

Charlestown Prison's appalling conditions had resulted in many riots by desperate and ill-treated prisoners. At 2:00 in the morning of January 18, 1955, less than four months after Ronnie had arrived there, the Cherry Hill riots began. For the next eighty-five hours, four armed prisoners held five guards and eighteen fellow prisoners hostage against the combined forces of the National Guard, five hundred state and local police, and prison guards in the Cherry Hill area of the prison where the most dangerous criminals were housed. The armed inmates had put their hostages in solitary confinement cells and promised that for every shot that was fired, one hostage would die.

The situation grew so dangerous that a National Guard officer moved in a giant army tank that had seen combat in World War II with his own promise that if any hostage was harmed, the tank would demolish the Cherry Hill section and everyone in the building.

On the third day of the siege, the prisoners agreed to negotiate with a seven-person citizen's committee to discuss the horrendous conditions of the prison and the rigid penal code in Massachusetts. After a day and a half of negotiating, the citizen's committee agreed to help the prisoners, although no deal was made before the riot ended. Later the same year, the prison was closed and all the Charlestown prisoners were moved to the much newer prison in Norfolk. On February 3, 1955, thirteen days after the riot ended, Ronnie, thanks to some sort of political pull, most likely arranged by goodly sums of money from Edythe's brother-in-law, real estate mogul Maurice Gordon, was one of the first prisoners to be transferred from Charlestown to Norfolk Prison Colony. While Ronnie was in Charlestown, I doubt any Blumenthals had a decent night's sleep.

At Norfolk, with an average population of 1,500 inmates, Ronnie was protected in multiple ways, by generous bribes to prison personnel and guards, as he had been in Charlestown. We all had heard awful stories about what could happen to a young, handsome new prisoner when he arrives in prison, but visits with Ronnie calmed our collective nerves and left us hoping and believing that Aunt Edythe and Uncle Barney would do everything humanly possible to protect our cousin from those horrors. While I had been considered too young to visit him in Charlestown, within a year after his move to Norfolk, I began to accompany my mother to visit him.

We Blumenthals could only write, visit, bake, and cook for Ronnie, but we hoped that Aunt Edythe's Gordon and Frank relatives, with their larger finances and more prestigious connections, would do far more. But cook we Blumenthals did! Continuously.

As the constant visits from cousins, aunts, and uncles began in this far-more-humane prison, reports from one to another seemed to indicate that Ronnie was settling in to prison routine relatively quickly and obediently. He appeared to be keeping busy where he was, furthering his education at the prison school, trying to earn the high school diploma that had eluded him at Brookline High School and at Huntington Prep, taking some college courses, recording books for the blind, organizing prison Passover seders. Most of all, he followed his attorney's advice never to attract undue attention. Sadly, attorney Herbert

F. Callahan died just three and a half months after Ronnie's trial ended and before he was transferred to Norfolk prison. On Wednesday, January 12, 1955, Callahan, age sixty-nine, who had handled thousands of criminal cases during his forty-eight years of practice, had just returned home from a long day in superior court defending a client charged with murder when he collapsed and died of a heart attack. To his dying day, Callahan had been proud that he never lost a client to the electric chair.

There was no question that Aunt Edythe and Uncle Barney had been willing to pay whatever was necessary, not only to defend their son but also to make sure Ronnie was safe and well-protected during his prison years. I thought it was amazing that my aunt was permitted to bring Ronnie expensive cashmere sweaters and pants so that he could wear them when she came to visit. It was obviously her plan that he would always be the best dressed prisoner in the entire prison. That much, she could control.

Since Ronnie had never managed to graduate high school and had no notable academic achievements at Huntington Prep, it was a pleasant surprise to hear him talk about all the different books he was reading on recordings for the blind, admitting for the first time that he was enjoying reading. I've often wondered if my cousin might have had some form of attention deficit disorder (ADD) that kept him hyperactive and his attention span limited. After all, while he had done well at military school from ages ten to twelve, he had later been unable to graduate Brookline High School and had done poorly at prep school. Perhaps in a prison cell, his every move dictated, and without the distraction of girls, cash, and cars, he was able to sit quietly and finally learn to concentrate on reading. Maybe it was a relief to be out of the pressure cooker of the life he was leading as a rich kid with money, with no ambition except to take over his father's liquor store. That is, of course, my very unprofessional opinion, for whatever it might or might not be worth. I know, the thought that a prison term would help a student with ADD is absurd. Still, Ronnie was reading. And we were all grasping at straws to find anything positive for him in the prison experience.

Years later, I wondered if the structure in prison, as well as the structure of military school, had been the only time when Ronnie functioned well, when he seemed to be able to control his negative impulses and destructive behavior. How scary and sad it was that one could say Ronnie was better off in prison than outside its locked iron doors.

While in prison, Ronnie was put to work, although not exactly at the hard labor the judge had mentioned—there was no breaking rocks, no chain gang. According to Ronnie's official prison record, his job was as follows: "Industries clerk, ass't Deputy Clerk (several years) and maintenance Truck driver, above average worker at all assignments." As for his education, the record lists "Several different correspondence courses." Concerning his spare-time activities: "His activities have naturally varied over the extended period of time at Norfolk ('55 to '64); has always kept busy with reading, studying, sports activities, taping for the blind, avocational work, Jewish services, etc." I found his work recording books for the blind admirable. Those books gave us plenty of topics for discussion during visits. The only negative comment about his conduct during his nine years at Norfolk was on May 28, 1958, when he was given a "Warning for Insolence to officer and lying." The description of his personality stated, "Subject has reportedly had some problems over the years of a personality nature, but has managed to overcome this with the passing of time." Perhaps since the brain's maturation process culminates around age twenty-five, Ronnie had simply gotten older and matured.

Still, "problems over the years of a personality nature" certainly sounded interesting, and I would love to have learned more about those particular problems. One of those "personality nature" problems ended up delivering him to prison and perhaps contributed to his inability to graduate high school. Was removing him from his home another way to solve these problems? Heaven knew he had a weird relationship with his mother that Barbara from Newton had witnessed. Unlike with his Brookline peers, college did not seem like an option for Ronnie as a way to escape from his parents. Perhaps he could never figure out another way beside enlisting in the military. While he may not have actively chosen prison as his new way of life, in many ways it did fit the bill for getting out from under the thumb of his parents.

While Ronnie's prison records do not indicate a great deal of time spent inside Massachusetts Correctional Institute at Norfolk's well-equipped prison library, interestingly, it was in this room where a far more celebrated prisoner, Malcolm Little, better known as Malcolm X, changed his life. Although Malcolm X originally began his twelve-year sentence for burglary at Charlestown State Prison in April 1946, his sister began a letter-writing campaign to get him transferred to the Norfolk Prison Colony, which had a reputation for inmate educational programs with ties to area colleges such as Harvard, Emerson, and Boston University. Her campaign was successful, and he was transferred to Norfolk on March 31, 1948, for the rest of his sentence. Paroled in 1952, three years before Ronnie arrived, he spent four years of his sentence at Norfolk, taking classes and being involved in the highly respected Norfolk Prison Debating

Society. Malcolm emerged as an educated man with a great love of reading and acquiring knowledge. No one could say the same thing about Ronnie, who never spent one moment on the debating team or in any of the Boston University or Harvard classes. Every time I visited Ronnie later on in his sentence, I thought of Malcolm and how fascinating it would have been to have met him in that prison visiting room during his years there. But their times at Norfolk never overlapped.

While Ronnie never underwent such an educational metamorphosis as Malcolm X, he did become interested in reading for the first time in his life. Ronnie also visited the prison machine shop and just about all of us who were part of his prison life ended up with wallets and pocketbooks he made and personally engraved. It wasn't until years later that we learned that our aunt and uncle had paid a sizable sum of money for the leather materials used in making those gifts.

My husband, Jack, who was a medical student at the time (we're now in the 1960s), kept the leather eyeglasses case, engraved on the front with a medical caduceus, that Ronnie had made for him. I had been visiting Ronnie for six years before I met Jack, who was more than a bit nervous the first time I brought him to Norfolk to visit my cousin. After I told Ronnie about Jack and showed him Jack's photo, Ronnie looked forward to meeting him. "I've got to approve him," he told me, probably only half-jokingly. That made Jack even more nervous about the prison visit, but the minute the two met, my boyfriend's nervousness disappeared. Of course, it was more than understandable that heading into a medium-security prison to meet your girlfriend's cousin, who is serving a life sentence for murder, might be a bit intimidating, but the truth is Ronnie had a way of making each of his visitors feel at ease. That was quite a feat considering the far from comfortable process each had to go through before being admitted to the visiting room.

First, there was the daunting check-in process, the initial step to visit Ronnie. After you waited in what was often a long line to present a driver's license or some other form of identification, and make sure your name was on Ronnie's visitor list, you had to put everything that you were carrying, except for some approved jewelry, into a locker. The locker key, along with the inmate visiting form, was about the only thing you were allowed to keep with you during the visit. Then you were led into the Visitor Processing Search Room, where you had to remove your belt, shoes, and coat. Hopefully, each visitor had carefully read the list of acceptable clothing and not worn any of the forbidden items, such as sheer, strapless, or halter tops or dresses or a skirt or dress shorter than two inches above the knee. Any clothing with offensive writing or images was not allowed.

After all your personal items were removed and placed in a box, you had to walk through a metal detector. If any metal was detected, such as the wire in an underwire bra, you had to go in a separate room where an officer would check you over very thoroughly. One time when I passed through the metal detector and set it off, it was the closest to a strip search I ever had to endure. The metal was in an unsuspected and very small clip in the back of my head used to hold my hair. It was not pleasant, but fortunately the problem was detected before a complete strip search was necessary.

After you went through the metal detector, you had to turn out your pockets, lift your arms, and show your hands, open your mouth, flip up your collar, uncuff your sleeves and pant legs, flip over the waist band of your skirt or pants, lift up any long hair, and show the officer the bottom of your feet (if you wore long pants you had to roll up the cuffs). If the handheld metal detector the officer used was set off again, you were in big trouble and had to go back to the end of the line to repeat the process all over again, which could take an additional hour. This happened to a friend of mine who wore an underwire bra when she came with me to visit Ronnie. By the time she was finished with the second search process visiting time was over.

When you were cleared to enter the prison you passed through an intimidating series of locked gates, as each gate clanged shut behind you with a noise that was enough to jolt already frayed nerves. To me, it seemed like a way of making sure each visitor got a taste of what it must be like to be imprisoned. It was important to remember that you were not allowed to use any bathrooms once you left the registration room, so if you had to relieve yourself after that, you had to leave the prison and forfeit the rest of your visit. Lastly, just before you finally entered the visiting room, your hand was stamped, which always felt to me like a mark of victory that I had succeeded at the difficult task of getting through all the checkpoints. I must admit, though, that I also muttered a prayer that the stamp wouldn't suddenly disappear and I'd be stuck behind the bars indefinitely.

At the end of the visit, you returned to the visiting room foyer to retrieve your articles before heading down the walkway to the steel door where an officer checked your hand stamp. Only then were you allowed to leave and regain your freedom. I always felt both relief and sadness at that exact moment. Of course, I was relieved to be out of that daunting place, but that feeling of relief was tempered by a sadness that while I went to a car and drove home, my cousin went back to a locked cell. Often, I allowed myself to think of the reason he was in that locked cell and how he had confessed to killing a woman who would never be able to live another day. Then I would take a deep breath and think about "maybe." Maybe Ronnie didn't kill that woman. Maybe someone else did. "Maybe" was a pretty powerful word, and I was always grateful to be able to use it, even if I was only tricking myself.

While I was used to the entire visitor's procedure by the time I brought Jack to the prison, I knew he was uptight after the process that got him into the visiting room. As was usual when Ronnie received visitors, he was already seated there when we arrived, wearing his usual outfit of a blue chambray shirt and blue slacks.

Sometimes he wore one of the cashmere sweaters my aunt brought him. I thought he looked better in the blue shirt and slacks, which accentuated his stunning blue eyes. He always looked neat and handsome, his small, shy smile lighting up his face. Even when Ronnie was seated, we could see that he was in terrific physical shape. I doubt that Ronnie ever exercised even one muscle of his body before he went to prison. Driving his convertible, sleeping late, eating crappy food, drinking too much—that was his lifestyle. I honestly believe that those prison years were the healthiest years of Ronnie's entire life. In prison, for the first time in his life he obviously exercised regularly, stopped drinking, read more than ever before, and appeared calmer and more relaxed. I know that sounds insane, but since I hardly knew Ronnie before we became well-acquainted during my visits, I saw nothing about him that ever indicated he was temperamental, moody, or difficult. I was also pretty naive about the kind of awful things that might happen to Ronnie when he left the visiting room. I assumed my aunt and uncle's influence and money protected him from the horrors of prison life.

When my cousins and I discussed our visits to Ronnie, none of us could remember any detail that Ronnie offered to let us know what happened when he was not with us. We all observed that he never mentioned the murder, often beginning a sentence with, "When I get home...." None of us ever pressed him for more information, as he always turned the conversation to our lives, seeming to enjoy hearing the most mundane details of life beyond the prison walls. We all felt awful when we walked out and left him there, but as the years went by, we were hopeful that he would indeed get out, and soon. The last thing any of us wanted to contemplate was why he was there. My cousin Dick told me when discussing our visits with Ronnie, "I certainly didn't bring it up," Dick said, "and he never offered to discuss it."

Obviously, I understood that prison was an awful place to be, but the Ronnie I saw there for two hours at a time was always kind and funny and a delight to spend a few hours with. While I dreaded the process I had to go through to get to the visiting room, I genuinely looked forward to each visit. Jack agreed 100 percent. Within five minutes of meeting Ronnie, the two of them were engaged in a discussion of sports, from which I felt, not unhappily, excluded. Ronnie appeared interested in every premed and medical course that Jack took and asked perceptive questions about them. You would not believe how he and Jack could dissect every move the Red Sox made. While I remained unusually quiet during that first visit, Ronnie smiled at me often and thanked me for the goodies I told him I had brought, including my mother's brisket, a regular part of every one of Belle Blumenthal Klasky's family visits, one for Ronnie and one for the "staff."

Brisket-wise, today, I have to admit that my brisket never came out as delicious as my sister's. Toby seemed to have inherited the Blumenthal/Klasky gene for cooking the perfect brisket. Maybe it's because she used far more than just four pounds of carrots. The problem is that when she made it, we ate so many of the cooked carrots before putting it on the table that we were too full to eat a single bite of the brisket!

After the brisket was properly distributed, I remained pleasantly sidelined for the visit, more than pleased to concentrate on studying the other visitors, as Jack and I sat across from Ronnie at the table for four to which we had been assigned. Occasionally I would marvel at the absurdity of the whole scene: my cousin, serving a life sentence for a particularly brutal murder, discussing anatomy with my premed boyfriend.

As the years wore on and my relationship with Jack became a permanent one, we often discussed our upcoming wedding with Ronnie. When we finally set a date of August 15, 1965, Ronnie was genuinely happy for us, and the three of us were hopeful that Ronnie's parole would come through and he would be home by then. Ronnie joked that the marriage would not be legitimate if he were not there to bless it in person. It was our hope that he would indeed be there, but I think, deep down, I always knew it was a pipe dream. By August 1965, Ronnie would have served eleven years of his sentence; parole seemed more of a possibility after thirteen years. Governor Endicott ("Chub") Peabody, who held office from 1963 to 1965, had worked hard to abolish the death penalty, and there was a possibility that he might be more sympathetic to Ronnie's chance of parole.

Indeed, right around the time of my and Jack's wedding, Ronnie's lawyers had him send a letter to a judge asking for an early parole, even though he still had more than three years to go before he would be eligible for parole. Although I am certain the lawyers wrote every word of the letter, I still find the letter interesting as it describes my cousin, to some degree, eleven years after he entered prison in this way:

> Undoubtedly the full data concerning my personal statistics, psychiatric evaluations, familial background, and institutional progress record are valid and available to you in the Pardon Board's copy of my casefile. Consequently, I shall, at this point only briefly summarize the factors which I feel are most important for your consideration in acting upon my new petition:
>
> My cardinal concern is for the health, welfare and happiness of my parents. I am an only child, there is a great deal of love and mutual respect between us, and they have suffered every hour of my confinement along with me. They are growing older, their emotional situations are anguished and adversely affected by my continued incarceration. Their health is at issue as a result thereof, and, finally, there is the ever constant fear that time might out distance us in our desire to be re-united.
>
> My father has been a licensed retail liquor dealer in the city of Boston since shortly after the "repeal" and is now at a point where he requires my presence and assistance in conducting his business. It is his hope and desire that I succeed in carrying on its operation and there again the

> question of time in regard to my availability is primary and it is questionable that he can continue alone until my release as scheduled. My mother and father both have to spend a minimum of 12 to 15 hours per day in their store.
>
> It is inconsistent to suppose that my own attitude, behavioral pattern, philosophy, and general outlook on life could be the same today as it was some nine and a half years ago when the offense was committed, and while I was laboring under a great emotional stress which no longer exists and never can in the foreseeable future. In this context I enumerate the following facts for your consideration.
>
> I have received various psychiatric tests, evaluations and therapy all of which is listed in detail in my casefile. I entered prison in my 18th year and the institutional index which I have compiled from that point until now is indicative of a fairness of resolve to conform even under trying circumstances. Further, achievements accomplished are reflective of a desire and drive for self-improvement and self-discipline.

The letter also mentioned the family's frustration with the publicity that, not unexpectedly, dogged Ronnie since the day of the murder:

> It is most significant that I make mention of this additional fact, that is pertaining to publicity.

> Ever since my initial arrest in July of 1954, the publicity via radio, television, magazines, and newspapers has been extreme. I realize that such media cannot be controlled but I also realize that although such sensationalism must be reported, this publicity has had not only and solely an adverse affect upon the mental and physical health of my parents but has also played a major role in the recent commutation hearings, as pointed out on radio, just a short while ago, November 26, 1963, on the radio program Frankly Speaking, by Executive Councillor John Costello. "In cases like that of Lorraine Clarke, John Kerrigan, and Blumenthal, a large amount of publicity can arouse the public, and this naturally would affect the Executive Council." And it is my opinion that this fact is also true of the Board of Pardons.
>
> It is apparent that the Board of Pardons has shown a genuine desire to afford me leniency, especially since they gave me an additional interview, subsequent to my initial hearing. But it would seem that their enthusiasm to this end has been governed by a "cloud of uncertainty." Of course, that is my own contention.

Certainly, everything stated in the letter was true, as my uncle had hoped Ronnie would take over his Boston liquor store and the extreme publicity in no way helped Ronnie with the Board of Pardons. Still, I wondered what was meant by the "great emotional stress" under which he had been "laboring," but it was certainly reassuring to read and to believe that this stress "no longer exists and never can in the foreseeable future." Perhaps he was referring to his father's affair with Ora. Since she was dead... the problem had gone away.

However, this well-written request, no matter who actually wrote it, did not succeed until two years later, when John A. Volpe became governor. Still, there had been hope my cousin would be out by the time Jack and I got married in August 1965, and, right up until the last minute, we held on to it. It had been hard not to put my arms around my cousin the day we disclosed the day of our wedding, but we knew better than to do that. Physical contact with an inmate was strictly limited at Norfolk Prison. Occasionally we managed a hand squeeze or a tiny hug when we entered the visiting room or were ready to depart, but that was all. Ronnie was always seated when we came in and never left his seat until we had left. My picture of Ronnie during all those years was of him sitting quietly, the sweet, half-crooked smile on his face, his hands, the backs of which were covered with light-blond, curly hair, resting on the table where we had just sat, making me believe, yet again and again, that those hands could never have murdered Ora Schonarth.

While the mystery of that murder never quite left the room, no matter where I was, I understood it would always be the elephant in the room. It was so easy to look at Ronnie as an innocent man suffering in a jail cell while important years of his life, years he could never regain, disappeared. But then there was Ora Schonarth, whose life had tragically ended that July day (or night). Sometimes it was best not to think about it. I just hoped that Ronnie would be home soon, having paid the debt that might or might not have been his to pay. And if he had indeed committed that heinous crime, that he had been rehabilitated, and it would never happen again.

As the years marched on, there were always visitors, as the Blumenthal cousins, especially Fred, Mel, and Dick, never hesitated to visit Ronnie, eventually even bringing their wives and kids with them. Like all of us, my aunt Etta's son Dick found it hard to remember exactly what he and Ronnie talked about during their visits. He recalled discussing experiences they shared when they were growing up. "We talked about their Nantasket house with the big porch that I visited a few times," Dick told me. "My mother was very close to her younger brother, Barney, and she adored Ronnie. When she came with me, she always brought her strudel. And when she didn't come, she sent me with some."

Dick also remembered an incident that happened outside the prison walls while Ronnie was at Norfolk. "I was visiting Boston and stopped in to see my uncle Barney. He seemed to be doing all right but insisted that he take me to a clothing store where he bought me a suit. He kept saying that since Ronnie was 'away' he couldn't buy it for him, but he wanted to buy it for someone. It was sad, but he seemed to get so much pleasure from getting that suit for me."

Dick's brother, Bob Halpert, who was six and a half years younger than Ronnie, had a similar experience. "When Ronnie was away, Uncle Barney took me to get a suit and an overcoat. I was a teenager at the time, but remember the store was a small, but very expensive place." Bob, too, visited Ronnie both at Norfolk and later at the Forestry Camp, where Ronnie spent his last year and a half of incarceration, often bringing my aunt Etta with him.

The reason Ronnie was there never left our minds. So many times I discussed it with Jack, especially while he was taking psychiatry classes in medical school, asking him if my cousin appeared to be a murderer. While we agreed there was no one-size-fits-all profile for what a murderer looked like, Ronnie's calm and easy demeanor appeared to be the total opposite of what one would expect from someone who, at age eighteen, had supposedly brutally murdered a woman three times his age.

The murder was a subject I rarely discussed with my mother. On our visits, when I was in junior high school, high school, and college, she was fairly upbeat during our hour-or-so drive to Norfolk. I knew she always reported back to her sister-in-law Edythe upon our return and that she visited Ronnie quite regularly, probably once every month or two, making certain no one else was using that time slot before she requested it.

On our arrival at the prison, once we had gone through all the channels to deposit the brisket, cookies, or other homemade goodies with the officials, and also during the visit itself, my mother continued to be her usual energetic, talkative self. There was no question she adored Ronnie, and he felt the same way toward her. The time flew during the visit, and I had no problem filling in any lags in the conversation with my own stories of school. My mother's smile remained on her face when the three of us said our goodbyes, but once we had cleared the last heavy steel door on our way back to the parking lot, empty food containers in our hands, her demeanor changed. Often, she simply sat in the driver's seat before even starting up the car and cried for a few minutes before she began driving, saying more or less the same thing: "It breaks my heart to see that beautiful boy sitting there, his whole life going by him. I don't know how Barney and Edythe can stand it."

The few times I tried to discuss the case with her, she closed the conversation quickly. "There's no sense discussing it," she'd tell me. "We just have to count the days or weeks or years until he comes home." So we all did, all the aunts and uncles and cousins and their girlfriends or boyfriends or husbands or wives making sure that we got to see as much of Ronnie as possible. We all agreed that not only did we feel as if we were seeing more of him in those visits than we ever had before, but that the Ronnie we were now seeing, despite the uncomfortable setting, seemed normal and someone we could not possibly, or ever want to, imagine killing Ora Schonarth. My father did not go to the prison very often, but my mother always discussed her visits with him, my father referring to his nephew by marriage as "the kid." My father did go before the parole board and spoke positively about Ronnie, explaining that he trusted him completely and that there would be a job for Ronnie at his East Boston steel company when he was released. Sure, Ronnie's father owned a liquor store in Boston, but if for some reason the parole board might not look favorably on Ronnie working in a liquor store, the steel company was perhaps a more acceptable option.

The true star of those thirteen years, as Ronnie changed from a teenager into an adult was my sister, Toby, five years younger than Ronnie. The day she brought her freshman college roommate, Florence Gold to visit Ronnie changed Ronnie's and Flo's lives irrevocably, not to mention the effect it had on my aunt and uncle.

Florence (Flo) Gold (left) and my sister Toby. In 1962, Toby asked her college roommate if she wanted to come along to visit her cousin Ronnie in prison.

CHAPTER EIGHTEEN

Flo 1961–1964

It was a lovely Saturday in November 1962 when my sister, Toby, mentioned that she was heading to see Ronnie at Norfolk Prison and that she asked her college roommate Florence Gold if she wanted to come along. I was still in high school when Toby took off for Mount Ida College in Boston and had immediately been impressed by her effervescent and pretty roommate, Flo, who, as expected, needed no encouragement to accept the invitation. That was pure Flo, always ready for a new adventure, full of energy and anticipation. A beautiful twenty-year-old with thick black hair and large, expressive brown eyes and a smile that always emitted warmth and friendliness, Flo had a string of male admirers. She also had a kind spirit that left her particularly vulnerable to needy creatures, human and animal. Somehow or other she had found a monkey that needed a temporary home, which turned out to be the dorm room she shared with Toby. Luckily, the visit from the monkey ended a long month later when Flo found an even better home—she had insisted on finding one without bars—for her needy companion.

The November morning that she left Boston and embarked on an hour-long drive to Norfolk Prison, Flo thought only about visiting her roommate's twenty-five-year-old cousin, Ronnie Blumenthal, who was most definitely living behind bars.

The last thing Flo expected to see when she made her way through the maze of iron gates, intimidating checkpoints, and seemingly endless body searches was a handsome blond man dressed in a blue cashmere sweater that matched his eyes. "It was his sweet smile that got to me," Flo said. "It was kind of a shy but friendly smile, and for some reason it just drew me in. Big time."

Toby was amazed at the instant rapport between her roommate and her cousin. A few of her high school friends had previously come with her to visit Ronnie, and she had always noticed the warm and friendly way he had treated them. With Flo it was different, not exactly the way she had expected the two of them to react. "It was like I wasn't even in the room," Toby said. "They only had eyes for each other."

At the end of the visit, Ronnie asked Flo if she would consider writing to him and maybe even come again to visit, something he had never asked of any of the previous female visitors Toby had brought with her. "Of course, I agreed," Flo said. "Ronnie seemed so sweet and was so nice-looking that I figured we could be good friends. And I felt sad that he was where he was. But I never expected it to develop into a romance of any sort."

That was exactly what happened. Flo found Ronnie's letters interesting and even funny. They were so natural that it was hard to believe he was writing to her from a prison cell rather than from a college dorm room. Flo tried to imagine what his cell must look like but found herself concentrating instead on the soft blue eyes and sweet smile of the man writing the letters. "He had the greatest sense of humor and always made me laugh. Plus, he made me feel special, as if he had known me for a long time, even though we had just met a few weeks earlier. And although I knew it was crazy, I felt as if I already knew him."

The next time Flo visited Ronnie she went by herself and was as comfortable sitting with him in a prison visiting room, surrounded by other inmates and their visitors, as she would have been if they had been sitting in a coffee shop together. "I never even considered the possibility that I would feel romantically attracted to Ronnie, but there was no denying that it had happened. Very quickly."

Soon Flo was making the visit to Norfolk as often as she could, usually twice a week, taking the place of his regular visitors, including his parents. "Understandably, my parents were far from happy that I was getting involved with a guy who was serving a life sentence for murder," Flo admitted. "They were simple, hardworking people. My father owned a small dry cleaning business in Brookline, and they lived a quiet, ordinary life. This was the last thing they wanted for their only daughter."

Ronnie's parents, however, felt the opposite. They could not have been more thrilled that this beautiful, vibrant college student who was even Jewish was spending time with their son. "Edythe and Barney practically adopted me," Flo told me. "And their lifestyle was the total opposite of the way my parents lived. They were teaching me manners I never knew about. Like how to fold the cloth napkin in a restaurant as opposed to the paper napkins I was used to at home. It was a whole new world for me. Before I knew it, I was being wined and dined, taken to Giro's, their favorite North End restaurant, where everybody knew them and where they introduced me as Ronnie's girlfriend. They just seemed so proud to have me with them."

Ronnie in prison.

As Flo found herself more and more attracted to Ronnie, she inevitably grappled with the reason he was in prison. She recognized it was the unspoken secret and that she could not ignore it forever. "We only discussed it once," she said, "and he assured me he didn't do it. And I believed him. We just never said anything else about it. Plus, he had already served almost eight years of his sentence. Foster Furcolo was the governor of Massachusetts [from 1957 to 1961], and he was supposed to parole him any day. Ronnie and his parents were pretty certain he would be paroled in the next few years."

Flo thought of herself as an individual who didn't follow the crowd, who cared about the underdog, someone who needed her help. Something about Ronnie made her forget where he was and why he might be there. He needed her, and she was falling in love with him. That was all that mattered.

The more Flo became involved with Ronnie, the more terrified and upset her parents became. "They would see me sitting home alone on a Saturday night while all my friends were out on dates and feel terrible for me. They couldn't understand what I was doing with my life. But it was even worse when they saw the way Edythe and Barney treated me. When they all met, it was awful. My parents had nothing in common with them, and vice versa. My parents were simple people who hardly ever ate out in restaurants and rarely went shopping. They had barely recovered from my dating a Catholic guy and now I was in love with a guy in jail. It was just all too much for them.

"But each night I spent with Edythe and Barney was fun. Barney was the sweetest, nicest man imaginable. Sometimes I would drive to his liquor store to pick him up before the three of us went out for dinner, and I would just sit there and chat with him before he closed up the store. Ronnie seemed so much like his father. He wrote me beautiful, romantic letters and I cherished every one of them, all handmade with loving words and cute pictures he drew on them."

As Flo and Ronnie grew more attracted to each other, and Flo's parents grew more panicked, Edythe and Barney became more hopeful that their son just might have a chance for a normal family life once he was released. Plus, even more important, thanks to the phenomenal Flo, at that moment Ronnie's spirits were high, which immeasurably lifted theirs.

The effect Flo had on Ronnie made his parents even more attentive to her. Edythe, in particular, could not have been more solicitous. "Edythe took me shopping to her favorite stores, Tilkins' and Dot's shoe stores, as well as some expensive places, and bought me lots of gifts," Flo said. "I was uncomfortable with all that attention and those presents, but there was no way to stop Edythe from showering me with them."

Edythe went further than merely bringing Flo into clothing stores. She brought her into both her family life and into the society affairs that came with that family status. "I went to her sister Dorothy Gordon's beautiful home in Newton," Flo said. "It was like a compound, with her daughter Lola's house there as well. It was just amazing to spend time at their pool and to have lunch there. Lola and her brother, Bobby, could not have been more welcoming to me. I was dazzled."

One of the most beautiful gifts Edythe gave Flo was a cashmere sweater with a mink collar. "Since I've always been an animal rights activist, I was not happy with the mink collar, but it was easily the most expensive sweater I had ever had," Flo said. "And to make it even more special, Edythe had her sister Dorothy line the entire sweater with lace. My mother could not have cared less about fashion, but Edythe loved it and kept saying how she had always wanted to go shopping with a daughter. Sometimes that made me a little nervous, but there was no holding her back. She even tried to teach me to knit. Since I have never wanted anything I made to look ordinary, I tried to knit a pair of different-looking argyle socks for Ronnie. My creation turned out to be a fiasco but 'Her Highness' completed them for me so they came out completely ordinary."

As Flo grew more involved with Ronnie, Edythe pushed forward with her intent to make Flo her "daughter," purchasing a blond-colored hope chest for her as a gift from Ronnie. Also called a dowry chest, this piece of furniture was to be a symbol of Ronnie and Flo's future married life together. Plus, it would be the perfect place to store all the delicate and lovely clothing Mrs. Ronnie Blumenthal would wear one day. Edythe had it sent directly to Flo's house in Medford. "I didn't know what to do with it," Flo said. "I knew it would upset my parents terribly, so somehow or other I got it to fit inside the walk-in closet in my bedroom where they would not have to look at it."

Edythe was profoundly delighted that Flo accepted the present, filling it with expensive pink lingerie along with satin slippers for her future daughter-in-law. "There was never any doubt that anything that made Ronnie happy made both Edythe and Barney happy," Flo told me. "And since I was making him happy, they simply could not do enough for me."

Shortly after Ronnie went to prison, Edythe and Barney sold their Beals Street home, obviously needing the money for Ronnie's legal bills, and moved into a two-bedroom apartment in the Jamaicaway Towers in Jamaica Plain, near the border of Brookline. Flo was a frequent guest there, dining with Edythe and Barney and often spending the night in a room they set up just for her.

Before Flo understood what was happening, Edythe enrolled her in the posh Mayflower chapter of the Boston B'nai B'rith organization. Edythe wasted no time involving her future daughter-in-law in a major charity event by casting her in an original musical production of *Some Like It Hot*, written by a B'nai B'rith member. Flo tried to get out of it, but there was no way Edythe would allow that. "Suddenly, I was singing and dancing in this charity performance, before a large audience, dressed in some sort of a tin-foil costume. Edythe and Barney, of course, came to the performance, and they were just so excited I was in it. I was easily the youngest person in the cast. I am usually outgoing and have no trouble talking to people, but getting up on a stage in front of a large group and singing and dancing was pretty scary to me. But I did it, even though I definitely screwed up my part. My role was small, but I was the only cast member in the show who received not one but two bouquets of flowers at the end of the performance. They were, of course, from Ronnie, with lovely notes attached to each bouquet, but at that time, that was pretty embarrassing. Still, I lovingly pressed those flowers into my scrapbook and held on to them for years."

No matter where Flo was, Edythe and Barney wanted to be part of her life. When Flo was involved in a minor car accident, resulting in whiplash, while driving to visit Ronnie in Norwood, they immediately took over, hiring a lawyer for her and settling the matter with her insurance company.

Inevitably, Flo found some prison visits better than others. Sometimes, the guards looked the other way when Ronnie and Flo held hands. "Other times, the visits were horrible, and I felt as if the guards were just waiting for us to do something wrong. Most of the time, however, Barney would shmear [bribe] the guards before my visits, which made things go better for us."

At each visit, the infatuated couple talked about their hopes for a loving future together. "I got completely sucked into those dreams, always hopeful that a connection the family had with one parole board member would bring Ronnie his freedom," Flo remembered. "It was almost impossible to look at his impish grin and not believe everything he said. I just loved the way he looked. He dressed so well, even in prison, and never looked like a bum or even a prisoner. I could not deny the titillating feeling between the two of us, as if every time we tried the forbidden acts of touching hands or leaning close to one another we were entering some special space where just the two of us existed. After those visits, I would often realize I had had no idea who else might have been in that room. All I had eyes for was Ronnie."

Several times, Flo brought her cousin's wife, Ellie, who was also her good friend, to visit Ronnie. "Ellie agreed that Ronnie looked like any well-groomed, good-looking college guy we might have met at a party," said Flo. "I had thought from the very beginning that his family was wealthy and would be able to get him out soon after we met. From the first time I met Barney, I thought he was sweet and lovable though pushed around by Edythe, who acted pretty hoity-toity. But I figured he could make things happen for Ronnie. Plus, there was some excitement, I must admit, in wanting something you definitely couldn't have. There certainly weren't any conjugal visits then since we were not even married."

Flo enjoyed accompanying Toby to Providence to visit our aunts, uncles, and cousins, all of whom knew about her and Ronnie and treated her warmly. "Aunt Etta and Aunt Marion were just so kind and friendly, and I felt as if I were part of this special, close-knit family," Flo said.

Flo's parents' resistance to her dating a man in prison continued to grow. In an effort to shield them from the barrage of letters Ronnie sent her, Flo had him send them to Ellie's house, where she later collected them. On February 14, 1964, Ronnie sent Flo an exquisitely engraved envelope with his own personal Valentine's Day message, which, like the envelope, was printed in beautiful gold script. She reread Ronnie's words over and over, relieved her parents hadn't seen that particular piece of mail, which she assumed Ronnie had paid an artistic fellow inmate to pen Ronnie's poem to Flo. It read:

It was written in the stars, dear

That sweethearts we would be

For I have given you my heart, dear

And you have given yours to me.

May our love shine on forever

Like the stars in Heaven Blue.

That's the prayer and wish I send dear

On this Valentine to you

Love, Ronnie.

It wasn't a complete surprise when I discovered that Flo had held on to so much of her Ronnie memorabilia for more than fifty years. Toby once told me that she believed that the love Ronnie and Flo held for one another would never be surpassed by any other loves in their lives. "They were each other's greatest loves," she said.

As the weeks and months turned into years, Flo and Ronnie began to have serious talks about what would happen when Ronnie was released. "It all sounded wonderful," Flo said years later, "but I could not help wondering how it would really be. What if once he got out, he wanted to date other women and lost interest in me? What would I look like to him when I wasn't just the only attractive woman sitting across from him in a prison visiting room? He'd been locked up for years. Wouldn't he want to date and enjoy being free in every possible way? And, even more importantly, how would he be able to support a family? Barney still had the liquor store, but it was small, and I wasn't at all sure it could provide incomes for two families. Ronnie would obviously have employment problems for the rest of his life because of his prison record. I could not have adored him more, but our future problems just kept worrying me more and more. I struggled to remain hopeful about getting married to Ronnie but always wondered about whether we would really hit it off once we knew each other in the real world and got past the lovey-dovey stuff."

While Edythe and Barney tried to assure Flo that everything would be perfect once Ronnie was home, her worries grew stronger. "I was fine for every minute of our visit," she admitted. "After all, he was a hot and sexy guy with a great smile and laugh. He could melt my panties off for sure. But the minute I walked out of the prison and got into my car, I could not stop worrying."

After more than two and a half years of this intense prison romance, as Flo struggled to hang on to her love for Ronnie and the belief that things would someday work out for the two of them, a bomb threatened to explode their tenuous relationship: Ronnie's latest bid for parole was denied. The parole board appeared more adamant than ever that Ronnie would not be released from prison any time in the near future. "I knew that Edythe and Barney were working hard behind the scenes to secure Ronnie's release, but there was no denying that, at that particular moment, their efforts weren't working," Flo said.

For the first time, the star-crossed lovers seriously discussed the almost-impossible task of making future plans together. "I think I was more heartbroken than Ronnie," Flo told me. "It was just such an unexpected decision that crushed all our hopes in one second. I never truly believed that Ronnie had committed the murder in the first place, so this verdict really shook me. I saw how hard Ronnie was now struggling to contain his pain when we discussed the situation, but I was honestly feeling even worse. He still hung on to faith that it would work out, but I just couldn't do that any longer. I really loved him and couldn't bear the thought of leaving him. But our situation just seemed hopeless. The unexpected failure of his parole bid and my parents' growing misery over our relationship were ripping me up.

If there had been some hope in that letter from the parole board, some possibility that Ronnie would be released in a few years, I might have been able to have stayed with him. But the letter seemed so final and so discouraging that I could no longer see our future together. I finally understood what had to happen. We had to end our relationship. What I was doing to my parents was getting harder and harder to accept. Deep down, I understood that we needed to break up, that so many nights I was way too sad and lonely, that our future together looked grim and hopeless. I still loved Ronnie and knew I always would, but that love had become an elusive longing that just wasn't within reach."

Flo understood that as hard as leaving Ronnie was for her, it had to be far more difficult for Ronnie at that particular time in his life. Yet he worked hard to assure Flo that she need not worry about him, that he would be fine and that all he wanted was for her to have a good life, with a husband and children and all the wonderful things he believed she deserved. He would always be grateful for all she had given up for him those past two and a half years.

"I could see how hard he was trying to make it as easy as he could for me," Flo said. "He was always so thoughtful about what I was going through. His letters were so sensitive, assuring me that he knew what had to be done. He said he would never stop loving me, but the way his future now looked, he had to let me go."

When Flo described my cousin's unselfishness and sensitivity, I was awed by her warm and loving words, but a part of me could not blindly accept them, and I could not connect them to the man my cousin eventually became. Had prison turned Ronnie, at least temporarily, into this near-perfect man? Or were his years behind bars teaching him how to pretend to act as if he were a good man? While I was doing research for this book, I showed Flo the police files and newspaper articles. No matter what I said to her about the murder to which he had confessed, she refused to believe the man she had fallen so deeply in love with so many years ago could possibly have committed a murder, never mind a brutal one. When she talked about Ronnie and the innocence she bestowed upon him, I was reminded of the master criminal James "Whitey" Bulger. Whitey was convicted of eleven vicious murders, but his longtime girlfriend, Cathy Greig, the woman who stayed on the run with him for eighteen years, refused to speak to law enforcement after their arrest, even though her words could have drastically shortened her own sentence of aiding and abetting a criminal. No matter what evidence was placed in front of her, she disregarded it. The man she loved faithfully could not have been a murderer. My cousin Ronnie was surely no Whitey Bulger, nor was Flo Gold a Cathy Greig, but both women would hold on to their belief in the innocence of the men they loved no matter what.

Flo, still deeply in love with my cousin, managed to walk, sobbing, out of the visiting room for what they both knew would be the last visit. "How I ever got to my car in one piece I will never know," she told me. "Nor will I know how I managed to drive away from the prison and return home safely. I was totally heartbroken."

For days and weeks after that last visit, Flo was tempted to return just one more time, but she knew she could not do that. It was over. It had to be. Although Ronnie had promised her that they would meet again, someday in the future, outside the prison walls, Flo feared that she might never see him again.

While Flo's parents could barely hide their relief that her affair with Ronnie was over, Edythe and Barney were almost as heartbroken as Flo. But Edythe didn't stop at heartbroken; she was furious. "It is an understatement to say that Edythe was pretty irritated at me for abandoning ship," Flo said.

Edythe (Ronnie's mother) and Flo in happier times.

My infuriated aunt quickly called Flo, demanding her to explain how she could have done such a cruel thing to her son. Why had she led him on only to desert him at such a difficult moment of his life, right when his parole bid had been turned down? After all she and Barney had done for her, how could she do this to their son? Barely able to deal with her own grief and guilt over leaving Ronnie, Flo could not handle any more calls from my aunt. Immediately, Edythe resorted to letter writing, insisting that Flo return every single gift Edythe had given her. There had been many, including a painted portrait of Flo that Edythe had commissioned from a photograph. Flo was not surprised that this was the one item that Edythe had not asked to have returned. As she explained in one of her seemingly endless letters to Flo, "Incidentally, I am not asking for the picture. I just mentioned it for you so that you will realize that there is no monetary feeling in this as I've told you when you were last here. But let me inform you that the picture alone was $80. My husband left the money so he should know."

Flo did return that painting. "It was not very flattering, and I certainly didn't want it," she said. "I have no idea what Edythe did with it. Maybe ripped it up and kept the frame?"

Flo agreed to give back the hope chest that she had kept hidden in her closet for the past two years. But getting rid of it, which her mother had never seen, was no easy task. She did not want to upset her mother, who, although relieved that her daughter's romance with a man serving a life sentence for murder was over, was now furious with the way Edythe was treating her daughter. So, Flo and her father managed to remove the piece of furniture from her closet when her mother was out of the house, place it in one of her father's dry cleaning trucks, and deposit it at Edythe's apartment at the Jamaicaway Towers in Jamaica Plain. As difficult as it had been for Flo to keep that chest hidden from her mother's eyes, Flo still felt a deep pain at seeing it loaded into the truck. It was as if yet another piece of Ronnie was now gone from her life, and it hurt.

When it came to the other items, Edythe continued to be more forceful in each succeeding letter. As one letter stated:

> Please don't let me have to write again to you concerning this. Ron had given presents to various members of your family and to also your relatives. I had completely forgotten about this until it was pointed out by my husband. I would also like any bottoms or tops of pajamas that you might have to make a pair. In short, please return everything except the ring and watch as

we believe that is just and fair to all concerned. I would also like the lounge set as it is part of the trousseau and like I told you which will all be put away untouched until it is seen fit to be used when Ron comes home.

I know you said last Friday over the phone that you had returned everything—well, you far from returned everything. You see, I knew at all times what Ron had made in there, even though you chose to keep it a secret from us, such as the lazy Susan, all the jewelry sets, etc. All these things were to be put away for future use and therefore I would like them returned as soon as possible. Along with everything that Ron gave you, I would like everything I gave you to be put away and I am sure a list doesn't have to be made out as you know very well what I did give you. As far as things that were my own, you sent some back and kept some, which I realized while unpacking the cartons.

There are slippers from Dot's that I paid for to put away as everything else was intended both from Ron and me. This is not done out of any animosity, believe me, but since it was a break, it should be done clean with no hard feelings. Please don't let me have to write again to you concerning this. If you choose not to come here, you can leave everything at your father's store in Brookline under my name and let me know

> when it will be there and I'll pick it up. As I've told you many times, I've put everything in Ron's dresser and the closet and there everything will remain until, please G-d, he comes home.

Reading Edythe's letters, Flo was overwhelmed with the vision of my aunt as a vengeful, nasty woman. Yes, Edythe was understandably crushed that her son was being dumped by the woman whom he loved, and she was understandably angry with Flo for abandoning him at a time when he was so low. The cruel words she leveled at Flo, however, seem to indicate that she never thought of Flo as a human being but rather as a gift she was giving to her son. It makes me all the more confused and critical of that particular mother-son relationship. Had Edythe's behavior with Flo put Ronnie more under her control than ever before? Obviously, there is nothing typical about a man's relationship to his mother when he is in prison, but my aunt's vindictive reaction to Flo's departure had to have left a strong mark on her son. As Ronnie sat in a prison cell, Edythe, in a sick way, might finally have had the full control over him that she had always wanted.

Each new letter from Edythe wounded Flo anew, but she was especially annoyed by what she considered Edythe's insensitive request for the pajamas. Edythe had given her the pajamas that Ronnie had worn before he went to prison, pajamas Flo had slept in so many times just to feel closer to Ronnie. She'd returned the pajamas, but not the peignoir set, which Flo defiantly placed in a drawer in her bureau.

Both furious at Edythe and still distraught over losing Ronnie, Flo spent a great deal of time composing a letter to Edythe, hoping to end the barrage of upsetting letters. Flo wrote:

Mrs. Blumenthal, At first, it was hard for me to accept so many gifts from you but after a while I really believed that you meant for me to have them with pleasure. You asked for their return as easily as you seemed to give them. It can only look to me and to others as though you bought me and then asked for a refund when our dreams and prayers didn't come through. You legally have no right to any of these items other than the cedar chest. I dislike trouble and decided to make things easy for you by returning the merchandise.

Thanks to your letters, my opinion of Ronnie is now quite different than before. My opinion of any man who would let anyone hurt the one he supposedly loves is quite low. I would never let anyone, with my knowledge, cause any sort of mental or physical harm to that person. I pray for his good fortune and for him to come home soon, but I do not wish to see him again.

The two of you seem to think that no one has feelings other than yourselves. You are mistaken. I never meant to harm you in any way and am sure that I didn't. I tried hard never to hurt Ron, but if I did then I'm truly sorry. And may the next girl get more pleasure from these gifts than I ever did. With the help of G-d, Ron will come home soon and be able to have as normal a life as he truly deserves. You are now the only one

> who can give him the strength and courage that he needs. Please never fail him.

After much thought, Flo finally decided not to send that letter to Edythe. She desperately wanted to say those things to my aunt but felt that her words might somehow end up hurting Ronnie, and that was the one thing she could not bear doing. Another item Flo defiantly kept out of Edythe's hands was the beautiful photo album that Ronnie had commissioned for them, with "Flo and Ronnie" elegantly carved in wood on its cover. "I managed to get off Ronnie's name," Flo said. "Then I used it as a family album for years."

While Flo could not help worrying about Ronnie and how she might have hurt him and what his life was like at Norfolk, she was hopeful that it was not intolerable after the breakup. "I am sure that Barney and Edythe buttering up the prison guards with food and favors helped his daily life," she pondered. "And I am sure that he was a model prisoner. No matter how things were at that moment, all our times together had been very sweet and special."

Many years later, Flo admitted, "Sorry, but to be honest, at the end it was time to cut the ties. I was so very sad but was also glad to have some normalcy back in my life. I ended up going to California with a couple of friends, but I will never forget the pain of saying goodbye to him that day."

CHAPTER NINETEEN
From Lockup to Liquor

Barney and Edythe react to the parole board's denial during the hearing held at the Massachusetts State House on November 20, 1962. The stoic Barney looks completely shell shocked, while Edythe's face registers a mother's complete anguish. After Ronnie's eight years in prison, she'd remained hopeful that Ronnie would soon be released. It would take another five years.

In November 1962, while Flo had still been a part of Ronnie's life, Ronnie's sentence had been officially commuted to a term of thirty-two years to life, making him eligible for parole after twelve years. In October 1966, well after Flo's departure from Ronnie's life, things began to look stronger for his parole bid. Jack and I had been married fourteen months earlier, on August

15, 1965. We had been deeply sorry that Ronnie wasn't able to be at our wedding, but we'd been hopeful that things would be a lot brighter regarding his possible parole. Right after the wedding, we left Boston for Washington, DC, where Jack began his third year of medical school and I began teaching English at a Maryland junior high school. We didn't see Ronnie until we came home for Thanksgiving in November 1966. By then, he'd been transferred to Massachusetts Correctional Institution (MCI) in Plymouth, a minimum security and prerelease facility that prepared inmates for an upcoming release. Located in the Myles Standish State Forest in South Carver, Massachusetts, near the northwest edge of Cape Cod, the prison, which could hold more than 210 adult males, allowed inmates who had eighteen months or less of their sentence remaining to participate in a work-release program within the surrounding community.

Walking into MCI-Plymouth, we felt as if we were visiting someone at a summer camp in the forest. It consisted of a cluster of low-slung buildings on the edge of a pond. According to its brochure, which I read before our visit, "Men in orange jump suits amble from building to building as security guards, some with dogs, stand watch. Everywhere along the two roads leading to the buildings there are signs: 'Department of Correction, No Trespassing.'"

Yet, we found visiting Ronnie there completely different and far less daunting and threatening from visiting him at the medium-security MCI-Norfolk prison. Jack always remembered Ronnie, one leg on a tree stump, dressed in jeans and a blue cotton shirt during our first visit there, looking stronger and more at ease than in the MCI-Norfolk prison visiting room. It was easy to imagine that the three of us were just having a pleasant visit in a forest park. Of course, we knew there were guards and wire fences. Still, it was undeniably one step closer to freedom and the real world for Ronnie, a thought that made the visit warm and relaxed.

Since the Forestry Camp was close to where the family of my cousin Mel's wife, Jacquee, lived, a visit to the South Carver institution held a double attraction for his family. "My mother-in-law lived in Kingston, right near Plymouth, which was where Jacquee and I had been married," Mel told me. "When Ronnie had been moved there, we went to see him as well and would bring our two oldest kids, Robert and Donna, with us and the five of us had a pleasant, easy visit."

Jacquee also remembered those visits as easy and enjoyable. "When we would go to the forestry camp, the guards were always present, but they were dressed in khaki uniforms, which blended in," she said. "Ronnie wore nice clothes since the inmates were allowed to dress as they wished on the weekends for visitors. Edythe would bring in huge baskets of food from Jack & Marion's or other well-known Brookline restaurants, and she would feed everyone who came to visit Ronnie. One time, our oldest son, Robert, was toddling around and one of the inmates knelt down to play with him. He had a pack of cigarettes in his pocket, and Robert tried to get them. Without thinking, I said to the inmate, 'Watch out, he's a pickpocket.' I had to laugh as I had no idea exactly why the man was there."

Cousin Fred also harbored positive memories of those visits with his wife, Sandra. "I was recently thinking about Ronnie in the Forestry Camp," he said. "My children, Jeffrey and Glenna, were six and three at the time. I asked Jeff if he had any memory of being at this camp, and he sort of remembered that we spent some time in a big room that resembled a cafeteria. That was all he recollected. Before we went, we explained to our kids that we were visiting our cousin at a camp. We would usually go in the spring or summer or fall, when the weather was nice, and stay about an hour and a half. When we left there, at some point we went to Edaville [a theme park] where they had a train ride and our kids played around. Everything we ever did when visiting him was as if he were at a school or a camp. Other than her first visit with Ronnie at Norfolk, Sandra had always felt comfortable. I visited him alone more times than when Sandra came with me. We both tried to block our minds as to why we were really visiting. For all my many visits to Ronnie, at the Charlestown Prison, at Norfolk Prison, and lastly at the Forestry Camp, I succeeded in pushing that awful question out of my mind. But I knew exactly why we were there, even if I did not dare to admit it. We were there because of what happened that night in July 1954. And we all knew it."

It was at the Forestry Camp where, thanks to his mother, Ronnie met Barbara Sickels. Barbara's widowed mother, Dorothy, had become friends with Edythe. Within weeks of their blossoming friendship, Aunt Edythe suggested that Dorothy bring her twenty-six-year-old, dark-haired, dark-eyed, slim daughter to Plymouth to meet her son, whom she promised would be "home very soon, with this whole awful experience far behind him." Needless to say, the fact that the daughter was unmarried made her even more attractive to Edythe. With Ronnie looking even more handsome and in better physical shape at Plymouth than he had been at Norfolk, Barbara was suitably impressed with the sweet, handsome, blond, thirty-one-year-old bachelor she met at the Forestry Camp.

Unquestionably, the soft-spoken, gentle Barbara was a far different type of woman from the effervescent, strikingly beautiful Flo, and Ronnie had no trouble making the change in his mind, if not in his heart. Sweet, funny, and increasingly more loving letters arrived in Barbara's mailbox, and her car quickly learned the easiest forty-five-minute route from Boston to Plymouth. For Aunt Edythe, the transition was easy, because this time Ronnie's girlfriend had a mother who looked favorably on her daughter's newest boyfriend. Edythe had apparently learned much from her relationship with Flo, on whom she believed she had lavished far too much attention, money, and pressure. Because Dorothy was her new friend and was delighted with the relationship, Edythe's job to ensure that her son would have a serious chance at a normal family life upon his release was far easier.

"Edythe was pleasant and warm to me," Barbara said, "yet I could also see how interfering she could be. But I understood what she had been through those past thirteen years and figured once Ronnie was released, her influence would fade. She would be so relieved her son was in 'good hands,' she would remove herself from every aspect of his new free life. I was wrong." So, for the final two years of Ronnie's imprisonment, Barbara, with the approval and encouragement of her mother and my aunt, was at Ronnie's side.

Still, Ronnie's road to parole required work. For the two years he was at the Forestry Camp his records showed his behavior to be "good to excellent." At the camp he took a personal management course through the Massachusetts University Extension program, in which he maintained a B average. He also completed the test series for his elusive GED, though the marks were still pending upon his release. I sensed that GED diploma was permanently intangible. Ronnie kept busy with reading, TV, cards, handball, weight lifting, and some socializing with other inmates, as well as attending Jewish services.

The prison records offer an even more complete view of Ronnie's personality during those last years of his imprisonment. They state:

> At Plymouth, a rather varied personality. Keeps to himself a good deal of the time for days at a time. Then would break out in community projects, cards, etc. Has not made many friends among the inmate body. He has always been polite in officer contacts, neat in personal habits and body. He has been willing and able to do any task assigned to him and has volunteered for any special assignment that may come up. In his own time, he has run the motion picture projector for the camp.

While Ronnie was obviously involved in almost the same activities as those in which he engaged at Norfolk, the personal management course was a bit impressive. Maybe Ronnie had big career plans once he was released. Or maybe he was figuring out how to improve his father's faltering liquor store.

Ronnie's reach for parole, of course, never ceased, although his personal circumstances certainly changed while he was at Plymouth. In 1966, when Ronnie wrote a letter to Governor John Volpe asking for a pardon, he mentioned his love for Barbara, to whom he was now engaged with a large and beautiful ring selected by his mother, stating:

> Though my suffering and confinement has been long and deep, it will never match the grief and continual deprivation that my parents have experienced for these many years. You being a parent

> can well understand the heartache and misery that only a parent can have when a child, especially an only child, is taken away. To mention the mental and physical adversities my parents have suffered will fill too many pages. I am in love with and engaged to a wonderful, wonderful girl, who has suffered with me, and stood by my side steadfastly for the past two years, never doubting, but with eyes to the future, for our happiness. My fianceé's (sic) mother has become another parent to me through our mutual love and devotion. Is it morally right for these people to be torn apart mentally and physically? If God can be just and merciful, surely man can.
>
> I humbly ask your insight and indulgence in this matter concerning my life and the lives of my loved ones. I pray you to see that my parole is restored and that I be allowed to marry, and live a normal life in society, and bring happiness and fulfillment to the lives of those who have devoted their lives to me.

It had taken a bit of maneuvering to finally get Ronnie settled in MCI–Plymouth, preparing for his upcoming parole. The parole board had given its approval for Ronnie's upcoming parole and transfer from MCI–Norfolk to MCI–Plymouth by a vote of 3–2 on September 27, 1966. Predictably, the newspapers never let up in their relentless coverage of his crime and the parole situation. Not unsurprisingly, eight days later, on October 5, 1966, the bid for his parole was revoked when Ora Schonarth's brother,

George Dwelley, opposed the release on the grounds that Ronnie could be a menace to society and might commit another crime, and Ronnie was transferred for a short time back to Norfolk.

However, Barbara Sickels did not turn away from the man to whom she was now engaged. If anything, she remained closer and raised his spirits whenever they fell. My cousin Fred remembered meeting her for the first time at the Forestry Camp and immediately liking her. "You couldn't help it," he said. "Sandra and I both felt she was such a real person and that she listened intently whenever anyone spoke. Plus, she had the best laugh of anyone we'd ever met."

Indeed, Barbara laughed easily and often during her visits to Ronnie, even when he was transferred for a brief time back to Norfolk. "I really cared for him," Barbara said. "Pretty much right from the beginning. I managed to overlook all the press about him and believed he was the man I saw every day at the camp. I had no doubt he had not committed that brutal crime. To me, he was a completely decent guy, and I was hopeful we would have a good life together when he was finally free."

Indeed, that is what happened. As the *Boston Record American*, which had relentlessly followed Ronnie's story from the day of the murder wrote, "On February 2, 1967, the Massachusetts parole board, by a vote of 3 to 2, granted a parole to the son of a prominent liquor dealer, Barney Blumenthal." Twelve days later the paper's front page announced, "Twelve years and four months after he began paying the penalty for the 'thrill murder' of a seamstress, Ronald S. Blumenthal 31, was freed on parole on Friday, February 17, 1967, from the Plymouth Forestry Camp in Carver. At 6:30 AM on that day, he walked out of the Forestry Camp. He was some 30 pounds lighter than the 220 weight he had weighed on entering prison."

It seems that would be the end of the story, followed by "And they all lived happily ever after." But it was not. At least it was the end of the Boston papers' sensational stories about the "thrill killer." Naturally, our family rejoiced at the news of the release, ready for the freed Ronnie Blumenthal's next chapter in life to begin.

CHAPTER TWENTY

Free At Last

I suppose no one should have been surprised that after having spent the years from ages eighteen to thirty-one behind bars, Ronnie struggled to lead anything resembling a normal and constructive life after his release in February 1967. Undoubtedly, the world had changed a lot between 1954 and 1967. From Bill Haley and the Comets to the Beatles. From the end of the Korean War to the Vietnam War. From crewcuts and conformity to long-haired hippies and rebellion. From an adult culture to a youth-oriented culture. From drinking to drugs. From enforced morality in movies to the end of the Hays Code, leading to movies like *Bonnie and Clyde* and *The Graduate*. I believe Ronnie sincerely hoped to reward his parents for having spent nearly all their financial resources on his attorneys and prison protection bribes by finding a lovely wife, raising a family, and helping revive the family liquor store with hard work and determination. Thanks to his mother, Ronnie's lovely future wife was, indeed, his ticket to this normalcy.

Fred remembered clearly the first time he saw Ronnie after his release. "He'd been released on February 17, 1967, and thirteen days later Ronnie and Barbara drove from Boston to Providence to have dinner with Sandra and me. I admit I was nervous and told Sandra that I thought it was a good idea we didn't serve any liquor. She agreed, but we were both pretty uptight when the doorbell rang. But within a few minutes, it was as natural as if Ronnie had never been away. He was calm and funny and very attentive to Barbara. And I could see right away that the gorgeous diamond ring on Barbara's finger had to have cost a lot more than he could possibly have afforded at the time. But, of course, we sincerely complimented it. I could also see that the four of us were going to be very good friends."

Indeed, seven months later, on September 24, 1967, Ronnie Blumenthal and Barbara Sickels were married at the fancy Belmont Country Club in suburban Boston. Barbara, who sadly died in June 2020, spoke honestly about the marriage. "I knew all too soon that this marriage wasn't going to work," she told me. "There were so many signs, but I just managed to ignore all of them. The sweetness I had found in Ronnie during his time in Plymouth and in the first few months of his release was quickly replaced with a sense of wildness, as if Ronnie just couldn't do enough and buy enough every day. But what bothered me the most was the drinking. It started slowly, but soon he was drinking way too much and not working anywhere as hard enough at the liquor store as he should. I knew I should walk away right then and there, but it seemed impossible. Ronnie had suffered so much the past thirteen years. How could I turn away from him then? But there was no doubt in my mind that I should have."

The wedding itself, at the posh country club, was nearly completely orchestrated by Aunt Edythe, excluding the nervous bride in every possible way. My aunt had waited more than thirteen long years for that momentous occasion, a chance to put all those awful years behind her family and start fresh and as close to normal as humanly possible. The last celebration she had organized had been nearly twenty years earlier, and she was determined to do whatever she could to bring back the adorable little bar mitzvah boy who had been the star of that night. Whatever she, Ronnie, and Barney had been through was now in the past. She was no longer the mother of a prisoner; she was the mother of a groom. She wanted every guest to see how perfectly the Blumenthal family was moving forward toward a bright new future.

Barbara Sickels Blumenthal was obviously an important part of Edythe's new strategy. "But it didn't take very long after Ronnie got out until I knew I was merely a fixture in her plans," Barbara said. "The wedding itself was torture for me. I kept telling myself to walk far, far away from Ronnie and Edythe and Barney, but I also knew I was in too deep. I think my favorite moment of the evening was when my cousin walked into the country club, wearing the same exact dress that Edythe had overpaid for. But my cousin was five-seven and had a figure to die for and looked positively gorgeous in the dress. And Edythe was short and plump and rather dumpy, and no one could ignore how different the same dress looked on the two of them. It definitely had to ruin Edythe's night.

"Edythe also drove everyone crazy about all these small details. We had this ridiculous argument about the sugar, whether or not to have sugar cubes, which Edythe definitely didn't want. It was crazy, but she kept badgering the staff about it. Like it really mattered what the sugar looked like. She certainly gave more attention to the stupid sugar than she gave to the bride."

Barbara was also furious over the guest list. "By that time, I had come to realize that all of Ronnie's friends were Mafia types, guys he had met in prison or since his release. And they all stunk of cologne. He insisted on inviting all of these guys to the wedding. That upset me terribly, but, as with everything to do with the wedding, there was nothing I, the pathetic bride, could do about it."

Fred remembered the wedding as being a big, fancy affair. "Truthfully, I was surprised I wasn't Ronnie's best man," he told me. "I was an usher, but I'd always thought I was his best friend. I have no memory of who was his best man. But I'm pretty sure it was someone I didn't know." But what Fred never forgot was that very large diamond engagement ring Ronnie had given Barbara while he was still at the camp in Plymouth. "When things went bad and they broke up, Barbara really needed money. I was able to sell that huge ring to someone I know who wanted that exact type of ring."

Before things went bad, however, the happy couple set off for a lavish honeymoon in Maui. As a convicted murderer, still on parole, only seven months after his release, Ronnie would not yet be allowed to leave the United States. Hawaii was the most glamorous and the most expensive location within the United States that he could choose for this trip. It was obvious from the moment that Ronnie got out of jail that there would be nothing but the best in his life after prison. No matter how much it cost, he would figure out a way to get it.

On their way back from Hawaii, Barbara and Ronnie had a stopover in Las Vegas, where Barbara won $300 on a slot machine. "Since we had spent far too much money on the trip," she said, "this $300 came in very handy."

Once they returned home, it was obvious to Barbara that the honeymoon was over in more ways than one. From the very beginning of their marriage she grew increasingly more concerned about Ronnie's drinking habits and the all-night drunken evenings with the "Mafia-type" friends she did not like. "I understood that his reentry into the world had to be difficult, and I pleaded with Ronnie to see a therapist," she said. "But he refused, and so I helplessly kept watching him make poor decisions, with his excessive spending and reckless friends who were making things worse. He seemed to have no semblance of morality, and there was nothing I could do to convince him that that was a dangerous way to act. The more he was with his former prison friends, the more I worried. And for good reason."

Despite Barbara's serious misgivings about the wedding and the marriage itself, the Ronald Blumenthals bought a fifteen-year-old ranch-style house, on Maryvale Lane in Peabody. A growing suburb of about fifty thousand, located fifteen miles northeast of Boston, Peabody had been a thriving community, with multiple tanneries for the area's shoe factories forming the linchpin of its economy. By the 1970s and '80s, the leather factories had closed and its workers were leaving the city. The Northshore Shopping Center in Peabody opened in 1958, one of the largest shopping centers in the area, drawing large groups of shoppers to its growing number of indoor stores. Ronnie and Barbara's house featured three bedrooms and one-and-a-half baths, as well as an in-ground swimming pool and lots of room for get-togethers, especially barbecues and holiday parties with the Blumenthal cousins. Fourteen months after the wedding, on Christmas Day 1968, their son Marc Frank (Edythe's maiden name) Blumenthal was born. Ronnie was ecstatic, as were the three grandparents. For Marc's first birthday, on a particularly snowy December 25, 1970, Barbara and Ronnie hosted a lovely party, complete with a special birthday cake with a horse theme for their adored one-year-old who loved "horsies." Just about every Blumenthal cousin who was living in Rhode Island and Massachusetts came and celebrated the special day. I remember standing with my cousins, marveling at the adorable Marc, shaking our heads at the fact that the cousin with whom we had spent so many afternoons in a prison visiting room now had a beautiful home, a pretty wife, and an adorable son. We were all also aware, however, of the excessive amounts of liquor being offered and consumed and of the fact that our cousin was plastered within minutes of our arrivals. It was a special day for him, though, so why wouldn't he want to celebrate and get a little drunk? Yet, when the party ended and we all got into our snow-covered cars and headed to our homes, none of us could get over the feeling that something was wrong.

Personally, I had little time that night to worry about Ronnie's heavy drinking. Immediately after getting into our car with Jack and our three-year-old son, Adam, I went into labor. Our second son, Joshua David (the middle name, like mine, Davida, for the uncle Dave Halpert I had never met), arrived at 5:13 the morning after Christmas.

Still, I will always remember what a fun party it was and how proud Ronnie had been of his son and his house and new life. Barbara was busy managing all the food, which was excessive, as was the display of alcohol. The adorable blond toddler who had turned one that day was the main attraction and cause for celebration. There was no doubt that Barbara's mother, Dorothy Sickels, a.k.a. Nana Dorothy, was very close to Marc, obviously more than my aunt was. You would have had to be blind not to notice that there was no love whatsoever between Barbara and her mother-in-law. Their body language told the whole story. At no time during the party did Barbara and Edythe come within six feet of each another. Luckily, the house was large enough to help them maintain that distance.

Both Barbara and Ronnie developed a close relationship with their next-door neighbors, Marlene and Wayne Cohen, in Peabody. That couple had three children, including a daughter close in age to Marc. "It was such fun to see the kids grow up together," Barbara said. "Marlene and I spent many cold winter days together with our babies and later as the kids grew up. It was like we were one big family. I knew Ronnie told Wayne about his background, but that didn't seem to hurt their friendship. But it was obvious Ronnie was drinking more and more heavily, and though Wayne liked to drink, too, I was just relieved he had one friend, a decent family man you couldn't help liking, who was nothing like the disgusting Mafia types he spent too much time with."

Ronnie worked at Hall's Liquor, but his work ethic turned out to be less than admirable, and Barney's store, which had been failing for the past few years, continued to slide toward bankruptcy. Still, Ronnie and Barbara somehow found the money to maintain their house, with its lovely swimming pool and modern furniture.

Rumor was that Ronnie had Mafia connections that he made inside the prison walls, which might have explained the money for the house and its upkeep, along with Ronnie's designer clothes and fancy new Cadillac. "Let me know what you want," was Ronnie's familiar refrain, an offer he was more than willing and able to fulfill. As I learned later, the rumor was a fact. Ronnie did have Mafia connections from prison, and those connections grew stronger with each year of his freedom. To say that it was a disappointment to witness my cousin's choices in his free life is a huge understatement. He'd seemed so grounded in prison, obviously because he had no choice but to follow the rules and behave. Outside the prison walls, he was a rolling rock that seemed to be gathering back dirt, headed toward any place but a constructive, positive lifestyle. While no one was able to put Ronnie on a more solid track, he was taking his wife and little boy with him for the joyless ride.

Although Ronnie spent more time with his prison friends, his cousins placed themselves in the middle of his path and did all they could to make him part of their lives. They organized dinners with Ronnie and Barbara at one another's homes and started a cruise fund for an upcoming trip together. For almost two years, six of the cousins sent Fred, who was an accountant by profession, five dollars every week, which he placed in the Blumenthal Cruise Fund. In June 1971, the cruise to Bermuda ended up costing less than $400 a couple. Although Ronnie did not contribute to the Cruise Fund, he managed, somehow, to come up with the $400. Since Jack and I and our two little boys were living in Hawaii at the time while Jack was in the army, there was, sadly, no way we could join them.

Over fifty years later, Fred clearly remembered that week. Ronnie and Barbara picked up Fred and Sandra in Pawtucket, and the four of them drove to New York City, where the ship set sail for Bermuda. The ship was far from fancy and lacked any stabilizers. "We were all told to grab a piece of fruit and go topside and keep our gaze focused on the horizon if we were feeling seasick," Fred said. "We were the first to head up there, but it didn't take long for the rest of our group to join us there."

My cousin Fred's wife Sandra, Fred, Ronnie's wife Barbara, Ronnie, my cousin Ruthie's husband Harvey, and Ruthie on the cruise ship leaving for Bermuda.

One day the eight cousins met in one of the lounges and played a board game with pennies. After the game ended, they put the pennies in a cup and walked single file through the ship telling any passengers they met that they had lost all their money gambling and were broke. They received a lot of change, including five dollars from one passenger. No one seemed to enjoy the game quite as much as Ronnie, who got the most money in his cup. "None of us had a care in the world for that whole week," Fred said. "Including Ronnie and Barbara."

While the cruise offered little entertainment, it did have a three-piece band that only knew how to play calypso music. During the three days on land, all of the couples rented scooters and toured the island. "The best part of the cruise was the food," Fred said. "I gained eight pounds. We all gained weight."

By that time, the cousins all strongly suspected things were not great between Ronnie and Barbara, but for that one week it seemed as though they could not have been happier with each other. From the moment the ship pulled away from the port in New York, Ronnie was fabulous fun on the cruise.

Horsing around on the beach in Bermuda.

He instigated games on the Bermuda beaches and joked around with other passengers in the bar, who laughed and played silly penny games with him. He frequently hugged and kissed Barbara, making her and the other cousins laugh at all hours of the days and nights. When cousin Fred, the official photographer of the Blumenthal family, sent some adorable photos to me in Hawaii, I felt jealous that I couldn't be there to share such a fun time. By some miracle, and perhaps including the love of a lot of relatives, there Ronnie was: thirty-seven years old, married to the smiling Barbara, their adorable three-year-old son Marc left in the care of Barbara's mother in the Peabody house, frolicking like a kid on the sandy beaches of Bermuda, his thick, curly blond hair covered with sand, the old Ronnie smile covering his handsome face. Photos showing him dressed in a white dinner jacket, his pretty, smiling wife in short shorts and tall white boots, posing in each photo, looking like any typical, happily married couple enjoying a fun cruise. No one who didn't know their history could ever imagine how a few short years ago the only way they could be together was in a prison visiting room. Or that Barbara and Ronnie weren't anywhere as happy as they now seemed.

Fun on the cruise. Ronnie and Barbara (right).

Indeed, the group of eight Blumenthals had a great time together, with just one problem. "Everything was paid for," cousin Bobby explained, "except for the liquor." While they all considered it a real treat to be sitting with Ronnie and Barbara each night, the liquor bill at whatever table Ronnie dined was far larger than at any other table. "But it was no big deal," Bobby said. "We just dealt with it."

Seeing those photos and hearing my cousins' stories blew my mind. I could not seem to stop staring at my cousin Ronnie. In every photo, he looked happy, no different than my other cousins. He and Barbara both looked equally as happy and normal, trying to capture a joyous, carefree week with the cousins they loved and who loved both of them.

From their earliest years, Fred had always been the closest cousin to Ronnie. He had been delighted with the cruise and had marveled at how much fun they had all shared. A close friend to Barbara as well as Ronnie, Fred knew that things were not always perfect between the two of them, and he always worried that Ronnie might take the wrong path. The week on the Bermuda cruise, however, gave him more faith that this marriage could work and that his closest cousin just might be able to create a good and loving life for himself. Deep down, Fred knew that it would be a miracle if all that happened, because miracles do not usually happen.

The fun times with the Blumenthal cousins had indeed been frequent during the first few years of Barbara and Ronnie's marriage. One such evening included a Thanksgiving weekend pajama party at cousin Ruthie and Harvey Levin's house in Cranston, Rhode Island, at which nine cousins arrived in their pajamas with their spouses. After lots of fun foods, we all spread out our sleeping bags in the Levins' living room and spent most of the night telling ghost stories and jokes, enjoying one another's company. The one sad detail of the night that I remember clearly was that Ronnie got more and more drunk as the evening went on. The rest of us eventually fell asleep, but Ronnie just passed out. Still, we all had to admit that until he passed out, he'd told the best ghost stories of any of us. I hated to admit it, but there was something unsettling and downright spooky about my cousin, who had confessed to a brutal murder as a teenager, terrifying all of us with stories about ghosts come to life and taking revenge. I, unlike Ronnie—who didn't wake up till late the next morning—didn't sleep well that night.

Lunches and dinners in restaurants with cousins, Cousin Club picnics, and parties in one another's yards kept all of us together as frequently as possible. So often at those fun celebrations I would look at Ronnie and remind myself how lucky we were that we were all together. Ronnie was sometimes quiet, but no matter what his mood, whether jovial or withdrawn, he was absolutely with us. We were determined not to lose him, not now that he was home with all of us.

CHAPTER TWENTY-ONE

Barbara and Flo and Helen, Oh My!

Back in Peabody, Ronnie's marriage grew more strained. We all knew and worried about it. Barbara was certain that extramarital fun for Ronnie became part of the neighborhood barbecues, along with alcohol and drugs, which were offered along with hot dogs and brownies. She watched her marriage to Ronnie dissolve into shouting matches. Their son grew more adorable, as well as quieter, with each passing year. As bad as things seemed in front of her, despite the trips and fun evenings with the cousins, Barbara had no way of seeing just how bad her marriage really was from the beginning.

Just a matter of days after his release from prison and his engagement to Barbara, however, Ronnie had managed to see the woman he considered the true love of his life, Florence Gold. By that time, however, Flo was married, though, sadly, not happily. In her heart, she knew that no other man in her life would be Ronnie, the man she could not touch but whom she had loved so dearly. Ronnie had waited far too long to be denied a chance to consummate their two-and-a-half-year prison-visiting-room romance. He wasted no time finding Flo at the doctor's office in Lexington where she worked. "He pretended he wanted to make an appointment to see the allergist," Flo said. "And the minute I saw him, my heart did flip-flops. He looked even more handsome and was more charming than I had remembered."

A few weeks later, Ronnie and Flo were finally together, and alone. Edythe had left Barney in 1968 and was living in an apartment in the Jamaica Towers while Barney was in a small room in a cheap hotel. I never knew exactly what happened to cause the separation, which, to my knowledge, was never finalized with an actual divorce, but my cousins and I assumed that Edythe had thrown Barney out. Perhaps they had stayed together, for the sake of appearances, only until Ronnie was released from prison and got married. Aunt Edythe finally had her son back, and the last thing she needed was an unfaithful husband with little money.

But if her son needed a place for any reason whatsoever, her apartment was available to him. Thus, it was in Edythe's apartment where Flo now met Ronnie. "I wouldn't have been surprised if she knew that I was coming over there to be with Ronnie," Flo said. "But she would do anything to make Ronnie happy, so she went out knowing he was having company."

Ironically, it was in Edythe's apartment where Ronnie and Flo finally consummated the relationship, with Flo in the beautiful negligee she had refused to return to Edythe. "I had picked out the nightgown at the Quincy Bargain Center," Flo said. "I loved that place, and Edythe happened to know the owner. I don't remember if I had worn it the night I got married. But I had always wanted to wear it with Ronnie. I must have told Mort I was going out with a girlfriend and told her what I was doing so she wouldn't call me. And then I drove by myself to Jamaica Plain. I just knew I had to see Ronnie."

Finally, years after they split up, they were indeed together, with no prison guard keeping them from even touching one another's hands. "How can I have forgotten even a minute of those precious moments of alone time with him?" Flo asked. "What I do remember is that it was great with him, that he was so sweet and gentle."

For Flo, it was an infinitely difficult and painful time, for she could not deny that her feelings for the sweet, thoughtful man she had fallen deeply in love with just four years earlier had never dissolved. She was pregnant, though, and there was no way she would leave her husband. Despite Flo's marriage and Ronnie's upcoming one to Barbara, Ronnie would not, again, abandon Flo forever. Determined to see her again, he arrived at her house sometime after the birth of her son. "We slept together three times altogether," she said, "and he even managed to borrow five hundred dollars from me, which I knew I would never get back. But I didn't care."

Ronnie's insistence that he would do anything to marry her was agonizing, but Flo knew that marriage, or even a long-term affair, could never be. It was simply too late for the two of them. She was a new mother to a baby son she adored, and nothing could tear her apart from him. She could not deny she and Ronnie had both moved on, and while prison gates had kept them apart all those years ago, a different set of barriers separated them now. "I may have thought of contacting him months later but didn't know where he lived, and I really wouldn't have wanted to cause any trouble. But, somehow, I must have spoken to him, or maybe Toby told me he had a baby. But it was over. This time for good. It had to be."

Aside from her relationship with Ronnie, Flo played a strong role in my family's life. In October 1960, when Flo was struggling with how to continue or end her relationship with Ronnie, my sister, Toby, convinced her close friend and former roommate to go out on a double date with her. Those days Flo rarely ventured outside her house very often. Yet, somehow, the details were worked out, and the two couples took off in a car, with Toby in the front seat with Flo's old friend Roger, and Flo in the back seat with Roger's friend Larry. By the end of the evening, Larry had decided he wanted to be in the back seat with Toby. The two men had a brief conversation out of earshot of the two ladies and the deed was done. Larry and Toby were together in the back, and Flo was in the front seat with Roger. While Roger and Flo parted for the evening with no plans to see one another again, things progressed quickly for Larry and Toby. By May they were engaged; by July 30, 1961, they were married. They stayed married until Toby's death in 2024.

Still, Flo often thought of the man she had so strongly loved, and long after she saw him for the final time she still tried to come to terms with what had happened in July 1954. "I often thought maybe Ronnie had had a breakdown and had actually murdered that woman," she said, "that maybe she had made a sexual pass at him, and, as an eighteen-year-old, he had simply lost it. Or that he knew what was happening with her and his father, and that Ora was a real bitch who had come on to him, too. Obviously, I have never been able to believe that this seemingly gentle, handsome man could do what I've read about. He might not have signed that confession, but what could have prompted a kid to say what he said to those girls? And, of course, the bloody clothing. I may never understand what happened, but I will always think that if Ronnie murdered her, then he was so traumatized that he never believed that he did. The mystery will linger longer than you and me. But I truly loved him."

Those words, "If Ronnie murdered her, then he was so traumatized that he never believed he did," coming from the only woman who most likely loved Ronnie, have resonated with me for a long time. Perhaps they were true. If so, then they did offer an explanation for why Ronnie never discussed what happened that July night in Ora's living room, as well as a rationalization of the life he led during all the years that followed. And Flo's following words, "The mystery will linger longer than you and me," were unquestionably true.

At eighty, Flo was still a beautiful woman, with brown hair streaked with red and blond, an infectious laugh, and an undying appreciation for life and all things fun. She had divorced Mort after twenty years of marriage. They had produced two awesome sons, Eric and Brian, and she and Mort remained good friends. As a matter of fact, they got together every week or so, with Flo cooking dinner for the two of them or going out to a new restaurant. She even attended his Harvard reunions with him. While Flo spent her summers south of Boston, enjoying her three grandchildren, she headed to Florida for the winter, dancing whenever possible and meeting interesting new people. Wherever she was, her red Kia Soul, with eyelashes painted around the headlights, along with her trusty bicycle on its roof, was never far away. It is still easy to see why Ronnie fell hard for this woman and probably never stopped loving her, even as he moved onward, often destructively, with other women.

Back in 1966, what Flo did not know, however, was that Ronnie already had another woman in his life, someone he had also met while he was in prison. Only that woman had not arrived to visit him. Helen Cortese was the daughter of a prominent mobster, Anthony "Bozo" Cortese, who had been a major figure in the Italian-Irish crime wars of the 1930s and 1940s. According to the same Boston newspapers that heralded eighteen-year-old Ronnie Blumenthal's sensational crime twenty-two years later, "Anthony 'Bozo' Cortese of Hanover Street was sentenced to two-and-a-half to three-and-a-half years in state prison when he pleaded guilty in Boston Superior Criminal Court in April, 1932, at age 23, to a charge of possessing dangerous weapons. He had been arrested on December 26, 1931, after a sensational gun battle in a Hanover Street building which resulted in the death of Frank Gustin and Bernard Walsh. He had three loaded revolvers on him at the time of his arrest." He was also arrested five years later, in 1937, at age twenty-eight, in connection with an armed robbery in Springfield, Massachusetts, for which he spent three years in prison.

No doubt, Bozo was dealing with pretty big gangsters. Before that 1931 gun battle ended his career, Frank Wallace, a.k.a. Frank Gustin, was a notorious South Boston gang leader, and Bernard "Dodo" Walsh was one of his henchmen. Apparently, Gustin and Walsh had invaded the bootlegging headquarters of a rival gang headed by Joseph Lombardi and started a feud over hijacking booze shipments. In the 1930s, Ronnie's great-uncle Ben Sass might actually have run into, or up against, Bozo Cortese. If nothing else, there was no doubt Helen Cortese came from criminal stock, higher up that ladder than Ronnie. With their ordinary family backgrounds, neither Flo Gold nor Barbara Sickels ever stood a chance against the infamous Cortese family and its daughter Helen.

While Helen's father, Anthony Cortese, died in 1955 at the age of forty-six, it was highly possible that Helen could have had been visiting a relative at Norfolk when she met Ronnie there.

Obviously, Ronnie understood that Barbara was a far more acceptable wife for his parents, who had no idea about Helen's existence. After all, Barbara had remained at his side for every day of his final two years in prison. The least he could do to repay both her and his parents for their devotion was to marry Barbara and produce an acceptable Blumenthal heir. It was all about keeping up appearances.

Ronnie remained married to Barbara for seven years, during which time they filled their house and Marc's life with screaming fights. While there were no instances of physical abuse, there was not, according to Marc, "one moment of affection between my parents."

Whatever love Barbara might have had for Ronnie during their prison courtship and their engagement after his release died very quickly. Despite fun times with the cousins, behind the scenes the smile on Barbara's face was nonexistent. "Truthfully," Barbara emphatically stated, "it didn't take long for me to come to believe that he absolutely murdered the dressmaker. And that he never recovered from what happened that night. I certainly did not believe that when I first met him and for many months after that. But when I got to see the real Ronnie and how cruel he could be, there is nothing I would not put past him. Or past his horribly controlling and downright nasty mother. I realize my opinions are those of a woman whose marriage has fallen apart and feels completely deserted, but the man I married was very different than the one I had met two years earlier. If he could have fooled me so completely, then he could have fooled anyone."

Still, Barbara held on to her affection for Barney, whom she had always found to be a sweet, kind man. Her feelings for Edythe, already poor at the time of the wedding, deteriorated into downright hatred by the time the marriage mercifully ended. "I always felt bad for Barney," Barbara said. "I remember one time when Ronnie was still away and his parents and I were driving together to a funeral. Barney sort of jokingly asked Edythe what kind of a funeral she would have for him, and she literally screamed at him that was the stupidest question anyone could ever ask her, that she could care less what happened to him after he died. Or now. It was an ugly scene. And just one of many that I got to witness as their daughter-in-law. From places other than the backseat of a car. As for Barney, he was always sweet to me, but I was sickened by the horrible way she treated him. No one could blame him for having that affair with the dressmaker.

"I'd heard the rumors that Barney had killed that dressmaker and Ronnie went to prison for it, and there were times I wondered if that could actually have happened. All I know for sure is that the Barney I got to know somehow never seemed to be in the room with us. It was like he was somewhere else. If he had allowed his son to take the blame for a murder he committed, or had a major part in, then, of course, he had to have lost part of his mind. So many secrets. And I was never told any of them. No wonder our marriage never stood a chance."

As for Helen, Barbara, who obviously knew nothing about her meeting Ronnie while he was in prison, insists she did know about her while she and Ronnie were still married. "He was sneaking around with her, and probably a bunch of other women, too, and I knew there was one particular woman who was doing everything to ruin our marriage, which was already shaky. But the two of us finally sort of did meet after the divorce. It happened one day when she and Ronnie were picking up Marc. Helen was slumped way down low in the front seat of the car, and I got a glimpse of her blond head. At that moment, I didn't feel any particular dislike for her. Which was amazing considering that she was such a homewrecker. But I guess it was an easy home to wreck."

While Barbara remained close with some of the Blumenthal cousins during her marriage to Ronnie, she had no idea what happened one night to explain why one particular cousin appeared to want nothing to do with her and Ronnie afterward. My cousin Mel and his family had been faithful visitors during Ronnie's years in prison, and Mel was pleased when Ronnie was released. In the years before Mel's family moved to California in 1970, Mel invited Ronnie to the frequent family get-togethers at his home in Providence. Mel remembers one party when Ronnie arrived with marijuana and was delighted to pass it out to anyone who might want to try it. His easy access to marijuana came in handy a short time later when my cousin Elaine asked him to get some for her. At that time, Elaine's thirty-year-old daughter, Hershey, was gravely ill with lung cancer and in a great deal of pain. Ronnie did not hesitate to provide exactly what his cousin needed. To be perfectly honest, I wouldn't be surprised if Ronnie pocketed some money from Elaine on that supposed mercy deal.

I remember that particular evening at Mel's house. I had gotten used to seeing Ronnie drunk but noticed that he appeared more stoned than inebriated that evening. He was funnier and easier to be with that night than he was when he had his usual one drink too many. I also remember talking to Barbara and noting that she wasn't the least bit stoned or drunk. She just looked unhappy, and I felt awful for her.

At another party, however, just before Mel and Jacquee and their four children moved to California, Ronnie's behavior was so infuriating to Mel that he refused to speak to him ever again. That night, Ronnie, probably drunker than usual, got way too flirtatious with Jacquee. When Mel was out of town on a business trip a few days later, Ronnie called and propositioned Jacquee, who was horrified by the suggestion. For Mel, this was such egregious behavior that there was no way he could even talk about it to Ronnie and express his anger. The fact that Mel and Jacquee were moving to California a few months later made it easier to avoid Ronnie.

Of course, we all knew that once Ronnie was no longer away, if you needed to get your hands on anything that wasn't quite legal, he was your go-to person. The idea that he could be so thoughtless and disgusting with one cousin and so thoughtful and kind to another is, I imagine, not all that surprising. While I know that people, especially troubled people, are complex, this was just another example of how little any of us really knew our cousin Ronnie.

While many of us did hear about Ronnie's kind gesture toward Hershey, a few cousins also learned and were shocked and disappointed in Ronnie's unbecoming conduct toward Jacquee. Whether Ronnie found out about Mel's fury was doubtful, and no one brought up that difficult situation with him. Cousins who knew about Ronnie's disgusting and unacceptable behavior went on the cruise to Bermuda with him and Barbara and rejoiced in how delightful he was every moment of that trip. In typical Blumenthal fashion, no one criticized Ronnie outwardly, either for his excessive drinking or his outrageous seductive behavior toward a cousin's wife. The attitude we had all maintained during his prison years remained the same. He was one of us, and, no matter what he did—or did not do, we weren't ready to let him go.

Not too long after the cruise to Bermuda, it was getting harder to deny that things were changing in all our relationships with Ronnie, as one by one we felt him drifting away from each of us. Each successive family get-together seemed more strained and less fun, and Ronnie's constant requests for loans become far too frequent and upsetting, especially since he never paid them back. None of my cousins had unlimited finances, and every loan was a big deal for most of us.

Eventually, what we had all suspected came to pass. "He had talked about going to Ohio for a possible new job," Fred remembered. "I thought it was a great idea. I knew things were difficult between him and Barbara. So I thought a change of scenery might be a good chance for him to pull his failing marriage back together and get a fresh start in his life. We were going to meet for lunch in Boston before he left, but he kept cancelling the plans and it never happened. But I wished him the best of luck with the new job. But when I learned that he had already left and hadn't taken Barbara and Marc with him, I was deeply upset. I knew that was the end of Sandra's and my relationship with him."

I doubt that it was a blow to Barney that his son was forsaking the liquor store and taking a job in Ohio. By then it had to be obvious that Ronnie was so useless in the liquor store that it most likely was a relief. For Barbara, the icy cold phone call from Ohio telling her to stay where she was, that Ronnie did not expect her and Marc to join him, was not a complete shock. Her suspicions about other women in her husband's life had been growing daily. Even though she had still harbored a small ray of hope that maybe a move to Ohio and a new job for her husband might change things for the better, Barbara admitted, "Still, I knew deep down that our marriage was over." As it turned out, Ronnie's new start fizzled from the very beginning. He returned six months later but not, unsurprisingly, to his life with Barbara and Marc.

Indeed, the many Blumenthal cousins who remained close to Barbara were delighted when, soon after her divorce from Ronnie, she found another man to love. The divorce had been far less tumultuous than the marriage since neither Barbara nor Ronnie had any desire to remain married. Whatever little money was received from the sale of the house or any of their possessions was divided equally. The new man in Barbara's life, we all had to admit, seemed a far better choice for her than our cousin Ronnie. John Hollister had recently graduated from Suffolk University Law School and was looking for his first job at a law firm. "He was the love of my life," Barbara said. "And he set a fine example of a good man for Marc." Marc, who was ten at the time, warmly remembered the wedding in March 1978. "It was a beautiful and amazing ceremony in a special dining room at Tufts Faculty Club," he told me.

Undoubtedly, the ceremony at Tufts University was quite different from the fancy affair at the Belmont Country Club just eleven years earlier. "John was in a military outfit, although I don't remember why, and Barbara was in a pretty cocktail dress," Cousin Fred remembered. "It was a warm, fun affair, and I was very pleased that Barbara had met such a really nice guy."

"I thought John was a genius," Barbara said. "He was a small-town boy who managed, all on his own, to go to law school, where he did very well. He had just graduated law school and had been working as a police officer during law school. He was in his late twenties when we met. John had never been married before, but had been in a long-term significant relationship before we met. John and Marc got along beautifully right from the beginning. I could not have been happier."

Through a friend, John was able to secure two decent law firm opportunities: one in Washington, DC, and the other in

New Orleans. Although he took the New Orleans job because it would be a quicker trek to partner, that partnership never happened. What did happen were frequent trips to Martha's Vineyard, where John's extended family owned two homes. "Marc and I both loved going to the Vineyard," Barbara said. "Those were very special times."

Times Marc spent with his father, however, according to Barbara, were "anything but fun." From the time of her divorce from Ronnie in 1975 until Barbara and Marc moved to New Orleans in 1979, Ronnie tried to see Marc on a relatively regular schedule, usually on Sundays. "Ronnie would pick up Marc supposedly to do fun and interesting things with him," Barbara said, "but he'd end up taking him to see his mother and falling asleep as soon as they got there. Poor Marc was stuck with two mental cases for the afternoon, his father and his grandmother. Fortunately, Marc had many chances to spend fun times with John's family during our marriage. I always felt that was the only way Marc could ever get to know a good, decent man."

Sadly, John and Barbara's marriage ended in 1985. "After seven years, John decided to leave me," Barbara said. "It broke my heart. I never recovered from that blow."

John insisted that he never stopped loving both Barbara and Marc, but his desire to have children of his own was too strong to remain in the marriage. As it turned out, after his divorce from Barbara, John and his new wife did have a son. "Barbara had originally said she definitely wanted us to have a child, but that was not true," he told me. "After so many childless years together, I understood she would never let that happen." John retired from law and became a clergyman in Mandeville, Louisiana, more than three hundred miles from Birmingham, where Marc lived, and remained in frequent contact with his stepson. Cousin Fred was deeply sad when Barbara's marriage to John ended. "All I can say is that when it came right down to it, Barbara just didn't have good luck with men."

While Ronnie's relationship with Flo had ended peacefully and his marriage to Barbara not quite so peacefully, his marriage to Helen, while far from joyful, lasted for thirty-five years until her death in 2011. The one true bright spot in Ronnie's life was the son born twenty-two months after his release from prison. While the other accomplishments following that release were, at best, questionable, nothing about Marc Frank Blumenthal could be considered dubious.

CHAPTER TWENTY-TWO
All Ronnie Left Behind

In 1935 when Ronald Sheldon Blumenthal was born, five short months after six members of the family died in a horrific car accident, there was an unspoken hope that the baby, born so soon after the family's loss, the embryo alive and growing in the womb when his cousins and uncle and grandmother died, would be the enduring Blumenthal hope. By the time Marc Frank Blumenthal was born, thirty-four years later, that hope had dwindled to little more than a faint promise, but, still, it existed.

On Christmas Day in 1969, the second and ultimately final hope for a Blumenthal redemption of any sort, this time for Ronnie Blumenthal, arrived. My cousin Ronnie became a father, producing a Blumenthal son, our generation's "golden child."

Nearly ten years after Ronnie died, it was that Christmas child who knew Ronnie Blumenthal better than anyone else, better than his parents, his two wives, or his once-devoted cousins, aunts, or uncles. There's no doubt that Marc was the person Ronnie loved the most, but Marc was also the one who would carry the scars of his father's "brand of fathering." For Marc, in his early fifties and married for more than twenty-five years to the love of his life, Michele Merritt Blumenthal, trying to comprehend this incomprehensible father is a task he was more than up to accomplishing. It was as though Ronnie left us a gift, a piece of what my cousin might have been if something inside of him had not prevented him from finding the path to a good and decent life.

As for that gift, there was a strong family resemblance between Marc and his father, both nearly six feet tall and fair-skinned with blond hair, blue-green eyes, and winning smiles. Except for twin quirky senses of humor, there is luckily little of Ronnie Blumenthal's psychological makeup in his handsome son. As Marc perfectly defined their resemblance, "I got Ron's skin tone, smile, hair color, and sense of humor. And possibly whatever genetically disposed mental anomalies come with being a Blumenthal."

Unlike his father, whom Marc nearly always referred to as "Ron," and rarely, if ever, as "Dad," Marc was honest to a fault, morally invincible, faithful, hardworking, sensitive to others' needs, highly introspective, and self-deprecating. He was also musically talented, playing the upright bass and participating for seven years in Loyola University's Youth String Orchestra. In contrast to his father, who, according to records Marc and I both searched, most probably never earned a GED, Marc was successful at academics from an early age through his postgraduate work.

Marc is the first one to admit that he was far from perfect. Honest, yes, but perfect, no. From the first time we began to discuss his father—Marc in Birmingham, Alabama, and me in Marblehead, Massachusetts—he let me know crucial details about who and what he was. "I suffer, and always have, with anxiety," Marc told me. "A few too many PTSD experiences probably, and no real parental help when it comes to coping mechanism. So, when real-life situations mount, it can send me over the edge."

Marc was equally honest about his parents' marriage. "I never saw one affectionate moment between the two of them. Mostly yelling and insults." When Barbara and Ronnie Blumenthal finally separated in 1973, even at age five Marc remembered that he wasn't at all surprised. "Ron was so incredibly absent that it wasn't a shock, and his lack of presence was assumed. At one point, he bought a Barbizon Modeling School and moved to Detroit. Before the divorce, I think. Anyhow, he told me about the separation at a duck pond in Newton. If memory serves, he was tactful. He didn't belittle my mother, though. That I do remember. The shouting matches between them on the phone after he no longer was part of the household, I remember as well."

Marc also recollected those first five years in Peabody with some delight, especially in regard to the Cohen family, who lived next door. "I loved the Cohens. My mom was close with Marlene and me with the kids. I know there was a lot of socializing on Maryvale Lane in Peabody, and I do remember pieces of Halloween and birthday get-togethers."

As an adult, Marc saw the relationship between the two families even more clearly. "Ron and Wayne Cohen stayed close friends until Wayne died from bowel cancer in 1996 or so. It was a huge loss in Ron's life. Neither man was close to an angel. Nothing romanticized on my end, but sad."

Having left Peabody for Newton when his parents were still together, after the divorce Marc moved to the Chapel Hill apartments in Framingham with his mother. "But Ron and I had some good Sunday visits then. It was so much more fun when it was just the two of us. Ron could be hilarious. He kept me in stitches, to be honest. Funny guy. He had an innate wit that was not congruent with his intelligence, which had always struck me. I don't mean to sound insulting when I say that. He was naturally funny, I guess. Had a knack for mimicry and impression as well. Told a good story. After one Johnny Walker Black, he was charming and witty. After five, he was sloppy, loud, and obnoxious."

Many of the stories with which Ronnie entertained his adult son revolved around his past romances. "I heard about some Sedra or Cedrea, the 'One Who Got Away,' according to him. Daughter of George and Helen, owners of Fontaine's Restaurant in West Roxbury. [Fontaine's opened in 1952 and closed in 2004.] Mouth-watering food. Known for its famous Topsy's southern friend chicken. Ron and I would go there weekly in the early nineties, when I lived there briefly, and it was two minutes from the Hebrew Rehab, where Edythe had moved when she seemed unable to care for herself on her own. So, we'd go visit 'Nana' on Saturdays, regularly, which, by the way, could be a little fun sometimes. He liked to make me laugh, and had that keen sense of humor, so he often could! But during Nana visits, he could go next-level comedy and have me in hysterics. Seriously.

"So, after Nana trips we'd go see George and Helen at Fontaine's. Johnny Walker Black to calm his nerves, boneless fried chicken and garlic mashed potatoes to calm mine. I was twenty-one or twenty-two at the time and could have had a cocktail; however, watching Ron knock 'em down, one after another, I had no interest. And still don't to this day."

Not only did Marc lack the appetite for alcohol that so defined his father, he had little interest in cars. Even later in his adult life, he did not have a driver's license and had no great desire to acquire one. The distinction between father and son regarding driving is all the more striking considering how Ronnie came alive when he was behind the wheel. From the time he got his driver's license at age sixteen, Ronnie seemed the happiest when he was exceeding the speed limit in one of his brand-new convertibles, often after having downed more than a beer or two. It is probably nonsensical, but when Marc told me about not driving, I could not help thinking about the Accident. Marc's father was named for the driver of the car destroyed by a drunk driver. Unlike Ronnie, who never hesitated to drive drunk and who nearly killed a teenage driver when he threw a firecracker into her car, could Marc have subliminally kept himself away from the wheel of a car?

Marc told me why he never got his license. "I don't drive," he said. "Not because of a suspended license or anything. I've just never learned to drive a car. Was in an accident with my buddy in tenth grade. He'd just gotten his first car, and he had picked me up to go to a Mardi Gras parade. Not two blocks from my house and an elderly lady neglected to stop at a stop sign and barreled into us, passenger side. Matt's leg was destroyed. I was fine, except for the mental scars, which became a phobia for the next thirty-six years. I've had friends give me lessons throughout the years, so I know how to stop, go, and turn. I've just never acquired my driver's license. Still a goal."

Perhaps it is possible that Marc was prescient about the dangers of driving. After all, his grandmother was pregnant with his father when the Accident occurred. His grandfather suffered great losses in that accident. While his father loved cars almost more than anything else in the world, Marc had an innate fear of them after being in an accident. More power to him for making such a decision and learning how to live his life without his own wheels. I can only imagine what my cousin Ronnie must have said to him upon learning that Marc did not want to drive, if he even noticed.

As a small child, however, Marc had loved being in his paternal grandfather's car when the two of them went off together. As for his paternal grandmother, as Marc grew older he rarely found visits with Edythe anything resembling fun. "After Barney died of a heart attack in 1976, when I was seven, there were just a few weekends sleeping at Edythe's," he said. "We played cards and watched TV. When Ron came, he'd mostly fall asleep on the couch. Then, later, infrequent visits to the Jewish Rehab nursing home to see Edythe when I'd be visiting from down South."

As a kid, Marc's life changed drastically when each of his parents remarried. His father was the first to remarry, to Helen Cortese in 1976. Well before that, an eight-year-old Marc had been aware of what was going on with his father and Helen. "They had carried on an affair through his and my mom's divorce. Good God, how sordid."

Although Helen's parents, Olga and Anthony (a.k.a. Bozo) Cortese, had divorced when Helen was young, Marc soon got to know the rest of Cortese family. "Not much was spoken to me about her parents or growing-up life," Marc said. "I'd heard her dad [who had died in 1955] was a crime boss. Helen's half-brother [Robert Fresolo], her cousins, and Ron were all connected to the extent that Ron, who'd been in touch with Helen while 'away,' had a small collections position lined up once he was released, collecting loans. Not full time, and maybe before his release, not certain.

"All I knew about was his full-time job with Barney, at Hall's Liquor. And I only came to know about the mob ties as I spent more Saturdays with him and his friends. Carmine and Bruno were first cousins of Helen's, and they would often be with Ron when he'd come get me for our day together. I received a few gold watches, a Rolex, and a couple of other items given to them as partial payoffs. Barbara would always find these articles of jewelry and go nuts. But everyone was super nice to me, I do recall that. All I know is that Ron wouldn't come off the forty dollars a week, or month, can't remember, for Mom and I, so screw him, to be honest. He personally afforded me zero."

Marc's resentment toward his father and the child support situation never wavered. "Dad and I never took as much as an overnight anywhere ever," he said. "He and Helen did, however, take several trips to Aruba, Bermuda, Jamaica, etcetera. The dude who couldn't come off forty dollars a week for child support, and before John came into our lives, wasn't interested in spending his questionable wealth on me."

When Marc relates those painful feelings to me, I cannot help but think of how differently Ronnie was raised, as if the entire world was handed to him. Private military schools, a fancy bar mitzvah, designer clothes, brand-new cars, and, of course, the way his parents stood by him during his years away, practically going bankrupt to keep him safe and eventually free and doing all they could to bring a future wife to his side.

I certainly wasn't close enough to Ronnie or old enough to see the day-to-day dealings of Ronnie and my aunt and uncle, and for all I know they were awful parents in every way possible. As all parents know, material gifts are no stand-in for love. As a child, Ronnie had to have seen the way his aunts and uncles treated his cousins. Somewhere along the line, I would have hoped that seeing his aunts and uncles in action might have rubbed off on Ronnie in terms of picking up some decent parenting skills. After getting to know Marc, I realized that my cousin lacked the ability to be a good and loving father. I felt that created a black mark on our entire Blumenthal family. We were all so loyal to Ronnie, supporting him emotionally for as long as humanly possible, but for his son, we all missed the boat.

Cousin Fred certainly tried. When Ronnie and Barbara made him Marc's godfather, he took that role very seriously, remembering Marc with checks on his birthday, keeping in close touch through Barbara after the divorce. He later admitted it wasn't easy, nor was he successful, being a good godfather to his great nephew. "We would always send him checks for his birthday, but for years he never acknowledged it," said Fred. "One year I made out a check to Marc Blumenthal, and he endorsed it by writing Marc Hollister, his stepfather's last name. For the past few years, I always send him an email on his birthday and anniversary. Other than when he was young, we were not ever close. I think the last time we saw him was when he and Barbara came to Orlando, many years ago. But recently, we have reconnected, and we email each other often, which Sandra and I thoroughly enjoy. It has been such a pleasure to get to know him again." Fred understood that Marc's childhood was far from easy, and he had never intended to give up on having a relationship with his godson.

For as far back as he could remember, Marc learned not to expect much positive parenting from his father. "Early on, I could 100 percent see where Ron had no chance at attaining the skills it takes to parent, much less live a productive day-to-day life," he said. "He had charm, wit, and charisma to spare but an unbelievably low emotional intelligence quotient, sadly. He could be quite affectionate and loving and showed it freely to me. Never raised a hand to me, but he was an alcoholic and a liar. He was also an adult child with a dark secret. I sympathize with aspects of these sad, terrible circumstances; it's what he was dealt. He wasn't up to the task, though. Plain and simple. Neither parent was, and I'm sorting much of that out now. Results and ramifications."

Marc considered himself lucky, however, to have met Helen's mom, Olga, as well as Olga's second husband, John Powers, who lived in Burlington, Massachusetts. "I knew John was some sort of a Boston publishing mogul, but he was also a super-kind person. He was maybe a little too pragmatic to me, when I needed more emotional empathy, but his heart was in the right place, 100 percent."

Helen also had a daughter from a previous marriage, Leslie, who was a few years older than Marc and with whom he got along relatively well. "Leslie was always with Ron and Helen," he said. "The three of them were very tight. I do remember Leslie starting smoking around Helen and Ron when she was fourteen, I believe!"

As for Marc's mother and Helen, according to Marc, "Oh, yeah, Mom totally did like Helen," he said sarcastically. "Based on zero meetings between them when I was a kid, and then only twice as an adult."

There was one particular meeting, however, between his father's two wives that Marc believes illustrated a good deal about the two women. In 2002, many years after the divorce, when Marc was on the academic staff at a holistic, remote-learning college, he had the opportunity to go to a naturopathic medical conference at Wheaton College in Norton, Massachusetts. Since he was living in Birmingham, Alabama, he was delighted that he'd be in Massachusetts for a week. "That meant I'd get to at least see Mom, who I knew would want to pick a night to meet and have dinner," he said. "I honestly believed that Ron and Helen would balk at the opportunity, out of pure nervousness.

But they didn't. So we went out, two of my colleagues who flew up with me, Mom, Helen, Ron, and myself. Mind you, Mom and Helen had not yet really officially met, and it had been about thirty years since the divorce at this point. So I'm sure *someone* had a Klonopin or two in 'em! Long story short, Mom and I had a super evening of food and kibbitzing with my two colleagues.

"But Dad and Helen were so fucking awkward, having not really experienced anything like that before. And, man, was Helen apparently pissed off. According to Ron, we had all tried to 'show off' and my coworkers were 'snobs' trying to make the two of them feel stupid. I'm sure that a simple discussion about the three of us sitting on the dissertation committee, or maybe something even more dull and benign, triggered them to hell and back."

In truth, Marc spared no mercy in describing his father's second wife, the woman to whom Ronnie stayed married, far from happily or steadily, for more than thirty years, until her death in 2011. In Marc's words, Helen Cortese Blumenthal was "an enabler, weak, small-minded, bigoted, with just the opposite ideals, creeds, and morals of anyone I respected or cared about."

One particular incident, Marc believed, accurately demonstrated his stepmother's attitude toward him. "Ron and Helen had picked me up at Nana Dorothy's [Barbara's mother, Dorothy Sickels] apartment. Nana and I had taken a trip to Child World, where I snagged a Malibu Ken. My friend Beth had a Barbie. I had a crush on Beth and believed that if I bought a Ken then our paired dolls would become star-crossed lovers, as would Beth and I. But Helen was appalled at the Ken doll and said I was going to grow up to be a 'fag,' as she put it, because I was quiet and played with dolls. She tore into me, telling me to get rid of the Ken figure and get barbells and a punching bag instead. I was eight! Fuck her."

It was shortly after Ronnie married Helen that Barbara married John Hollister. In 1979, when John took a job with a law group in New Orleans, Marc, who was in the fourth grade at the time, moved to New Orleans with his mother and stepfather.

Marc's views of his stepfather could not be more opposite from his feelings for his stepmother and, sadly, for his father. "John is the human equivalent of pragmatic, kindhearted, and honest. He was, if possible, a one-eighty flip of Ron. 'John 'n' Ron: A Tale of Two Dads,' is the story of a young boy's journey into cognitive dissonance. There's so much about John that I could relate that I wouldn't know where to start and stop. I truly love John. We had very little conflict beyond that of a new stepdad situation. I could be a jerky eight-year-old, but hopefully not often."

For the eight years of his mother's marriage to John, and the four years before that, from ages six through seventeen, Marc felt blessed to have such a decent and good man in his life, but he understood that John had to have been a bit of a thorn in his father's side. From the time Marc and Barbara moved to New Orleans, the frequent weekends for Ronnie and Marc ended, replaced by phone calls and short visits whenever Marc returned to Massachusetts for a visit. According to Marc, "I think it ate him up."

John was more specific about the phone calls. He remembered one particular call during the summer when Marc went to Massachusetts with Barbara to divide a month between Ron's house and her brother's house. While they were driving to Boston, John called Ron and told him very clearly that he had to stop phoning Marc when he was drunk. He tried to explain that those drunken calls happened all too often and left Marc deeply upset, and it took a long time to calm him down after they hung up. "I told him that if he didn't stop doing that, he would lose Marc as a son," John said. "Which would be my gain. Ron screamed and yelled and carried on and pretty much told me to mind my own business. The next night, right after Barbara delivered Marc to his father's in Boston, I got a phone call very late at night, and there was a very soft little voice saying he needed to talk to me. It was Marc, and he had waited until Ron went to sleep to call me. He told me Ron had been very angry and had yelled at him and told him that I had told him bad things. Marc was clearly very upset, and it bothered me greatly that a little boy had to hear such things. I calmed him down, and when we hung up I knew from then on that Ron had lost his son and I had won him."

As it turned out, shortly after that late-night call, Marc joined his mother at his uncle's house for the rest of the monthlong visit. John understood that it might well have been too much for Ron to have a little boy in his life. That was fine with him. He didn't have to worry about Marc for the rest of the visit.

Yet, Marc hung on to some pleasant memories of times spent with his father. "Before we moved to New Orleans, like when I was five, six, seven-ish, Ron and I'd go to the Stoneham Zoo, my fave," he told me. "The solo visits, just he and I, were much different than spending time at Helen and Ron's. Once they married and cohabitated, the focus was less solo with he and I together, just the two of us on Sundays, and more time at their condo. When I moved to New Orleans, it meant only summer trips up to Massachusetts. At that point I would go to work with him and, well, work! He had a string of jobs after liquor sales, managing convenience stores and a couple of liquor stores. I would work the register and bag stuff. It was pretty cool, actually."

As the years went on, Marc understood even more clearly how different he and his father had become. "That was becoming apparent as I grew up. Morals, ethics, ideals; all so different," Marc said. "I was being raised by two pro-education, left-leaning, racially tolerant individuals, and that was a polar opposite of what I would experience at Ron and Helen's. I was very, very quiet anyway, but almost mute when around them. Helen would quip that it was stupid that I was playing violin [bass, actually]. Why not learn to box or play football? Simpleminded thinking by simpleminded folk. So, it was eye-opening to live those divides."

It was only during Marc's summer trips to Boston that he found an opportunity to spend time with his father. "We were together during commutes to and from work, as well as time at work. All decent experiences. But he was jealous of John's and my relationship, and that caused even more issues as I got older. Drunk calls became the norm, as did the terrible things he'd say. John or Mom intervened a couple of times, which led to some loud phone calls between John and Ron or Mom and Ron."

Marc later understood how jealous his father was of John, of his stepfather's intelligence, education, and role in his life. "Unlike John, Ron insulted my seven-year participation in Loyola University's Youth String Orchestra and anything that he didn't understand. He was completely delusional throughout our relationship, believing that he really needed to be raising me. He asked about school, but I wouldn't say he had a vested interest in my life. I think he would have liked to have had that innate interest, but he couldn't mime it. It wasn't there."

What was especially wonderful about John, besides the calm and honesty and normalcy that he brought into Marc's life after the endless shouting matches that defined his parents' marriage and the nastiness he felt from his father's second wife, was John's extended family. One of Marc's greatest joys was spending some of the summer at the Hollister family cabin in Oak Bluffs on

Martha's Vineyard. "The family also had a tiny, tiny beach dwelling right slap on Gay Head Beach," said Marc. "John would take two weeks off in August to fly in to Logan, and then we would catch the ferry to Woods Hole."

Marc managed to spend some summer vacations up north with his mercurial father. "Those times, Dad would walk onto the plane to retrieve me when I was younger. I also flew up alone during a spring break [Mardi Gras vacation] for five days or so. Then, Ron and I had some good times. Not being a baseball fan but knowing I was a ravenous follower, he would score Sox tickets for either the two of us, or sometimes his old friend Herbie and his daughter Kerry would join us. Herbie was my barber and performed my first haircut. He was a prison mate of Ron's, and they stayed friends until a falling out in the early nineties. No clue what happened."

I can't help but smile when I think of Ronnie walking onto the plane to collect his young son, imagining the old, sweet Ronnie smile when he first caught sight of the blond little boy who so clearly resembled him. It seems like such a normal father-son interaction that I would imagine any passenger or flight attendant seeing it could not help but smile as well.

Yet, the image of Ronnie and Marc at a Red Sox game brings me mixed emotions. Of course, I was pleased to hear of my cousin's sensitivity in providing his son with such a special night for the two of them. I also remember how the only questions Ronnie had for his guards during his 1954 summer and early fall days at the Dedham jail before his trial were about baseball scores. Those times he seemed oblivious to what was happening around him and to him, but baseball mattered. When he was older, he had apparently lost his love for the sport, but still he took his son to a game.

CHAPTER TWENTY-THREE
Revelations

Edythe and Barney with their grandson, Marc.

It was during one of those summer trips to Massachusetts when Marc was twelve when he and his father had what Marc called "the talk": Ronnie's explanation of what happened to him from ages eighteen to thirty-one. Marc believed he was very young, perhaps as early as four years old, when the subject was first mentioned, but more seriously when he was twelve. "We were in the den of his and Helen's house," Marc related. "She wasn't there. Obviously by arrangement. He began by telling me that I was free to ask him anything when he finished, and that he would be honest in his answers. I listened, and the big question, of course, was whether he did it. I asked and he answered, 'I took the rap for Barney.' But then, in the same breath, he also mentioned blacking out the memory and his not being sure. He kept repeating he was open to any questions that I may have had. Due to the nature of our relationship, I didn't feel that sort of freedom, though that was on me, and I really had nothing to ask at the time. Nor was I in shock, as the plan to tell me as a preschooler, then again as an adolescent, must have been spot on. Certainly, there had been some little mentions when I was younger of Ron being "away," though they must have been fleeting as I barely remember them.

"Quite honestly, I don't think Ron spoke much about day-to-day life in Norfolk. That's where he said, again, that he was 'away.' According to him, he was rewarded with good behavior, and often. I know there was a Forestry Camp towards the end that Barney was able to make happen.

"At no time during that conversation did Ron lose his composure, or even seem upset. Not in a sociopathic way. He simply wasn't shaken at any point during the conversation. All may have seemed fishy to me, if I recall. The 'blacking out memories' notion never sat well."

Hearing Marc utter his father's words, "I took the rap for Barney," sent me into a tailspin. Never had I or my cousins, my mother, or my aunts ever had such a "talk" with Ronnie. Somehow, we had all managed, sadly, to avoid it. Yet every one of us had already heard that story about "taking the rap" for Barney, but it had all been just hearsay, until we had "proof" of some sort from Marc. It had not been an outright confession, and Ronnie took it back a few seconds later. Still, Ronnie had uttered those words.

I well understood that my mother's theory had always been to blame "the dressmaker," and the two of us had never delved any further into the subject of exactly what happened. By the time I had caught up with Marc, my mother had been gone for more than twenty-five years. I wished more than ever that she was still alive and I could repeat those words to her and hear her reaction. Truthfully, I could pretty much imagine what she would say: "That's ridiculous, Phyllis. My brother, Barney, was the sweetest man on the face of the earth. And he adored his only son. Ronnie was just fooling around with Marc. Marc completely misunderstood what his father was saying. The murder was practically an accident. That dressmaker said something to Ronnie that made him crazy for a minute, and he killed her. It should never have happened. And he never meant it to happen. But Barney could never have killed her. Any more than he could have let his son go to prison. And that is that."

I repeated the story to my cousins soon after I heard it from Marc. Now, none of us could ignore it. We had all heard that theory discussed by friends or acquaintances and discussed it amongst ourselves. Knowing that Ronnie had spoken those words out loud to his twelve-year-old son gave them a new sense of authority. Ronnie was no longer alive by the time Marc and I discussed "the talk," so now it was just out there, and each of us could do with it whatever we pleased. As for me, I could not completely discard Ronnie's first statement, nor could I believe that Barney had been the murderer. Something else had to have happened that night. Someone had helped Ronnie murder Ora Schonarth or had pushed him into it.

I also understood how those words must have affected a twelve-year-old's relationship with the complicated and bewildering parent who had spoken them. By age twelve, Marc had already been disappointed and perplexed more times than he could remember by the man he called Ron. Now, that same man had laid a huge bundle of more confusion at his feet. Marc knew that on the day his father had turned nineteen he had gone to prison for what would be thirteen years for a murder the grandfather, no longer living but whom Marc had always loved, had committed. Or he *might have* been the murderer. What a load, indeed, my cousin had just dropped on me.

I can't imagine that Ronnie had ever looked forward to "the talk." What father could possibly want to tell his son that he had gone to prison for thirteen years? That he had murdered a woman? How could he ever face his son after uttering those words? His son was living in another man's house by then, so their relationship was already fraught and broken. Of course, he would want to try to save some face. Barney was dead, so it wasn't a big deal to put the blame on him and have his son look at him not just as a murderer but as a son who had sacrificed his life to save his father's. There was no way I could believe that theory. What the hell did I know for sure about my cousin Ronnie, anyhow? Certainly, a lot less than his son did.

Naturally, twelve-year-old Marc discussed "the talk" with his mother soon afterward. As expected, Barbara had nothing good to say about Ronnie or Edythe, so he found her relatively supportive of his feelings of confusion. "Of course, she was biased," Marc said. "But I honestly can't remember her exact response. And it's not as if she knew anything more than I. She probably got a similar story."

Marc never discussed it again, until more than ten years later, with his wife, Michele. When he mentioned it to a good friend in Alabama, however, the friend found the first newspaper article of the murder that the fifty-year-old Marc had ever seen. "When he showed me the 'Thrill Kill Kid of Brookline' newspaper article," said Marc, "I was pretty shocked. I found online the *Brotman Blog* [a blog called "A Family Genealogy" created by Amy B. Cohen from 2013 to 2023], which included mention of the victim's family. But now, for the first time, all of the details were in print. I think I went pale when I read the article, and Michele became immediately concerned. Until she learned what I'd just laid my eyes on. I wasn't disturbed or horribly upset, but was like, 'Whoa!'

"I'd only ever heard about strangulation. So, the stabbings and bludgeoning were new concepts to me. But the gruesome crime didn't shock me at all. I think it's due to the fact that I was never close to him. I endured him but did not love him as one loves a parent. Or at all, actually. Hey, I can build and put up walls like an effing brick mason. He was a recipient of such a wall."

Marc is adamant that the knowledge of Ronnie's time "away," as well as the circumstances surrounding it all, never freaked him out. "It didn't bring a sense of shame to me, nor a sense of personal tragedy. It wasn't a cool badge I wore, either. He and I didn't have that kind of closeness to where that would be a factor for me about my father. His whole story, as I now understand it, is high drama at the least and a powerful lesson in twisted, family dynamics.

"There are hundreds of small 'indictments' I could 'charge' him with, but all that energy spent delving into negativity isn't necessary at this point. You got the important shaping points as far as his and my relationship goes. I would have loved to have a neato dad who taught me things, molded me, shaped me into a man, all of that, but I was dealt Ronnie 'The Thrill Kill Teen' from Brookline. My cross to bear. Or...my matzah to crack. There, that's more appropriate."

It wasn't easy to hear Marc talk so disparagingly about his father and his entire family. Even when he added a bit, or rather a crumb, of humor. I must admit a combination of guilt and sadness that once Marc and Barbara left for New Orleans when he was so young, most of us cousins lost contact. As Marc's godfather and a faithful friend to Barbara, my cousin Fred kept in close contact with the two of them. Yet, even though the Blumenthal family had such strong feelings about never losing another family member, we lost Marc, an innocent bystander in a sordid story, a kid who could have used the support of a loving family no matter where he lived. That was just plain wrong.

Indeed, Marc had more than one thought about his own particular family dynamics, which I found intriguing. "Hmm, it's conjecture," he said calmly, "but I can guess that Edythe was a monster to Barney, with verbal belittling in front of their son. Her use of guilt tactics most likely twisting young Ronnie's head up, with Barney probably cowering. It's all just twisted.

"Ron probably suffered from a personality disorder. I don't think he had classic depression or anxiety; however, the power-drinking through the seventies, eighties, and nineties was in essence to cover something dark, painful, and uncomfortable. A state of Edythopia. He may have had a uniquely rare mental disorder that only Edythe could unleash on another human. Joking, but not really, because we know how sick and destructive she was. He didn't really present as narcissistic or particularly borderline, but instead a level of 'little baby who wants *his bottle*'!

"Anger. Repressed everything, and probably quite a bit of anxiety and maybe PTSD from bludgeoning and stabbing someone. I know I would."

While Marc found it almost impossible to believe his gentle grandfather could have been a murderer, he does not consider it out of the question that his paternal grandmother could have pushed her son into action against the murder victim. That thought certainly goes along with the idea that neighbors noted in the police reports in 1954 that Ronnie and his mother visited Ora together shortly before the day of the murder. Of course, those same reports mentioned eighteen-year-old Ronnie telling a friend that he would do whatever needed to be done to protect his family.

Marc was far from the only family member to give credence to such a thought depicting Edythe's involvement in the murder. Cousin Mel, who admitted that he went to visit Ronnie during his imprisonment mostly to please our uncle Lewie, admitted that he was no great fan of his slightly older cousin Ronnie. Of course, the scene involving the grown-up Ronnie propositioning his wife later on colored Mel's attitude toward his cousin. "He was spoiled as a child, sent away to military school, lazy, arrogant, and not repentant," Mel said. "And when he came out of prison, he had delusions of grandeur about what he could do for a living. I only met Barbara a few times. I'm sure life was not great for her."

Mel also offered speculation about his aunt's involvement in the murder. "Edythe may have found out that Barney was having an affair and told Ronnie to admonish or threaten the woman, and he may have gone to her house and things got out of control. If Edythe herself had participated, I would expect the police would have found clues, e.g. fingerprints, that she was there. I can't understand why Ronnie would brag to those two girls about doing it."

Marc always knew that there was no love lost between his mother and Edythe and that Barbara would have no trouble believing such a scenario. "I believe the word my mom used the most when discussing Edythe was 'destructive.' She told me a story of a Christmas/birthday family get-together at our Newton house. Edythe was present, and, according to Mom, who witnessed this bit of insanity from across the living room, Edythe slowly emptied her glass of red wine onto the freshly cleaned carpet. Having known that my mother had spent half a day doing a carpet cleaning treatment."

Marc felt no love for the woman who so clearly mistreated his mother. He had no trouble continuing to psychoanalyze his father. "As a young adult, I connected the dots pretty well," he told me, "and could see where a young man, an only child, spoiled yet neglected in the most fundamental ways, could be internalizing the hurt, letting it manifest into rage. But where he *had* feelings, he didn't know much what to do with them. He was angry and eighteen until he passed. Sprinkle in some eternal guilt, and there he is. Not a sociopath, but woefully immature and searching. This is the shit I've endured for decades. It's more his absentmindedness than being cruel or whatever."

Marc was more than amazed when his father suddenly exhibited a change in his political outlook. "At some point in the late nineties, and for whatever frickin' reason, he became a staunch liberal? Spouting off racial awareness and snowflake sentiment, he dove full-force into things Democrat. He even, like, read a book, something like the Clinton bio. I can think of no cause for this awareness."

While John Hollister was part of Marc's life, he was both willing and able to provide a far less twisted version of parenting than the one Ronnie employed, and he urged family counseling to try to undo whatever damage that twisted parenting might have caused his stepson. "When a kid has been through as much chaos and weird stuff as Marc had been through, a good measure of just keeping one's head down and hoping the shrapnel will fly over is only to be expected," John said. "Barbara and I had started this course of counseling because we feared that Marc would be having trouble as he inevitably had to come to grips with a knowledge of Ronnie's problems and deficiencies as a father. It was intended to be a sort of mental health vaccination. There was never any discussion with Ronnie about this counseling."

Perhaps not unsurprisingly, during the four years Barbara and John were dating and the eight years they were married and living together, John could not recall even one discussion between Barbara and Ronnie about Marc's welfare. Their phone conversations were usually quite short and restricted to things such as arrangements for Ronnie to pick up Marc or drop him off. "I always put that lack of interchange down to the circumstances of their separation and the way Ronnie just called Barbara out of the blue and had told her not to plan to move to Ohio with him," he said.

John had his own opinion of Edythe and the negative effect she might have had on her only grandchild. "By the time Barbara and I started dating in Framingham [in 1974], Edythe had thrown Barney out and he was living on his own. A few times Edythe dragooned Ronnie into agreeing to have Marc come visit her, which is how Barbara and I drove, at least a few times, to wherever she was living to drop him off or pick him up. It was after those visits that we would hear some of the strange things

Edythe had done and said to him, and that was how I picked up that, even at the young age of five, Marc was figuring out that something was off about his grandmother."

To be more specific, John recalled examples of "Edythe's classic pattern of 'pull toward/push away,' just as she had always exercised toward Ronnie and Barney, combined with a heavy dose of passive-aggressive manipulation. Her standard technique seemed always to include snide put-downs, 'O, woe is me!' drama, and masses of psychological projection, accusing the other person of doing precisely what she herself was actually up to. That was what was so fascinating about Marc's being able to see through that at the tender age of five." John was personally relieved when the visits to Edythe tapered off, and he was equally relieved that Edythe never made a trip to New Orleans, not even for Marc's bar mitzvah in 1981.

John was aware, however, that the relationship between Marc and his grandfather was loving and important for both of them. "Barney, on the other hand, would drive out to Framingham every Sunday, pick up Marc, and take him somewhere, just the two of them," John said. "Marc looked forward to his visits with his grandfather. Barney obviously doted on Marc, and the two of them had a fine time together."

After Barney, who had died at the age of sixty-nine on January 3, 1976, his liquor store having gone out of business years earlier, his shiva (the Jewish period of mourning) was held at my sister's house in Lexington. Toby was not quite sure why that happened. "I guess no one else could do it, not Ronnie or Aunt Edythe, and our parents were living in Florida, so I had it," she told me. Perhaps it was because Toby was likely the only cousin who had any favorable feeling toward our aunt. At the shiva, Edythe played the role of grieving, loving widow, which, even Toby knew, was ridiculous. Still, it was sad that our uncle had been so alone when he died. He had certainly led a difficult life, watching his son locked up in prison for thirteen years, obviously knowing that his affair with the dressmaker had to have been a major factor in the murder. How much I wish I had been able to sit down and talk to my uncle about his childhood on 7 Overhill Road and the effect of the Accident on his life, on losing the older brother with whom he always been close, but that never happened. No one imagined that life with Edythe had ever been pleasant or easy, even when, thanks to Edythe's sister's and brother-in-law's wealth and fame, they had been socially prominent. There is no doubt that Barney died a broken, lonely man, a fact that disturbed Marc.

"What's bugged me for decades," he said, "is the fact that Ronnie was making decent money, buying Cadillacs and Lincoln Town Cars and taking Helen, pre- and post-marriage, to Caribbean Island trips and Aruba and the like, but his father, who always stood by him, was living in the Avery [located in The Combat Zone, the name given to the adult entertainment district in downtown Boston in the 1960s] in a room with a bed and shared bathroom or some shit. A welfare hotel. I mean... really? It's choices and behavior like that where all I can do is shake my head."

It was indeed sad that the one pleasure later in my uncle Barney's life, his only grandchild, was not at the shiva, nor were either of his son's two wives, Barbara or Helen. Even Flo, who had adored him during the years she was involved with Ronnie, was absent. The cousins were there, however, as were Barney's sisters, Marion and my mother, Belle, and his brothers, Lewie and Hy. It's weird, but neither Toby nor I can remember if Ronnie was there. Most likely he made a very quick, unremarkable appearance during the week. Thanks to my sister, the memorial week for Ronnie's father was far more loving and respectful than the last few years of his life had been. Barney's "grieving" widow Edythe died twenty years later, on October 27, 1996, at age eighty-five, at the Hebrew Rehabilitation Center in Boston, from the effects of a stroke. By that time, Toby was living in Florida and did not have a shiva for our aunt, and no cousins attended the funeral.

My cousins Naomi and Bob recalled inviting Barney and Ronnie to their Thanksgiving dinner a few years before Barney's passing. Marc was in New Orleans with Barbara at the time, and Ronnie appeared to have been separated from Helen at that moment. Unfortunately, a snowstorm hit Rhode Island that day, but Ronnie still drove in from Boston with his father. Ronnie had stopped over at the house of cousins Phil and Ann Ruth in Pawtucket for a quick visit and a drink before they all headed to Bobby and Naomi's house in Providence for dinner. No one remembered much about the dinner, except that Ronnie had little to say about Marc, who must have been about ten at the time. Naomi and Ann Ruth felt bad that Marc wasn't there as they were sure he would have enjoyed spending time with their sons, David Halpert and Jack Brown, who were close to Marc's age. Both Naomi and Ann Ruth, although they were Blumenthal cousins by marriage, were devoted to the family and worked hard to plan occasions when we could all be together. They had hoped that that particular Thanksgiving dinner would have been a chance to cheer up Uncle Barney and make sure he knew that he had nephews and nieces who loved him. Fortunately, the snowstorm ended during the afternoon, so Ronnie, who did not appear too drunk, and Barney were able to drive home safely that evening.

A few years later, in the summer of 1981, Naomi and Bob invited Ronnie to come to their new home in Plum Island, off the shore of Newburyport, Massachusetts, to a celebration in honor of their first grandchild, Kayla Faye. It was the baby's first visit to Plum Island, and her ecstatic grandparents could hardly wait to show her off to all their friends on the island. Ronnie arrived alone, carrying a large box of Italian pastries. "He immediately set himself up as a bartender, passing out drinks from our small supply of alcohol," Naomi remembered. "I am sure he served himself first, but that didn't matter to Bob or me. We were just so pleased he came."

While Marc, sadly, had all-too-little contact with his Blumenthal cousins, one of his "favorite persons on the face of the earth" was his Nana Dorothy, his maternal grandmother, who joined Marc, his mother, and his stepfather in 1983, when her roommates of many years decided to move to a retirement home. "We were very, very close, from my birth till her passing," Marc said. "Dorothy Sickels was a down-to-earth, kind, thoughtful, giving, and peaceful person. She brought peace to me, anyway, in a period of chaos that outlines my early life. She and my mother were close, and I now realize that Dotty probably worried about Mom more than I could ever realize in those days. Nana never spoke an ugly word about Ron. She was supportive when I was upset about an episode with him but showed no outward or ostentatious displays of anger toward Ron like Barbara did."

Before he moved to New Orleans, Marc would sleep at his nana's house at least a couple of weekends a month, and those were times he treasured. "I loved it when Nana moved in with us in 1983 and was heartbroken when she passed three years later. She'd lived through my shitty, obnoxious, depression/anxiety-ridden teens, passing when I was nineteen."

John Hollister also had only praise for Dorothy. "Barbara once told me that when she was walking into the wedding with Ron, her mother told her, 'You don't have to go through with this,'" he said.

Of all the regrets Marc might have had about his childhood, the strongest was his decision to turn down a scholarship to Loyola as a music major. When he'd been a fifth grader, he'd been selected to join the University of New Orleans at Loyola Youth Symphony, and he stayed with the symphony all the way to tenth grade. Despite the numerous performances he participated in for more than five years with the Youth Symphony, his father never attended one single concert, nor did he express any interest in Marc's musical ability. His stepmother, Helen, disparaged Marc's musical interests. Until Barbara and John separated, John was Marc's strongest supporter of Marc's pursuit of his musical talents. For many of those years, John helped out with getting Marc and his bulky bass to rehearsal three times a week as well as making it to all the performances. Had John and Barbara's marriage lasted longer, Marc might have made a different decision about the scholarship opportunity.

CHAPTER TWENTY-FOUR
Regrets

Ronnie made it to New Orleans only once during Marc's childhood, to attend his son's bar mitzvah service, on December 12, 1982, a far simpler affair than his own three-day bar mitzvah celebration thirty-four years earlier in Brookline, Massachusetts. The only Blumenthal cousins invited to Marc's celebration were cousins Fred and Sandra, who were Marc's god-parents. Many other Blumenthal bar mitzvahs were held around the same time as Marc's, but none included Marc and Barbara on their guest list. When my son Josh celebrated his bar mitzvah more than two years later, in April 1984, only Ronnie and Helen were invited to the affair, just as they had been invited three years earlier to our older son Adam's bar mitzvah celebration in June 1981.

No invitations to either bar mitzvah were sent to Barbara and Marc, and Ronnie made no attempt to have us invite his son to either event. I have only myself to blame for that. Marc and Barbara were so far removed from my life by then that it never even occurred to me to put them on our guest list. I knew it would not be a terrific idea to have Barbara and Helen at the same affair, but how sad it was that we allowed little Marc to be collateral damage in that unpleasant marital situation.

As it turned out, just having Ronnie in attendance at Josh's celebration turned out to be a giant mistake, one I will never forget. The scene at Josh's bar mitzvah party in April 1984 affected many of my Blumenthal relatives, but none more than me and my husband Jack. The party was a relatively fancy dinner dance at our synagogue. That night, as Jack and I excitedly visited each table of our friends and relatives, I noticed a commotion taking place at one of the tables we had not yet visited. The band was playing and the social hall was quite noisy, but I knew that something unpleasant was happening at one particular table a bit of a distance away from where we were standing. From across the room, it looked like a few of my male cousins were standing up and holding on to a man. As Jack and I approached, I saw that those cousins were literally dragging Ronnie, who was visibly and disgustingly drunk and grumbling loudly, out of the room.

I knew immediately what had happened and was heartsick. The same cousin who had been so sad that he hadn't been able to attend our wedding, who had managed to come to our older son's afternoon bar mitzvah celebration three years earlier and had smiled for the photo sitting next to his unsmiling wife, Helen, had now dissipated into a raging drunk. I knew, as all my cousins did, that Ronnie's drinking had gotten worse in those years and that, while he might have been relatively sober during an afternoon celebration, an evening affair with free-flowing alcohol and a large crowd of people would be his downfall. I got one last glimpse of my white-haired and red-faced forty-eight-year-old cousin as he was physically removed from the building, his equally drunk wife, Helen, stumbling behind him, and I wanted to cry. It would be the last time I ever saw him.

Ronnie, bottom left, at my son Adam's bar mitzvah on April 21, 1980. His arm is around his second wife, Helen, and he is seated at a table with our cousins and their spouses.

I had felt such a wave of pleasure days earlier when I'd made out our table arrangements and had seated Ronnie and Helen at table number four with the rest of my Blumenthal cousins. He might have missed many family gatherings for the years he was in prison, but each time he joined us for weddings, bar mitzvahs, birthdays, holiday celebrations, and simple cousins' get-togethers, I rejoiced in his presence. But no more. My cousin was losing his grip on reality. He drank more and more, his marriage looked shakier and unhappier, his son lived far away in New Orleans and was hardly ever visible in his life, and heaven only knew what he did to support himself financially. The night of Josh's bar mitzvah, I saw the faces of my cousins Bobby and Phil when they returned to their table. I saw the sadness and anger as they forced themselves to smile and offer Jack and me their congratulations. We were losing our cousin Ronnie again, this time for good.

At the time I hoped that Marc was blissfully unaware of the slights my husband and I made by omitting him from those two celebrations. In the long run, it turned out to be a blessing that Marc was not a guest at the bar mitzvah celebration of his second cousin Josh, where he would have witnessed his drunk father being manhandled out of the temple. All he remembered about his own bar mitzvah was that his Torah portion was Genesis 40 (the main part of a bar mitzvah celebration is that the boy reads from the sacred scrolls, called the Torah). "I butchered the Havdalah [a special candle-lighting ceremony] chant/sing thing," Marc admitted. "I did it for the party and gifts!"

John, an avid calligrapher and, at that time, very much a part of Marc and Barbara's lives, hand-addressed each bar mitzvah invitation and was far more involved in every aspect of the event than was Marc's father. Marc remembered well that his father was, indeed, there. "Ron was staying at the La Quinta Inn where Mom had him served papers for his forty dollars a month child support. She warned him from the get-go that he had to start paying child support, so she said, 'Fuck it,' and followed through. I heard about that one for years! How many times I heard Mom bellow over the phone, '*Forty fuckin' dollahs a month, Ronnie!*'

"Another sort of legendary note is that Ron fell asleep during my Torah portion. He could be audibly heard snoring." At that, Marc sighed. As for Helen's absence, there was no surprise or sadness for Marc in that respect. Just relief. "She did not come. Just Ron."

Cousin Fred, who was close with Barbara, was the only Blumenthal cousin in attendance for Marc's special day. He hadn't seen Ronnie since eight years earlier, when Ronnie left briefly for a supposed job in Ohio, angering Fred by not taking Barbara and Marc with him. "When Sandra and I approached him at the bar mitzvah that morning he looked surprised," Fred recalled. "We acted as if nothing had happened in the past. We spent the whole afternoon with him visiting different places of interest. Really had a good day and were looking forward to spending the evening with him as well. We were surprised when he didn't show up for the evening party. He did not appear to be drinking at any time when we had been with him that afternoon. He looked okay."

Fred never had a chance to meet Helen. "When we [Fred and Sandra] were living in Rhode Island just before moving to Florida, Ronnie and I had spoken at length about the old days, etcetera, and set up a date for Sandra and me to meet him and Helen for dinner," Fred said. "I gave him my Florida phone number, but he never called." In 1988, seven years after Marc's bar mitzvah, Ronnie called Fred to tell him that Barbara's mother, of whom Fred had always been fond, had died. Fred, who, of all the Blumenthal cousins, was the most loyal to Ronnie, never saw Ronnie again after that bar mitzvah day.

Marc had another opportunity to get to know his father better, however, when, in 1990, at age twenty-two, bored in Birmingham and looking for a change, Marc and a good friend moved to Boston. Again, I felt a stab of regret when Marc related this trip to me. I was living a few miles north of Boston at the time and went into Boston three times a week to teach at Boston University School of Journalism. How easy it would have been for me to have met Marc and taken him out for dinner one night.

The truth was I had little to do with Ronnie at that time and would never have expected him to tell me anything about the son of whom I knew very little. Any memories Marc had about being with the Blumenthal cousins so many years earlier must have faded. Had I bumped into Marc on the streets of Boston in 1990, we would never have recognized each other. Sure, I might have thought, *Wow, this young man looks like a younger version of my cousin Ronnie,* but I would have walked right by him.

At the time Marc moved to Boston, Ron was separated from Helen and living in a one-bedroom apartment in Stoneham into which Marc and his friend Todd temporarily moved. "He was sort of a bachelor," Marc said. "Though he was not seeing anyone except Helen. We'd hang out sometimes. He was drinking pretty heavily at that point. We didn't get along too bad as I chose not to be argumentative with him."

Ronnie was working at Pastore Seafoods and found jobs for Marc and Todd there, Todd in packing and Marc in the business office. "At this time Ron was a drunk, after work, but not during, showing his ass to Todd almost upon arriving," Marc told me. "It was uneventful at Ron's, as we three worked like 6:00 a.m. to 4:00 p.m. Back at the apartment, it sucked. Ron was like a sixteen-year-old, trying to impress two young men who barely even drank."

Marc rarely, if ever, drank alcohol, even later in life. Indeed, the lure of alcohol never reached him. Perhaps it was the years of watching his father drink too heavily. Perhaps he finally got the message: Alcohol, from bootleggers to rumrunners to drunk drivers to failing liquor stores to destructive drunk men, was the nemesis of the Blumenthal family.

Just a few weeks of watching the nightly antics of his drunk father convinced Todd and Marc that the arrangement would never work. "We hurried up with our saving so we could get the eff out of his one-bedroom place," Marc said. "We found a dump in Quincy. I found a new gig that November; Todd got fired and basically moved back to Birmingham in December of '90. I made it another year and a half in Boston."

Unfortunately, even in his own place, Marc found himself forced to spend time with Ron, even when they were not working together. "Mostly on Saturdays. No real choice, it seemed, as he'd pout if I didn't want to. We'd visit Edythe at Hebrew Rehab, then Fontaine's for lunch. Maybe back to his apartment."

Marc was blunt about those times, which surely did not bring him and his father any closer. "We did not bond over anything. He was not someone I'd choose as a friend or acquaintance. He was drinking pretty much until he had a minor heart attack in the fall of 1990 and had a pacemaker put in at the Lahey Clinic. Then the drinking kinda dwindled down. There were no withdrawals or things associated with alcoholics. It was seamless, except actually dealing with the emotional aspects that caused him to drink beyond reason. Most lunches were me prompting him to tell stories or whatever, to keep from hour-long silences."

At one such lunch, Ron informed Marc that he'd spoken to his lady barber about hooking Marc up with her friend. "I stared blankly, I think," Marc said. "He was let down that I had zero interest in being blind-dated via his vapid hair person. Ron was thrown into an existential crisis over his linguini. 'Is there something *I should know*, Maahc?' I let him know that it wasn't a conspiracy and that I just didn't care to be set up with his hair person's BFF. I was pining for a girl I worked with at home, but I wasn't going to placate right then. I toyed with him a bit longer before I assured him of my heteroness. I still think he didn't believe me till Michele." Marc had no memory of doing anything remotely interesting or pleasurable with his father during those two years, besides eating or watching television.

Even though Helen and Ronnie were not living together during that time, Ronnie was not seeing anyone else and would still go out with Helen three to five nights a week. Marc remembered another woman, however, named Joy, whom his father dated for about a year in 1982, during one of his earlier breakups with Helen. "I met her one evening. She seemed okay. Dad built her up to be 'fat 'n' ugly,' probably as a prank, I guess, as she wasn't fat or ugly. I laughed and nodded my approval over the fact that I'd been 'had by dad.' Yuk yuk yuk."

Ronnie had more than one story to offer his son about women in his life. This one involved a cute girl who was the cashier at the Pilgrim Pantry in Medfield, which he managed for a year or two. Marc remembered that story well. "Helen caught wind of this and followed them, stealthily, to the hotel. Helen proceeded to find this poor girl at the hotel lounge and dragged her by her hair to the parking lot, where Helen struck her down with vengeance and rage. Then Helen and Ron got back together for a couple of years. Wow! Sure impressed me," he added sarcastically.

Though Barbara was certain that Ronnie was using cocaine during that time, Marc only recalled one occasion when he actually saw that happen. In late 1991, when Marc got accepted to the University of Alabama at Birmingham, knowing all his friends were back there, he decided to head back south. Although Marc considered leaving his father, the best part of the plan, Ronnie took it poorly. "He pouted and threw a low-grade temper tantrum at a McDonalds. Dumbass."

In August 1997, six years after Marc left Boston, Ronnie made his first trip to Birmingham, this time for Marc's wedding, another important event in his son's life in which, as was the case at his son's bar mitzvah in 1981, he took no part. At that affair, sadly, no Blumenthals other than Ronnie and Helen were in attendance, not even our cousin Fred. I heard about the wedding several years later but had a hard time even imagining what Marc might have looked like at that time. Still, I assumed he looked a lot like his father at age twenty-five, but since Ronnie had been in prison during his twenties it was hard to conjure the correct image in my mind. Marc was so far removed from my life at the time of his marriage, as he sadly was with the rest of my cousins, that I gave the whole concept little concern. Since my own sons were years away from marriage, I paid no attention to weddings of any sort. I wish I could turn back the clock and change my behavior, but all I can do now is continue the special relationship with Marc, which this book has provided me.

For Michele, however, getting to know her fiancé's small family back in Boston had understandably been a bit complicated. "I was nervous, wanting to make a good impression and so excited about seeing Boston," she said. "I loved Marc and wanted his family's acceptance."

Initially, Michele found Barbara warm as well as funny. She knew Barbara had raised Marc to be a good person and was grateful to her for that. "They used to talk on the phone daily, so I figured things were better than they were," Michele said. "But when we were together in Boston, it was obvious things had changed drastically between Marc and his mother. She wasn't the same woman I'd heard talking to him in the past. Now, she was talking to him like he was stupid, even telling me something disparaging about him. At first, I'd try and defend him, thinking she just didn't have all the facts. Then a couple of times I told her not to say those things to me, and, finally, I gave up and just ignored her as best I could. It was obvious her behavior was bothering and confusing Marc, who had recently begun seeing two different sides of his mother."

In Boston, Michele also visited Ron and Helen. "Marc had told me some stories about growing up, a little about the murder and prison. And about Helen's family's mob ties and how they met. At their house, I was so out of my element. All the gold and mirrored walls. I remember the meal was a sausage pasta dish. It was uncomfortable conversations of mostly small talk."

For the most part, Michele found Ronnie to be pleasant, mostly when Helen was not with him. "I'd seen photos of Ron when he'd been at the prison camp, and he was handsome and beefed up from the physical outdoors work," she said. "He was much older when I met him and he had those real bushy eyebrows older men get, and he was different-looking than those older photos."

Michele never found Helen's company pleasant or comfortable. "She was just cold. She would be civil, but there was absolutely no warmth. It was pretty obvious when the four of us were together that she considered Marc another woman's child. Not hers. I knew she had inherited some money, either from her father or mother, and their house was expensive, but I also saw how they piddled away the money she had inherited."

Marc and Michele were married on August 31, 1997, in the rose garden at the Birmingham Botanical Gardens. "Ron and Helen flew down for the wedding," Marc said. "He was pissy about having to rent a tux and also about the flight cost. At one point when I was discussing tux rental, he came out with, 'You can have us or a wedding gift, kid.' I said a gift would do and hung up on him. He apologized for being shitty."

Marc found it both hilarious and typical that Ron and Helen rented a Lincoln Town Car and booked the most expensive room at the Embassy Suites. He was far from surprised that they never gave a wedding gift.

Marc never hesitated to ask Barbara to walk him down the aisle, alone, just the two of them. His father wasn't very sick at that time, though he had a heart condition and diabetes. He never considered wanting his father at his side walk.

Barbara walks Marc down the aisle at his wedding in Birmingham, Alabama, on August 31, 1997.

"Ron sat at an outdoor table with Helen, who was wearing a heavy coat in one-hundred-degree heat," Marc remembered. "Ron would just look around, bored, until I'd wander back over to talk to them. He wasn't drinking then, so it was bottles of water for him. Would have been cool if he'd been friendly to Michele's side."

Helen, Ronnie's second wife (left), Ronnie, and Barbara, Ronnie's first wife (right) at Marc's wedding. It was one of the few times Barbara and Helen ever met.

Marc had forewarned Michele's family that his father would be uncomfortable and nervous about the entirety of the crowd. "He didn't know or wasn't in touch with anyone there," Marc said. "I know there was an introduction to my in-laws and I'm sure he was nervous but polite. He kibbitzed with Mom for a bit and had Helen there. But he sure as shit wasn't walking around shaking hands and introducing himself. But his mood was decent. And Mom seemed like her old self. She was great. Actually, the whole event was unbelievably great."

Here, Ronnie was all smiles seeing Marc getting married, jokingly waving around a bottle of nitroglycerin, his heart medication. Coming to live with Marc at the end of his life, fifteen years later, there were no smiles at all.

John Hollister had been divorced from Barbara since 1985, but he'd always remained close with Marc and arrived at the wedding with his new wife, Debby. Barbara chatted comfortably with both her ex-husbands and their wives. "She had zero hard feelings toward Helen," Marc said. "And she had always found it odd and laughable that Helen would physically shrink down in her seat when they'd pick me up for Sundays, as a child. Mom pitied her."

Michele wasn't surprised that Helen and her new father-in-law spent most of the rehearsal dinner under the deck, smoking and keeping to themselves. "Still, there was probably some racist stuff going on with my relatives. After all, they were from the segregated South." She knew their attitude didn't have anything to do with her new father-in-law's prison background. "None in the family knew about his past. But some anti-Semitism could well have been lurking not too far under the surface."

Five years after their wedding, Marc and Michele drove to Boston to lend a hand to Barbara, who was having medical and personal problems. During that visit, Marc and Michele learned that Ron and Helen had talked her daughter, Leslie, into selling her condo, and the three were going in together on a McMansion. Ron took them to see his new oversized house, which was under construction. As it turned out, not unexpectedly, that house and Ron and Helen's shared plans with Leslie didn't end well for any of them. The expenses for building the house and its upkeep were impossible to handle, as was the business of their living together under one roof.

What Marc considered the most important and memorable part of that trip was the visit with his mother, one he never expected would be their last. At that point, his bond with his mother had been declining rapidly, and he found everything about her difficult. It was as if the temper and unpleasantness she had held in place for many years was now stronger and more visible than ever.

A year after his mother's death in 2020, Marc was still deeply conflicted about their relationship. "Mom gave me a set of good values, the respect and care for people of different races, creeds, and culture. Being a minority, too, also knocked home some of those values. It's just that beyond sharing culture (seasonal theater, symphony, and ballet tickets) and good human values with me, my relationship with my mother was fraught.

"'She weren't right in the head,' as they say down here. Rage, anger, and projection were what I was treated to. She was physical at times when I was way smaller than she was. She was loving as well, and I can't say I walked on eggshells too much, but it was bad. John feels guilty now, not having been aware as he worked late all of the time. But our conversations recently have revealed how troubled he is by this fact. I never once have blamed him for not stepping in or being there."

Marc was also quick to offer examples of his mother's positive influences on his life. One of the most important ways she gifted her son was through her love of reading. "She read to me until I was about seven or eight, at which point I could tackle larger words. Our guest bathrooms, from as early as I can remember, had books sitting on the toilet back. And it's carried over throughout my life. Books make me happy."

Still, after that visit in 2005, the idea of seeing Barbara and staying at her apartment had little appeal to Marc. "Years earlier, I would have been so excited to go hang with Mom for a week, but she had changed, and it had become far more difficult to be with her. And I made the tough decision not to put myself in the position of being there and going through what I'd go through, especially after she stopped driving. Long story short, Mom had relied on her little brother, financially, since she and John split. Her career path yielded little, and he bailed her out for years. But I blame her, in part, and when I'm feeling blamey, for not giving me the full balance I needed growing up. I'm a fucking mess of an adult. Not a felon, not a substance-abuse victim and don't drink, save for an anniversary glass of wine to appease Mich [Michele]."

Needless to say, hearing Marc speak so honestly made me, yet again, feel sad and guilty. His conflicted feelings about his mother are understandable. But Barbara did not have an easy life herself. She had been in the wrong place at the wrong time. Single, pleasant-looking, living with her widowed mother near my aunt and uncle, with few other men knocking at her door, she was ripe for the plucking, and my aunt easily plucked her. Not surprisingly, marrying a man who had just finished serving a sentence for second-degree murder caused unending havoc in Barbara's life.

CHAPTER TWENTY-FIVE

Trying to Put the Pieces Together

Perhaps Ronnie could have been a decent father to Marc if he had begun fatherhood a bit longer than just two years after his release from prison. Flo made a far better decision to end her relationship with Ronnie when she did. Perhaps it would have been better for Ronnie, Barbara, and even Helen for my cousin to have emerged from prison, thirty-one years old and single, and then slowly find his way back into the world beyond the prison walls. He'd been locked away for thirteen years, entertaining guests in a prison visiting room, a young man growing up and dealing with other inmates. His every move was regulated and controlled by the prison officials. While he had been a rather wild kid before he began his prison term, in prison he was held back by rules and fears of having extra time added to his sentence for any misbehavior whatsoever. His family did everything humanly possible to protect and encourage him during those years, but not one day during that time could be considered normal. How could he possibly emerge, his punishment over, and easily begin a normal life? A psychologist trained in helping inmates adjust to a world without bars and searching for the reasons that put them there, along with a steady job and quiet time to readjust to a new life, might have helped. That, unfortunately, was never Ronnie's plan. Seen from the outside, a wedding, a wife, and a baby would fix all the problems of the past. Perhaps Ronnie's internal thoughts were to consume enough booze and bed enough women to make up for all the time lost from July 1954 to February 1967. While Ronnie never committed murder again, a chance for a normal and good life was close to impossible.

Innocent victims once again suffered for Ronnie's new "crimes" after prison. More than anyone, I blame Aunt Edythe for what happened to an unwitting Barbara after she met Ronnie. I doubt that my aunt sincerely liked Barbara anywhere as much as she adored the vivacious and beautiful Flo. When Flo took off, my aunt wasted little time finding her replacement. More than anything, Edythe personally needed the fancy wedding with the Jewish bride beside her handsome, free son for the world to know that her family was just fine. What had happened on July 27, 1954, and the thirteen painful years in prison had been nothing more than an aberration, a time to be erased from the Frank, Blumenthal, and Gordon family histories.

Barbara never stood a chance against my aunt. Ronnie never stood a chance of being the right husband for her. Marc never stood a chance of emerging a happy kid from that poorly arranged marriage.

What had happened to the long-held Blumenthal belief that after it had lost six family members in a tragic accident it would never lose another one? Years had obviously passed since Aunt Etta's delicious Sunday dinners at 7 Overhill Road. Where were all the Blumenthal relatives when Marc, the son of the

Blumenthal who was supposed to ease the pain of the family's tragic loss, was in such mental distress? He was far away, not just in a different locale, but in every possible way. We should not have lost him for so many important years of his life.

My memories of times with Marc were regrettably few. I remembered one Blumenthal summer get-together at Narragansett, Rhode Island, when Ronnie and Helen brought Marc. He was around ten and happily played baseball with his cousins. My cousin Bobby, the most ardent foodie of us, which makes sense since he was Aunt Etta's son and grew up with delicious home-cooked meals, declared Helen the star of that day. "She didn't have much to say to anyone, but she brought some incredible Italian specialties with her," he told me. "And I made sure I was right there when she took them out of her cooler." Indeed, although I never ate any of those delicacies or had any memorable conversations with Helen, I recalled it as a lovely day, typical of the annual Blumenthal late-August picnics on the grounds of the pristine Camp JORI (Jewish Orphanage of Rhode Island) in Wakefield, Rhode Island. It was the only one that Marc attended.

Several years before the summer family picnic, Barbara, without Ronnie in tow, brought Marc to my sister Toby's house in Lexington for some type of Blumenthal family gathering. I especially enjoyed looking at the photo taken that day of Marc, probably no more than three or four, sitting at the kitchen table with five of his male cousins, his blond hair standing out among his dark-haired tablemates. Toby remembered everyone there was delighted to see Ronnie's son, who so belonged with all his cousins. Marc was two months younger than my nephew Dana and very close in age to my two sons as well as to three of my cousins' sons. He fit right in with all the little Blumenthal kids. Even later in life Marc cherishes those memories, while regretting how few there were. His memory of that one day at Toby and Larry's house, so many years ago, was incredible. It broke my heart to think he was there only once when he had such a good time and would love to have returned.

"I vividly remember Toby and Larry's rec room," he said. "It was amazing, with all kinds of machines. They had an air hockey table and a bumper pool table, too! On the far back wall they had a couch and coffee table, with a record player and speakers in the surrounding area. Moving toward the stairs, were the air hockey and roller bowling game thing. The floors were multicolored, game/matting-textured, and red, white, and blue. I had a blast."

I was amazed to hear about his interest in his father's family, which was surely far greater than Ronnie's. "I have a fascination with photographs and would always ask to look through the bags and boxes of pics. Including the Blumenthal family. I especially remember Aunt Etta. I think I even remember going to her funeral. I must have been five at the time." Truthfully, I doubt that Barney or Ronnie would have brought such a young child to the funeral, but since I wasn't there, I cannot say for sure.

Indeed, there were far too many other times when Marc was absent from Blumenthal get-togethers and celebrations and he slid from our view. No matter where he was living, we should not have allowed that to happen, especially when we later found out that his childhood and adolescence were far from easy. Perhaps some loving relatives could have made a difference. Grateful that writing this book brought me into Marc's life after so many years of ignorance, I have no intention of letting him slip away again.

When Barbara entered a Boston nursing home so many years after those Blumenthal family gatherings, I was grateful that I was now in close touch with Marc. Unfortunately, things between Marc and his mother had deteriorated. Marc was exasperated that even a phone call to his mother was nearly impossible. Because Barbara slept poorly, if at all, and left her phone off the hook most days, Marc rarely had a decent conversation with her. When he was able to connect with her, she didn't make sense, or, if she did, she would be angry at him. He was miserable after the calls and struggled to figure how to manage to get up to Boston to visit her.

When I learned from Marc that Barbara's Boston nursing home was only an hour from my home, I was shocked. I had lost touch with her too many years earlier and was anxious to see her again. With the help of a kind nurse who woke a sleeping Barbara several times during the day, I managed to talk to her on the phone, as had my sister, Toby, and my cousin Fred. Neither of them had known exactly where Barbara was until I'd gotten the information from Marc, and each had, with difficulty, somehow orchestrated a phone call with her.

On my three calls with Barbara, I found her a bit confused but otherwise anxious to talk and full of memories of the times we'd been together many years earlier. Surprisingly, and totally incorrectly, she told me she'd been certain my mother had been angry with her. My mother had died more than thirty years earlier, and nothing could have been further from the truth. My mother always thought Barbara was a lovely woman and was elated when Ronnie married her and terribly disappointed when they divorced. She saw Marc a few times before he moved to New Orleans and was thrilled with her grandnephew. Somehow, with great difficulty, we shielded my mother from seeing her nephew Ronnie miserably drunk at several family affairs, including my younger son's bar mitzvah celebrations. She was sharp enough to see that Ronnie was running into problems after he came home from prison, but she always said her "poor nephew" had suffered so much that we all had to be extra forgiving toward him. I never understood why Barbara thought my mother was angry with her, so I attempted to assure her, with minimal success, that she was wrong, that my mother was never the least bit impressed with her nephew's *second* wife and told me more than once that Ronnie had made a drastic mistake and that "Helen could not hold a candle to darling Barbara."

Some of my discussions with Barbara were indeed a bit hard to follow, and it was obvious that she suffered from dementia along with her physical problems. But in other discussions, she was strikingly articulate and sharp, her memory about Ronnie clear and intense. Still, it was so good to have connected with her that I could have talked for hours if she hadn't gotten tired after fifteen or twenty minutes. On our last call, I set a date for the following week to visit her and could hardly wait to see her. Marc was both pleased and surprised at my success and made his own plans to drive to Boston with Michele to see her a few weeks later.

Then COVID arrived, and the nursing home shut its doors to all visitors. Neither I nor Marc got to see her. From then on, her phone was off more than ever, and any calls became scarcer and more unpleasant. The only communication I had with or about Barbara was with the friendly nurse who had awakened Barbara the first time I called.

When Barbara Sickels Blumenthal Hollister died from pulmonary and cardiac causes on April 25, 2020, at the beginning of the pandemic, she was alone. Angry with himself for not having tried harder to get to see her before COVID appeared, Marc was crushed by her death and further frustrated that he could not even come to her funeral. Yet, Marc felt as if he learned more about his mother after her death than he knew during her life. "One of the more interesting aspects of my mom's passing was the revelation that she had some type of mental illness," he revealed to me. "I learned that from a few folks who came out of the shadows, and from John who woke me up to some stuff. She had taken a drug called Elavil several years back when I was, like, in my sophomore and junior and senior years of high school. She claimed it was to stave off headaches and smoke less cigarettes. But I learned it is an antipsychotic medication to stave off 'crazy,' for fuck's sake! I am aware of the milligram dosage she took because I took 'em too. They were not microdoses, which can be used successfully. Follows a pattern of untruths, gray areas, and sneakily throwing me off paths. Happened to John, too.

"Undoubtedly, I probably have a combo platter of challenges from both my parents. My mom hid her real, deep-seated issues from me, and I know they were many. Things that literally ate her up [bladder, lung, and breast cancers and a main aortic explosion] till she passed. That added to the serial molestation I suffered from an older neighbor teen as a young kid, having my innocence and youth plucked from me before I even hit puberty, which I later learned is a particularly destructive event, leading to all sorts of fun developmental repercussions."

Though Marc was reticent to discuss these painful events, he will never forget them. "I also know that none of that defines me, that I am Marc, and have a solid grasp on my strengths and weaknesses, as well as a grasp on what I need to do to avoid stress-induced cardiovascular disease or cancers. I truly believe that my mom's darkness, secrets, and rage manifested the awful diseases she experienced. Mind-body and all. I studied and taught it; it's real."

However, it was not Barbara Blumenthal's death that drastically changed Marc and Michele's lives. It was Ronnie's.

CHAPTER TWENTY-SIX

The Final Sentence

Helen Cortese Blumenthal's death on March 21, 2011, became the catalyst for great change in Marc and Michele's lives. Marc knew Ron had been getting progressively sicker, with his diabetes often out of control, as well as his bladder cancer diagnosis and heart problem. As much as Marc disliked Helen, there was relief knowing that Ron was hundreds of miles away in Boston and only a part of his life in Birmingham, Alabama, via telephone. The last thing Marc wanted was any more contact with his father other than an occasional brief phone call, preferably no more than once a month.

Still, from a distance of nearly 1,200 miles, Marc tried to be somewhat helpful. Understanding that his father was lonely, ill, and unable to get around much, Marc suggested that Ronnie write about his life in a journal and send the entries to him via email. It was more an exercise to give his newly widowed, bored, and ill father something to do instead of sitting alone day after day. It was not an attempt to learn more about his father, about whom he could not care less. Too many years had gone by, too many moments when his father had disappointed or angered him, to suddenly turn their relationship into anything resembling a warm, loving, father-son bond. Marc could not imagine Ronnie writing anything particularly revelatory, especially since he had never related much about his childhood and was never the least bit anxious to discuss the relatives whose photos he'd piled neatly in a box in his closet. Maybe those emails would offer some answers to Marc's unanswered family questions. Maybe, by some miracle, they would open a door even a sliver into the confusing and confused man who was his father. Following is one such email from June 27, 2011, that Marc sent to his father.

> Starting off easy here. Please give as much detail as you can. Also, please add any memories that you may think of while answering these. I am going to do this project semi-interview style, meaning that I may ask you questions regarding something that you may have answered.
>
> Please tell me a bit about your birth (date, city, hospital), then a brief introduction about your Mother and Father (names, occupations, heritage/bloodline eg: where are their parents from? Europe? Where in Europe?

In response to Marc's request, Ronnie surprised his son by sending the following three emails, which offered at least a minute insight into his childhood, a subject they had rarely discussed. On June 27, 2011:

> okay let's get started with this. My birth date is October 1st 1935, just at the end of the depression

era. The hospital was The New England Hospital for Women and Children. This hospital is no longer in existence. My parents were born in the USA, mother from Boston and father from Providence, RI. At the outset of their marriage my mother was a homebody and my father was a bootlegger and ran a drugstore with his older brother, Uncle Ruby, in Providence. Both parents were Jewish.

My grandparents on my mother's side were both from Russia. Her father Philip (sic) was a Cossack [In truth, there were no Jewish Cossacks. It was the Cossacks who perpetrated the pogroms on the Jews] and Fannie was a homebody. On my fathers side, Philip was from Germany, our family name being Savage and my grandmother Rose was from Russia. I did not know my grandmother Rose as she was killed in the car crash that wiped out five (sic) family members. I think you have the paperwork on that event. I knew Philip vaguely. We, my parents and me lived with Philip and Fannie Frank for several years.

On July 9, 2011, Ronnie sent this next email:

Subject: continuing on

I am quite sure that there may have been more children planned, but due to a medical problem, Edythe could not have any more children.

I know that she had a thyroid operation after I was born and I think that was the situation.

Going as far back as I can remember, the first house we lived in was my grandparents, The Franks, and that was located in Roxbury. In the late thirties and early forties, the Jewish population in this state, was settled in Roxbury, keeping in mind that there were some gorgeous homes in Roxbury. I know I went to some sort of school when we lived there. Then my father bought a house in Brighton, and then another house in Brighton. I went to school in Brighton until about the fourth grade. My cousin Marty also attended the same school, it was named the Alexander Hamilton.

My life in those days was simple, after all, how much trouble can a person get into at that age! I also was attending Sunday school, which is when I faced my first incident with authority. It seems that I took ten dollars [about $175 in 2024 dollars] from my mothers purse, not realizing that there was really nowhere that I could spend that money at my age.

I have recollections of WW 2 taking place and Barney was an air raid warden for our area. I remember sirens howling from time to time and people were frightened by all that was going on. It was almost at the end of the war when I first started thinking about military school.

> Once again, we bought a house, this time on the Brookline-Brighton line.

I was probably more fascinated with the information in this email than Marc might have been. I couldn't help wondering if the theft from my aunt's pocketbook could possibly have been the catalyst for my aunt and uncle sending their one and only adored son off to military school at age ten for "reasonable strict discipline." How interesting it was, though, that a man who had been convicted of a murder at age eighteen focused on telling his son about a simple robbery involving ten dollars from his mother's pocketbook when he had been no more than ten years old. Ronnie seemed so innocent and so reflective in the email, as though he thought back over his life with simple warmth and pleasure.

On August 6, 2011, Ronnie continued:

> Subject: the story
>
> Okay, here we go!
>
> My cousin, Bob Gordon, was going to military school and came home for Christmas vacation. We spent some time together and talked about Riverside. It all started to look good to me so I sent for some more in depth information. At this time, I brought up the subject with my parents about their feelings on this subject. If I remember correctly, my age at this time was nine. My folks had no objections to this, so I wrote to the school for an interview, which was the way things were handled. Every summer the school sent an officer to the northeast,

> doing interviews. WWII had nothing to do with decisions. Had my interview and was accepted started Riverside in the fall.
>
> Edythe and Barney were good parents. Barney was working long and hard hours at our store and Edythe was doing her thing, playing cards mahjong, etc.
>
> Will continue anon
>
> Love, Dad

I wondered what Ronnie could have been thinking when he wrote those emails to his son. He had previously revealed so little of himself to Marc, preferring to talk about his successes with women rather than trying to detail his childhood or attempting to learn even a little bit about his son. Ronnie's discussion of how a nine-year-old kid from Brookline handled the application to Riverside sounds a bit hard to imagine. Obviously, that is the story Ronnie wanted to tell his son.

Yet the part of the email that hits me the strongest is Ronnie's descriptions of Edythe and Barney as "good parents." Of course, in many ways they were. They offered their son every possible material gift he could have desired. They stood by him during his darkest days, managing to provide the funds for thirteen years that kept him as safe as possible in prison. Yet again, Ronnie told his son, the son whom he told that he "took the rap for Barney," that his father was a good parent.

As for his mother, how could he honestly have meant that? Just the vengeful, nasty way his mother had treated his adored Flo after their breakup should have been upsetting to Ronnie.

Edythe had claimed to have loved Flo like a daughter, bringing her into her family in every possible way. Yet the moment Flo and Ronnie realized they could not continue their relationship, that it was unfair to Flo and her disapproving parents, the "good parents" turned on her. Ronnie had to have seen his own mother's cruel desire for revenge, forcing Flo to return every item she and Ronnie had ever given her, the degrading letters she had written Flo, all had to have shown her son the way her personality could change if things did not go her way. Good parents indeed. With the mystery of July 27, 1954, infiltrating Ronnie's life from age eighteen on, those two words seemed even more ludicrous in regard to his mother. Indeed, Edythe was such a complicated character, a woman cheated on by her husband, who had never been provided the type of life to which she had felt entitled, a cold, brittle woman described by one of Ronnie's teenage friends as always "trying to act young." Indeed, Edythe was anything but the typical protective Jewish mother of the 1950s. There was nothing good about her mothering.

To Ronnie's credit, he had a good recollection of where he had lived and what schools he had attended. Since I was searching for any clues about how and if my cousin had turned into a violent murderer at age eighteen, I regretted that he did not reveal any thoughts or feelings on what his younger years might have been like. I was personally disappointed that Ronnie had not used those rare mail exchanges to open up to his son, to have talked about his failure as a father and as a husband, or about the years locked in a cell, or even to have come clean about the Incident that delivered him to that cell. Those were the stories that I am certain Marc, along with me, for certain, would have wanted to read. Maybe my cousin was simply unemotional and not interested in sharing any feelings or thoughts about his childhood with his only child. It occurred to me, not for the first time, that my cousin simply was not introspective or sensitive to others' opinions or maybe just not that bright. Most of all, Marc's simple words about his father being "an alcoholic and a liar" resonated in my mind. While I do believe Ronnie made an honest attempt to open up to his son about his childhood, it was difficult, if not impossible, to accept anything my cousin said as honest.

While I was writing this book about my cousin, I consulted a well-known Salem, Massachusetts, psychic to see if I could learn more about July 27, 1954. The first session resulted in a "visit" from my cousin. The man who appeared told the psychic he was my family and was glad to see me. He was relaxed and, according to the psychic, had a kind spirit. I should have walked out then, but I stayed a little longer since he had something to tell me. He wanted me to know he had to protect his family. Those words were eerily like what Ronnie had told a girlfriend the night before the murder.

At my second visit, the psychic saw an attractive, dark-haired woman with red lipstick and a nice shape and great skin. I wondered if that could have been Ora Schonarth. But a more beautiful dark-haired woman, someone younger than the first woman, soon arrived and seemed more anxious to stay. She wore red lipstick too. Ronnie was happy to see the second woman and said she had a compassionate heart, was young-spirited, and she'd made his life a better place.

In my third and final session, the psychic saw signs of the mob; in particular, the Irish mob. That made little sense since Helen's father and cousins were connected to the Italian mob. As for his son, Ronnie wanted me to know he wished he would have stuck around longer and been there for his son emotionally.

The psychic also saw racetracks, seedy joints, and lots of drinking in my cousin's former world. He was dressed fashionably in expensive-looking pants and a pale-yellow silk shirt. He had an excellent physique. But over and over, the same words were coming from our visitor: "*No remorse.*"

When I questioned about Barney or Ora or even Edythe, she suggested I book another session to see if we might be able to reach one of them. Ronnie was manipulating this session and didn't to want to share the stage with anyone. But he told me not to worry about him. I decided not to book another session. This psychic may well have had some ability to enter the spiritual world of the dead. Or perhaps she had read details about the well-known murderer. How was I to know? I left shaking my head, feeling confused and dissatisfied. I barely understood or knew my cousin when he had been alive. I wasn't particularly certain that the man who had apparently come to see me via the psychic was anyone I knew.

When I mentioned the psychic session to Marc, he said she apparently knew her craft and may have had some powers. And that nothing she revealed about his father surprised him. Except that he doubted that Ronnie had any desire to have been a better father. "That ability simply did not exist in Ron," he said. But he had his own opinion of the murder victim who might or might not have showed up for the session. "I mean, she *was* having an affair with a married man. And knew as much, right? Oy." He didn't think I should try to connect with Ora. And I didn't.

Marc's opinion about his father's final emails was blunt: "I felt like he was rewriting his history the way he'd like to remember it with some of those replies, but who knows? We never made it to the big stuff."

Indeed, it wasn't long after Ronnie's last email recounting this not-particularly revealing family history that the final chapter of Ronnie's life began, one sadder and possibly more awful than his prison sentence; one for which every living Blumenthal must take some measure of regret and guilt.

It all began with one phone call. Less than a year after Helen died, Ronnie called his son to tell him, "Your old man needs you, kid. I'm fucked." Indeed, Helen's daughter, Leslie, had had enough of her stepfather and decided it was time for Ronnie's son to step up and get him the hell out of her house. I must admit that at that time I had no idea what was going on with Ronnie. I had heard that Helen had been ill but did not know she had died. My husband, Jack, had reached out to Ronnie a few years earlier to see if he could offer any medical advice, but Ronnie had never returned any of his calls. We'd heard that Ronnie also had some medical issues, but, again, Jack and I had been unable to reach him. To our knowledge, neither had any of our cousins. In retrospect that seems so sad, but Ronnie had faded into the background for so many years, especially after my son Josh's bar mitzvah, that it seemed more and more unlikely that he would ever come back into my life. Indeed, the Blumenthals had given up on him, the very thing we had all been taught never to do to a member of our already decimated family.

While we had all turned our backs on Ronnie, at that time he was depositing himself in the midst of his son's life, the one person who had the strongest reason to turn his back on him, the person he had disappointed so many times. Yet, once Helen's daughter, Leslie, gave Ronnie his walking papers, Marc had no choice but to set out to perform the impossible: to provide whatever necessary care he could to make his father's remaining years as positive as possible and maybe even, miraculously, to develop some sort of a father-son bond. In the hard, cold reality of what the past fifty-one years of his life with his father had been, Marc held no such illusions. Haunted by what had happened to his adored papa, who died in a crappy rented room in Boston's Combat Zone in 1976, Marc was honest about his feelings after Leslie's call. "He sure as fuck expected to be taken care of when Helen died and Leslie tossed hm out. I was expected to save him from the likely outcome that he wouldn't save his own father from. Ugh!!!!"

When it was all over, as Marc put it, it sounded so simple: "There was no obituary. He died here in Birmingham, with Michele and myself." It was anything but simple, however.

From the outset, Marc admitted that moving his seventy-seven-year-old ill, depressed, and cranky father from Massachusetts, where he had always lived, to a house in Alabama, practically a foreign country to Ronnie, was a plan doomed to fail, especially based on the misinformation Marc had been given. Had Leslie been honest about Ronnie's health, Marc would have delivered him straight to a nursing facility either in Massachusetts or Alabama.

From what Marc was able to discern after he and Michele arrived in Massachusetts to collect Ronnie, his father suffered from myelodysplasia, a form of blood cancer, along with diabetes neuropathy, a heart condition, and painful back issues. Before they hit the road for the three-day drive to Alabama, Leslie unsettled them with stories of the years of intimidation and bullying she had experienced from Helen and Ron. The two had used Leslie's inheritance of over $30,000 from her grandmother Olga to build their dream house in Wilmington. Soon, unable to pay even their electric bills, they were forced to sell the house at a great loss and buy a far smaller one in Billerica. It is not hard to understand why Leslie felt no love for her stepfather and no reason to care for him in his present state.

On March 21, 2012, the one-year anniversary of Helen's death, the three remaining Blumenthals of that line left for Alabama in what turned out to be a miserable road trip. Ronnie was argumentative and grumpy from the outset and became even more so when Michele realized his neuropathy rendered him unable to feel the accelerator or brakes correctly and had to oust him from the driver's seat. Uncomfortable due to degenerative back problems, as well as a catheter due to his bladder cancer, Ronnie needed to sit on a thick towel, which needed frequent changing. Things only got worse when they finally reached Birmingham. The plan was for Ronnie to rent Marc's neighbor's empty house. The house, unlike Marc and Michele's home, had no stairs and seemed the perfect place for Ronnie to have some independence and for Marc and Michele to have some distance from their sullen and unwanted guest.

From the beginning, the plan was fraught with problems. Ronnie had promised to smoke only in the screened-in back porch, but he broke the promise the first night he was there. Because walking soon became more difficult, he constantly smoked in the living room, burning holes in the rugs. At least Ronnie wasn't drinking any longer, taking only the prescribed meds, including the morphine tablets, that Michele picked up for him along with groceries and whatever necessities he required. Ronnie spent all his time in the oversized La-Z Boy chair they had brought from Boston in a small U-Haul. He required daily care with his meals and catheter. The only slightly pleasant times for the three of them were when Marc and Michele brought over dinner the nights they were not working and watched Ronnie's favorite shows or pay-per-view movies with him on the large-screen TV he had also brought with him. There was no one else in Ronnie's life, and he used the phone only to call Marc and Michele or, later on, the fire department. Ronnie grew progressively worse, physically and mentally, each day. Marc and Michele knew for certain that Ron was not going to be able to function on his own for long and would expect far more than nightly visits and food and medicine deliveries.

Then the falling started. At least once a day, Marc or Michele got a call from Ronnie that he was on the floor and needed help. Because Marc didn't drive, he had to get a ride from work as soon as he could. If Michele was home, she would meet Marc at Ronnie's and the two of them would pick up Ronnie and set him back on his La-Z-Boy lounger. After a while, Ronnie began calling fire and rescue. When he was no longer able to walk or even hoist himself up on the bed, he lived and slept in the lounger. Michele began dropping off all his meals, trying to control his diet, but to no avail, as he had no interest in anything resembling healthy food items. He had only his oversized television, which was on all day and all night, for company.

Listening to Marc's descriptions of those difficult times, I sensed his frustration along with his guilt. It was as if some barely known, sick relative had been delivered into his and his wife's lives, making every day insufferable.

Things continued in that manner for three weeks until one especially hideous fall, a scene Marc never forgot. "We had been calling him and he didn't answer his cell for more hours than was normal, so we drove over," he said. "We found him on the floor. Blood everywhere. His catheter bag had exploded when he'd fallen out of his chair again. It was 'a blood bath.'"

Marc called fire and rescue, who, after refusing to transport Ronnie to a hospital several previous times, finally saw how seriously ill he was. Ronnie could barely answer the required mental check questions. Immediately diagnosed with a dangerously low white blood cell count and an equally deadly urinary tract infection, he was transported to the seventh floor at St. Vincent's Hospital, a ward, according to Marc, "for those who they didn't believe would be around long." Indeed, that early May day was Ronnie's last day at the rented house, or anywhere in the "free" world.

Marc and Michele made daily visits to the hospital around their work schedules. Ronnie was not an easy patient, but Michele was able to work with the social workers and professionally handled the myriad problems that arose from his erratic behavior as well as his declining physical condition. To everyone's surprise, however, Ronnie fought hard and recovered some of his strength. "He was either asleep or awake and crabby once he had begun feeling a little better, though still with serious health issues," Marc said. Behind the scenes, however, the discussion centered around Ronnie no longer being able to care for himself, a fact that had obviously been going on for a year.

As soon as he heard this news, Ronnie became both angry and despondent. "All he could see was that he was going into a grisly home, similar to the one where his mother had been dumped at," Marc said. "He had been so resistant to going to a facility that he'd hid his constant falling. When he went to rehab after the last hospitalization and knew he wouldn't be going back to that house, he was scared. We tried to make it as positive as we could, but that was his greatest fear, a nursing home."

I can understand Ronnie's fear of being placed in a nursing home, where the doors would be locked and his freedom to move around wherever he desired would be removed. His physical condition basically prevented him from moving anywhere without assistance, except to the bathroom, but still, up until then, he wasn't in a nursing home and mentally knew he had the freedom to come and go as he pleased.

Knowing it would involve a tough battle with Ronnie, Marc and Michele made appointments at nursing homes that fit Ronnie's limited budget and eventually settled on the Golden Living Center. Not unsurprisingly, Ronnie could not understand why Marc and Michele would not let him live with them. "My answer to him," Marc said, "was that neither Michele or I were trained nurses, and he needed twenty-four-seven care. He had quite literally begun splitting himself rectally from a year of falling on his butt. A condition needing multiple/daily nursing care."

Despite Ronnie's anger and frustration, Marc and Michele moved him to the Golden Living Center, into a private room with a massive plasma TV. "We visited the next day, and he was lucid and mean," Marc told me. "Bitching about the bill-paying while he'd been hospitalized. I read him the riot act , and we left abruptly after making sure he had everything he needed, at least for that visit. I got a call at 5:00 a.m. that he'd had a heart attack and died."

Marc considered the resolution he and Michele made a few hours after that phone call the most difficult decision of his life. Once it was made, however, there were equal amounts of relief and guilt. Even nearly ten years later, Marc was haunted by that day and its ramifications. "We met a gentleman in the bereavement room to discuss arrangements. But Ron had zero dollars except for a forthcoming Social Security check. We had no real choice except to let the city have him and bury him in an indigent site. Or go into deep debt for a funeral and burial. There were a couple of packages, but no. It eats me up, but more due to fears of my own passing. Being poor as we are, all of that."

Thus, Marc's troubled relationship with his father was, by most accounts, over. The fact that he had been a part of his father's degrading and sordid final months of life, however, ultimately forced him to consign his father to a pauper's grave, almost as if Ronald Blumenthal had never lived, leaving an even deeper mark on Marc than the years of what had been described by his stepfather as a "twisted version of parenting." Marc, indeed, was far from the only relative rendered guilty and ashamed by Ronnie's final journey and ultimate resting place.

Cousin Fred was one of the few Blumenthal relatives genuinely distressed by the situation. After Barbara called to inform him of Ronnie's death, Freddy made calls to some of the Blumenthal cousins to see if anyone wanted to pitch in for the burial expenses. All his calls were fruitless. "I wasn't surprised by the refusals," Fred said. "I wish I could have done it on my own, but I couldn't. I knew the other cousins were fed up with Ronnie's lies."

Unfortunately, Ronnie had borrowed money from most of the cousins in the past, money that had never been paid back. In addition, none of us had heard from him for years and had no idea he had been so sick or had moved to Alabama, where he was under Marc and Michele's care. The burden of that lack of communication rested equally on Ronnie's shoulders and those of all his cousins.

Fred's last conversation with Ronnie had taken place fifteen years earlier, in 1997, just before Fred moved permanently to Florida. The two cousins talked over the phone for an hour, discussing old times and making plans to get together with their wives somewhere between Providence and Boston. "We had a date set for a few days before Sandra and I were to move when he called to cancel," Fred said. "That was the last time we ever spoke. I had always hoped things would have been different between us, but it wasn't meant to be. The ball was in his court, and he never played it. I turned the other cheek so many times and would have forgiven him for anything, but he never came through. I knew he had never stopped trying to impress everyone, but he still mattered to me a lot. I'd always thought his life was a tragedy caused by his parents and Edythe's family's money. But he was my cousin and my friend and I loved him."

Cousin Mel did not share that love. "Fred asked if I wanted to contribute to his burial," he told me. "I didn't. The last time I'd seen Ronnie was at a cousin's party at our Providence home in June 1970. I had no idea about his medical problems until at the very end. I heard he was very sick." The fact that Ronnie had propositioned Mel's wife, Jacquee, after that 1970 party easily explained Mel's lack of desire to see his cousin again or pay for his burial.

Cousin Fred's brother, Phil, who was, as was I, nine years younger than Ronnie, had his own complicated feelings about his older cousin. His reason for visiting Ronnie in prison, he conceded, was to take his mother, Marion, Barney's sister, to see her nephew. "I had no interest in seeing him myself, and truthfully all I remember was the Forestry Camp looking like an outdoor camp with freedom for all," he said.

Things had changed for Phil and his wife, Ann Ruth, after Ronnie got out of prison and married Barbara. "At the beginning, we had a mutual love and closeness then," Phil said. "He was easy to be with, and we always enjoyed his company." However, one particular family gathering had pushed Phil to cut his cousin out of his life. "But as the years passed and he married Helen, I felt nothing toward him, and I finally lost total respect for him when he got drunk at Josh's bar mitzvah. I am not the type of person who wants to extend myself to people who cannot give back friendship or emotion. Again, I cannot speak for any other cousins, and this is how I live my life. I knew other cousins tried very hard to keep in touch with Ronnie, but Ann Ruth and I felt drained by trying to deal with Ronnie's erratic behavior and simply gave up."

Cousin Bobby, Aunt Etta's son, and his wife, Naomi, had previously stayed by Ronnie's side for many years, traveling on the 1971 cruise to Bermuda and staying in close touch with Ronnie and Barbara. They attended Barbara's wedding to John Hollister, yet tried hard to get to know Helen and spend as much time as possible with Ronnie and his second wife. Even gentle and forgiving Bobby eventually reached his limit. "Ronnie did it to himself," he said regretfully. "We would call him and he would not call back. And when he did finally call, he would make up excuses not to get together, even with just me. I honestly think he was losing it."

Cousin Dick, Bobby's equally kind and compassionate older brother, always had a special affinity toward his slightly older cousin, though he, too, on a limited budget himself, declined to pay for his cousin's burial. "We were all buddies and close contemporaries growing up; Fred, Mel, Ronnie, and I, all a year or so apart," he said. "Though Fred and Mel and I lived in Providence, and Ronnie was in Boston, he was always one of us."

Dick last saw Ronnie in the early seventies, when they were both approaching forty and many years before Ronnie's death. "I was living and working in New York," Dick said. "He was visiting New York, and the two of us met for dinner at a nice restaurant near Central Park. He looked old that night. He was only a year older than me, but he looked so much older. I could see the wrinkles all across his face. But he seemed fine, and it was wonderful to reacquaint ourselves. I had seen him a few years earlier when I'd gone to see him take off from New York on his cruise to Bermuda with the other cousins. But now, at dinner, he just seemed much older."

For years after that dinner, Dick worked hard to stay in touch with his cousin, but he was never able to tie Ronnie down to another time to meet. "He kind of disappeared from my life after that dinner. I did continue to call him at least a few times each year, and we occasionally spoke, but he never initiated a call to me. One time when both he and Helen were having some health problems, we had made another set of definite plans to meet in Billerica, but at the last minute he cancelled. He said Helen was too sick. That was the last time we spoke." Shortly after that phone call, three years before Ronnie's death, on October 12, 2009, Dick sent the following email to his cousin:

> Subject: Re: greetings
>
> Dear Ron & Helen,
>
> I have some sad news. Uncle Hy passed away yesterday. The funeral ceremony and burial are both scheduled for Wednesday [October 14] at graveside in the family cemetery at 11:30 AM. I believe the cemetery is called Lincoln Park and is in Warwick, RI. I am not able to give directions since I don't remember the names of the roads but have been there enough times to be able to find it by rote. If you plan to attend I suggest you look for the cemetery on the Internet and get directions from them. I will be there with Karina and I know that my brother and Naomi will be

> there as well but I doubt whether any other cousins will be attending except of course, Roberta and Bill. Meryl passed away a couple of years ago and Irma is disabled in a nursing home. The rest are too far away to be able to travel to R.I. on such short notice. I would love to see you again even if under sad circumstances.
>
> In any case, I hope you are both well and even though we haven't recently communicated I think of you often.
>
> Best regards and with our love,
> Karina and Dick

It was sad reading Dick's email as I remembered the losses of my strong World War II hero Uncle Hy and his daughter, my cousin Meryl, along with my cousin Irma's deteriorating condition. I recalled Uncle Hy's funeral well, the sorrow at losing the last of my mother's Blumenthal siblings and the pain of looking at the six headstones already at the family cemetery plot in Warwick. How many times had I already been there with my mother and, most often, my Aunt Marion and laid pebbles on the headstones, as is the Jewish custom. Seventy-four years passed by the time I attended my uncle Hy's funeral there, but the tears shed on October 14, 2009, by the remaining Blumenthal relatives were as fresh as they might have been had I been alive in May 1935.

Dick saved Ronnie's response, which arrived one day later, the last email he ever received from Ronnie. "I just can't get rid of it," Dick said. "It's the last thing I have of his."

Subject: RE: greetings

Hello Dick

Just read this second or first part of your communication.

I would love to be there but Helen has her radiation session at 9:30 every day and it would be impossible to get there on time and am really sorry that we will not get the chance to see you and Karina.

Please stay in touch

Ron

While Fred continued to strike out on his list of possible donors for Ronnie's burial cost, he never contacted me or my sister, Toby. Or Cousin Bobby. "I just ran out of energy," he said. "And I knew that Ronnie had become a stranger to every cousin." That statement was hard to grasp but impossible to fault. Years before he died in the Golden Living Center, Ronnie was gone from our lives. What we had never thought possible had happened. We had not just lost six relatives in a car crash; we had lost a cousin who was still living. We had never completely abandoned trying to understand exactly what had happened to that cousin on July 27, 1954, but we had given up on holding afloat that one relative who had drifted far, far away from all of us. Shame on us, on all of us.

For Marc, the entire event of his father's last three months of life, from the day Ronnie called to say he needed help to the decision to bury him in an unmarked indigent site, was torturous.

"I'm not sure how I thought things might play out with him once we took him to our home," Marc told me. "But it never dawned on me that it could be so bad."

One can only wonder what Ronnie was thinking when he realized the end was near. Perhaps the murder on July 27, 1954? How could he have erased that from his mind? Marc always wondered if that was why his father drank so much after his release. "Perhaps the drinking was a mind eraser," he said. "But who knew what he could have been thinking at the end? Perhaps he was thinking of Helen. Or thinking about how he resented Michele for talking me into sentencing him to a nursing home. I think he went and heart-attacked himself out of an abject upset. I felt instant relief. Is what it is."

While I was pleased but a bit skeptical of Marc's feeling "instant relief," I found his use of the words "sentencing him" to the nursing home poignant. His father had been sentenced nearly sixty years earlier, on his nineteenth birthday, on October 1, 1954. That time he received a life sentence to prison. After eight years it was commuted, and he was paroled after thirteen. His final sentence arrived on June 14, 2012. This time, after a mere twenty-four hours, he commuted it himself. He'd been locked up once before, and, according to his son, he had somehow willed his heart to stop to make sure it wasn't going to happen again.

POSTMORTEM

The story of the Blumenthals is more than a story about a tragic car accident and a murder. It is about my family, one of the millions of families who arrived here as immigrants at the end of the nineteenth century, wanting nothing more than to raise their children in America, free, strong, and able to practice their religion and earn their own living in the new world. And yet it was our fate that somehow a curse found its way inside the core of this family.

We managed to navigate our way through these two unexpected and devastating events. And although we endured great unhappiness, we emerged as a genuinely happy, cohesive, and resilient family following the Accident. However, the Incident proved too much for several of us. It destroyed Ronnie's and Barney's lives and left Marc to deal with the broken pieces.

What I knew for certain was that the 2012 death of the man who served thirteen years for the murder of Ora Schonarth was noticed by only two people, his son and his daughter-in-law. No newspaper that had once displayed headlines such as 18-Year-Old Thrill Slayer and Death Sentence for Blumenthal carried his obituary. The many relatives who had loved and cared for him with food, visits, and letters during his years of imprisonment, as well as when he first came out, didn't offer to help pay for him to have a decent burial. His beloved Flo did not know of his final years. For her, the memory of the sweet, gentle man still lay, untouched and cherished, inside her. She had not seen the deterioration that the others who had loved him had witnessed up close. For them, their love died before Ronnie passed. There was no consideration of laying him to rest in the Blumenthal plot in Rhode Island where the six markers with the year of his birth, 1935, forever stood. Without doubt he wasted all that familial affection, drinking too much, borrowing too much, lying too much, caring too little. Maybe he couldn't help it. Maybe, when you are locked up in prison from ages eighteen to thirty-one, having spent much of those thirteen years with the soul-killing thought that your father's deeds had caused your incarceration, then maybe you don't emerge with your soul intact. Maybe the knowledge that you had killed another human being was a soul killer. Maybe Flo's words were true, that if Ronnie murdered Ora, "then he was so traumatized that he never believed he did it."

So many maybes, so much guilt, so much sadness. One vicious murder; two lost lives.

I'm not a psychiatrist, nor am I a detective. I'm just Ronnie's cousin who happens to be a journalist. While I might not be able to solve definitively the mystery about who killed Ora Schonarth, I can see how Ronnie Blumenthal, with the help of his parents, destroyed his own life. I have always been astounded by the newspaper reports of how Ronnie showed little if any emotion to that sentence, in the courtroom or back in his jail cell. Some wondered if he actually understood it. Fifty-eight years later, his body and spirit broken, his bank account empty, his second wife dead and his son and daughter-in-law distanced, he understood exactly what was happening. This time there were no loved ones to console or support him. No mother to bring him cashmere sweaters. No father to keep paying for lawyers and sympathetic guards. No Aunt Belle to deliver the brisket. No Cousins Fred or Mel to bring their children. No Uncle Lewie driving from Providence to visit his adored nephew in prison, bringing Aunt Etta and her freshly baked strudel. No beautiful Flo to fall in love with him. Now there were only that alienated son and daughter-in-law, who had no choice but to impose this sentence, two relatives who had neither the means nor the love to care for him in their home or to provide a proper interment. Ronnie Blumenthal's story began with a celebrated birth four and a half months after a car crash and six deaths. It was punctuated with the baffling murder of an innocent woman. It ended in an unmarked grave.

Since July 27, 1954, no one ever heard Ronnie mention Ora Schonarth's murder, except to tell his twelve-year-old son that he had taken the rap for his father. Decades later, that same son wondered what happened on that day. "Who knows? You could even imagine Edythe being part of the scene," Marc mused, believing as I did that his grandmother Edythe was tough enough to have had a role. "It's all just twisted. His self-esteem and overall possible low opinion of himself all tied up in Edythe's abuse and his evil deed. Too bad he never once considered therapy. But I guess he felt he was all good."

As for Marc's grandfather, despite his father telling him he "took the rap for Barney," Marc could never imagine any possible role for him in the actual murder scene. "The Papa I knew was a kind and gentle soul, who did not set out to hurt anyone. He could never have been at fault for what his son did that night.

And as for his affair, it was understandable, considering who he was married to."

I disagreed with Marc on that statement. The kind and gentle man *was* at fault for what happened to Ora Schonarth, just by bringing her into the family's orbit. As I stated before, my uncle brought that woman into his family's lives. Yes, she was his family's dressmaker, but he made her his lover and possibly, according to neighbors who saw Ronnie enter that woman's apartment more than once in the late evening, that same woman was also his son's lover. The thought of Edythe pushing her son into action against the murder victim also concurs with the idea that neighbors noted in the police reports in 1954 that Ronnie and his mother visited Ora together shortly before the day of the murder. Of course, those same reports noted Ronnie telling his friend Esther, "It's worth going to the electric chair to save my family. I asked her to give him up—I mean my father—but she only told me to mind my own business."

Marc and I were not the only family members to give credence to the idea of Edythe urging her son to take care of their family problem. Cousin Mel offered his own similar speculation about our aunt's involvement in the murder. "Edythe may have found out that Barney was having an affair and told Ronnie to admonish or threaten the woman, and he may have gone to her house and things got out of control." Perhaps it went even deeper than that.

So often I thought about heading to Birmingham and doing whatever was possible to locate Ronnie's grave. I visited the Blumenthal family cemetery in Rhode Island enough times to picture vividly all those graves engraved with the date of May 14, 1935. Shouldn't Ronnie's grave be beside those final resting places? They were, after all, his three first cousins, his grandmother, and his uncle. Should I find that grave, wherever it was, merely to mark it with the name Blumenthal? I knew that would not happen. I would never put Marc through the trauma of searching out his father's unmarked grave in the pauper section of some Birmingham cemetery.

I cannot, try as I might, say with utter conviction that my cousin, alone, with his own hands, and with no outside impetus, murdered Ora Schonarth. I throw blame, perhaps unwarranted, on others: on his mother for never being anything remotely resembling a decent, loving parent; on his father for spoiling him far too much and carrying on an affair with Ora Schonarth; on the vacant lifestyle that never shaped him into a responsible human being. And, perhaps, on a curse that began with a group of bootlegging brothers and cousins and continued on through a fatal drunk driving accident, landing on an unborn Blumenthal fetus, coming back to haunt our family eighteen years later. Ronnie was flawed and unable to handle any sort of mishap. He was lazy and inconsiderate of others. Paradoxically, he was handsome and deemed the Blumenthal miracle that followed the hideous car accident. His chubby, smiling, beautiful face generated smiles from all the relatives who loved him for what he represented rather than for what he truly was. This young man, unworthy of the love the rest of the Blumenthal family bestowed upon him, cracked and committed a crime as awful as the one committed by a drunk Connecticut driver, and certainly worse than the original sin of bringing in and selling illegal booze to thirsty Rhode Islanders.

Yet, for reasons I cannot easily explain, I hold on to an infinitesimal particle of love for my lost cousin. I can only hope that, wherever he is, he rests in peace. I also hope that Marc—perhaps far more like "Papa," the grandfather Marc loved as a child, than resembling the man he persistently calls "Ron"—suffers no guilt for his father's pathetic final sentence.

Perhaps the seeds of the curse were unknowingly sown on January 17, 1920, when Prohibition went into effect and some of the young Blumenthal (and Rosenfield and Sass) men began to figure out how to profit off of it. It first flowered to claim six lives on May 14, 1935, and bloomed again on July 27, 1954, to claim another. Over ninety-two years—and three Blumenthal generations—have passed since that second installment of the curse. On June 14, 2012, with the pitiful death and shameful final resting place of my cousin Ronnie—perhaps the third and final installment occurred, as bad things tend to come in threes. In writing this book, I have now concluded, with gratitude, that with the passing of Ronnie, the curse of the Blumenthals is finally over.

What I have learned from my Blumenthal relatives is that no family can prevent a curse. However, love can help dispel a curse. It can keep family members together and make them more determined than ever to hold on to one another.

THE END

CURSE OF THE BLUMENTHALS

Questions

1. Do you think Ronnie killed Ora Schonarth? If it wasn't Ronnie, who might it have been?
2. The Accident was a tragedy that was multiplied because of the many victims, causing generational trauma. How can a family get over a traumatic moment, or does it become a lingering dark cloud, seen by family members as a curse?
3. Aside from Ronnie, which character was the most complex or intriguing to you, and why?
4. Were you affected in any way by Marc's words? "I listened, and the big question, of course, was whether he did it. I asked and he answered, 'I took the rap for Barney.' But then, in the same breath, he also mentioned blacking out the memory and his not being sure."
5. Were there any characters in the book deserving of forgiveness? Who was not?
6. Guilt and innocence are the flip sides of the same coin. In *Curse,* who is guilty? Who is innocent?

7. What role do alcohol and alcoholism play in the book? Is it fair to blame alcohol as the root cause of the Curse?
8. Did you find examples of anti-Semitism in the stories of the Accident and the Incident?
9. How do you think the Accident would have been treated legally today?
10. Belle Blumenthal was greatly affected by the Accident and the Incident. What were the lingering effects of these two events on her life?
11. Families keep secrets. How do secrets influence the Blumenthal family over the generations?
12. Immigrant and first-generation American families are often close-knit, either living together as extended families or living near each other. Is there an address in your family that played the role that 7 Overhill Road did for the Blumenthals?
13. What can you find in Ronnie or his background that might make him more of a sympathetic character?
14. In *Curse,* the Blumenthal cousins can be said to perform the role of a chorus in an ancient Greek tragedy. Which of the cousins made the greatest impact on the rest of the family and why?
15. While in high school, Ronnie had a lot of girlfriends. Let's consider the women in Ronnie's life: his mother Edythe; his girlfriend Barbara, who broke up with him while he was in the Army Reserve; his first fiancée, Flo; his first wife, Barbara; and Helen, his second wife. What kind of influence and effect did each one have on his behavior and life?
16. Ronnie is a complex and enigmatic figure. Do you think Ronnie became a husband and father because that was

what society—and his mother—expected of him? How did he handle the pressures of fatherhood and marriage? Would he have been happier or better off if he'd never gotten married or fathered a child?

17. Marc couldn't choose his parents. Has he been a victim his entire life? How has he tried to cope with the issues brought upon him by his parents?
18. Burial is an important ritual in Jewish culture. Do you think it was cruel or understandable that none of the cousins, besides Freddy, would help pay for Ronnie's burial?
19. Do you believe in family curses? Do you think the Blumenthal family was cursed? Why or why not?

ACKNOWLEDGMENTS

For Marc Frank Blumenthal, my dear cousin, who gave me his memories and his heart.

For Robert Krock, my friend, who lent me his brilliant mind and his editorial skills.

For my cherished Blumenthal cousins: Fred and Sandra Brown, Mel and Jacquee Lipson, Dick Halpert, Toby and Shelly Smolokoff, Ruth and Harvey Levin, Phil and Ann Ruth Brown, Naomi Halpert, and Larry Bondy.

For the Blumenthal cousins we have lost: Barbara and Allen Halpert, Morty Blumenthal, Irma Krasner, Elaine Silverman, Barbara Blumenthal, Toby Bondy, Bobby Halpert, Karinna Halpert, and, of course, Ronnie Blumenthal.

For my treasured friends who listened, over and over, to my never-ending stories about the Accident and the Incident.

To BJS, the Wisest Woman in the World.

With deep appreciation to Doug Grad, my extraordinary agent. We met at *Brutal* and joined forces again for *Curse of the Blumenthals*. From the first sentence I wrote for *Curse*, he was with me, understanding what I wanted to say and making sure I did it in the best manner possible, to display my family, its warts and joys, and to prepare it to leave its cocoon and face the world.

With gratitude for all the unnamed but never forgotten researchers who offered their time and expertise, without whom I could never have written this story.

PHOTO CREDITS

Page xi	Courtesy of Robert Krock
Page 2	Courtesy of the author
Page 7	Courtesy of the author
Pages 12–15	Courtesy of The Providence Journal—USA TODAY NETWORK via Imagn Images
Pages 24–25	Courtesy of the Willimantic Police Department
Page 31	Courtesy of Dick and Bob Halpert
Page 34	Courtesy of the Willimantic Police Department
Page 48	Courtesy of the public domain
Page 54	Courtesy of the author
Pages 58–62	Courtesy of the Clerk of Family Court, Providence, RI
Page 75	Courtesy of the author
Page 76	Courtesy of Fred Brown
Page 81	Courtesy of the author
Page 88	Courtesy of Naomi Halpert

Page 93	Courtesy of Mel Lipson
Page 98, top	Courtesy of The Providence Journal
Page 98, bottom	Courtesy of The Jewish Herald
Pages 117–118	Courtesy of Marc Blumenthal
Page 134	Courtesy of The Boston Herald
Pages 141–142	Courtesy of The Boston Globe
Pages 143–144	Courtesy of the public domain
Pages 152–154	Courtesy of the Brookline Police Department
Page 165	Courtesy of The Boston American
Pages 206–207	Courtesy of The Daily Record
Page 208	Courtesy of The Boston Globe (Globe staff photo by Charles McCormick)
Page 229	Courtesy of the author
Page 233	Courtesy of the author
Page 243	Courtesy of the author
Page 249	Courtesy of Edmund Kelley, Boston Globe via Getty Images
Pages 266–268	Courtesy of Fred and Sandra Brown
Page 299	Courtesy of Marc Blumenthal
Page 315	Courtesy of the author
Pages 323–325	Courtesy of Marc and Michele Blum enthal

ABOUT THE AUTHOR

Photo by Jennifer Shore Photography

Phyllis Karas, the author of a dozen books, taught journalism at Boston University and was a stringer for *People* magazine. She is the coauthor, alongside Kevin Weeks, of *The New York Times* bestseller *Brutal: The Untold Story of My Life Inside Whitey Bulger's Irish Mob*. She coauthored, with Kiki Feroudi Moutsatsos, *The Onassis Women: An Eyewitness Account*, the subject of a *Dateline* NBC special. An award-winning journalist, her work has appeared in *Vogue*, the *Miami Herald*, the *Boston Globe,* and *Boston Magazine* among others, and she wrote a popular column, "Wit, Wisdom and Woe," for the *Boston Herald.*

An alumna of Boston University and George Washington University, Karas and her husband, Jack, a retired physician, are longtime residents of Marblehead, Massachusetts. She has two sons and three grandchildren.